"*Selfish Prayer* chroni... modern day paladins who personi... ...warrior ethos of placing the mission first, never accepting defeat, never quitting, nor leaving a fallen comrade. Emmett and his fellow soldiers brought their dedication, courage and experience from main street USA to the deadly mountains, valleys, and villages of Afghanistan, saving countless lives and changing Army Medevac forever. Those who are entrusted to increase the survivability of our service members-politicians, doctors, medics, and commanders must read this book and sustain the paradigm shift initiated by these seasoned veterans."

Max Santiago, Deputy Commissioner (Emeritus), California Highway Patrol

"SSG Emmett Spraktes is an American hero. There is much to learn from the rescue that resulted in his being awarded the Silver Star: 'Don't get hunkered down,' 'look down field,' and 'keep moving' is sound advice on the battlefield, as it is in a busy emergency department. SSG Spraktes was honored for saving the lives of five heroes in the Watapur Valley in Afghanistan on July 17, 2009. His real legacy, however, will be the thousands of lives that will be saved due to his advocacy for increased training of military air rescue personnel."

Gary W. Tamkin, MD, FACEP
Medical Director
California Highway Patrol
Associate Clinical Professor of Emergency Medicine
University of California San Francisco School of Medicine

"*Selfish Prayer* is the story of a soldier's deployment to Afghanistan. It is a glimpse into a branch of service often under-recognized by those who tell the military story. It is a story of courage, strength, and heroism; as lived and told by a humble, honest, and sincere man. For all who respect the sacrifice made by our armed services, this is a must read book."

Kevin Green, Assistant Commissioner, California Highway Patrol, Retired

"*Selfish Prayer* not only explains how to save the physically wounded, but shows the invisible scars soldiers carry that others cannot see—the emotional and psychological injuries caused by the trauma of war. Spraktes has the courage to share his soul and gives first-hand accounts of how to cope with and survive the emotional wounds that injure first responders and military personnel called upon to serve when war or disaster strikes. Every American citizen, politician, and military commander should read this book..."

Todd Langus, Psy.D., Trauma Specialist; former police officer, dr.toddlangus@gmail.com.

SELFISH PRAYER

How California National Guard DUSTOFF
Changed the Face of Army Medevac amid Chaos,
Carnage and Politics of War

SSG Emmett William Spraktes
with
Victoria M. Newman

Copyright © 2013 SSG Emmett William Spraktes
All rights reserved.

ISBN: 1484856767
ISBN-13: 978-1484856765

Library of Congress Control Number: 2013908671
CreateSpace Independent Publishing Platform
North Charleston, South Carolina

For the eight

SELFISH PRAYER

How California National Guard DUSTOFF
Changed the Face of Army Medevac amid Chaos,
Carnage and Politics of War

TABLE OF CONTENTS

Preface	xi
Foreword by Major General David S. Baldwin	xiii
Part One – Nine-Line! Nine-Line! Nine-Line!	**1**
1 – My Father's Legacy	3
2 – Police Officer, Patrolman, Paramedic	9
3 – A New Mission	27
4 – Righting Wrongs	45
5 – We're Not in America Anymore	61
6 – Study at Bagram	69
7 – Combat Hoists	83
8 – Building Trust	93
9 – Afghan Police Officer	109
10 – Critical Care Transport	115
11 – Seven Minutes in Hell	123
Part Two – The Killing Season	**141**
12 – Spinning Plates	143
13 – Chapadera	151
14 – Stetsons and Spurs	159
15 – Ten Miles from Jbad	163
16 – Loss at Barge Matal	173
17 – Walmart and Other Morale Builders	181
18 – Selfish Prayer	193

19 – Routine Career Call 219
20 – Riding the Hero 227
21 – Sauvetage 233
22 – Benson and Stead 239
23 – Ambush at Ganjgal 245
24 – Landings, Lasers, and a Ronald Reagan Moment 259

Part Three – Abandonment and Retribution **269**
25 – Let the Terrorist Fly 271
26 – Keating 279
27 – Reintegration 291
28 – Results from Bagram 305
29 – How Did This Happen? 317
30 – The Siren's Call 323

Endnotes 328
Glossary 329
Bibliography 339
Acknowledgements 353
Author Information 357

PREFACE

Selfish Prayer is about a group of soldiers who save lives for a living. We are older than the average soldier, we have civilian jobs that we love, and we're a little warped around the edges because of our life experiences. Every one of us is motivated by love for our brothers in uniform, but sometimes this love manifested makes us act like assholes—caustic and impatient. It's called tough love—it's not who's right, it's what's right.

Selfish Prayer recounts the 2009 Afghanistan deployment through medevac eyes. We performed many rescues and medical procedures and had calls that to this day haunt us in the night. We fought death with our rubber-gloved hands, and mourned silently as some breathed their last. We witnessed extraordinary bravery by those with whom we served.

Selfish Prayer documents another battle—to give Medevac flight medics a greater voice, more education and training so they will be better equipped to care for patients on the battlefield. In between war, rescues and politics, we conspired to follow a careful plan to document and compare EMT-Basics to EMT-Paramedics and their corresponding mortality rates. This in-theater study was to prove to the decision makers there was indeed a significant problem.

These stories are true. They are not exaggerated. All recollections and opinions reflected have been recorded, verified by documents and witnesses, and in some instances, recorded on camera. Victoria and I followed up on details that didn't mesh and rechecked stories, some from several sources.

Selfish Prayer is controversial. Some stories don't line up with other published accounts. I assure you, the reader, if I couldn't corroborate the story, it wasn't included.

Thanks for reading,

SSG Emmett W. Spraktes

FOREWORD

Casualties are an inevitable fact of war. To defend our principles and way of life, men and women put their bodies and lives at risk, and they trust they will receive the greatest possible care when injuries occur. That care depends upon brave, courageous soldiers like SSG Emmett Spraktes, who fly into hostile areas and risk their own lives to save those on the ground.

A National Guard citizen-soldier who is also an experienced California Highway Patrol officer and paramedic, SSG Spraktes brought a level of expertise to his tour in Afghanistan that was uncommon among flight medics at the time, but which has since become the Army standard. There are service members throughout this country who hold a special gratitude for SSG Spraktes and the lifesaving care he provided them in Afghanistan. But those lifesaving actions pale in comparison to the improved care that service members will receive in years to come due to the example he and other California National Guard flight medics set during their tour.

Cal Guard medevac personnel had long been aware that the level of care provided by most US Army flight medics fell short of the standard SSG Spraktes and his fellow unit members deemed sufficient. They believed service members who put their lives on the line to defend this country deserve at least the same quality of care received by citizens who dial 911 at home, and the men of Charlie Company, 1-168th General Support Aviation Battalion (Medevac), refused to sit quietly and allow brave US service members to die needlessly.

Prior to deploying in support of Operation Enduring Freedom, SSG Spraktes and his fellow Guardsmen decided they would take it upon themselves to create a positive change in the way the army takes care of its soldiers. In addition to their daily duties responding to distress calls in hostile areas, the men of Charlie Company agreed to record data on the patients they transported, which would ultimately prove the Cal Guard citizen-soldiers outperformed their active-duty US Army counterparts, resulting in a 66 percent lower risk of death within 48 hours for severely injured patients.

Since the publication of this data, the army has changed its standard to measure up to the criteria proposed by Charlie Company—and every US soldier who deploys in the future owes them a debt of gratitude for increasing the likelihood of their safe return home. As the leader of the California National Guard, it is a source of great pride for me to know that a Cal Guard unit effected such an important, lasting, lifesaving change throughout the active and reserve components of the army.

I am also grateful for their selflessness and persistence, as I know this did not come easily or without sacrifice. For some of the men of Charlie Company, the quest for improved soldier care began long before the wars in Iraq and Afghanistan began, and they encountered resistance at every turn. Going toe to toe with officers who preferred the status quo, which had been in place for decades, posed a risk to the careers of SSG Spraktes and his Charlie Company brethren, but thoughts of personal gain and status never entered into the equation.

Led by their hearts, their sole focus was to save more lives, today, tomorrow and in every engagement the US takes part in for the foreseeable future. Theirs is a legacy of selfless service and doing what is right—and even more so, of forcing the US Army to do what is right for its own members. These men embody the values we in the Armed Forces endeavor to uphold. They are a credit to this nation, and I am honored to serve with them.

Major General David S. Baldwin
Adjutant General, California National Guard

On July 1, 1964, in the heat of the Vietnam War, Major Charles Kelly (call sign Dustoff) responded to a hot zone to pick up soldiers wounded in combat.

The enemy was waiting and unleashed a barrage of heavy fire. Major Kelly was advised to withdraw immediately, but his answer was, "When I have your wounded..." He was killed on the spot.

Because of his unwavering commitment to the soldiers on the ground, all future air ambulance missions were referred to as Dustoff.

It is the result of accepting this commitment that all US Army medevac have adopted as their credo,

"When I have your wounded..."

PART ONE

Nine-Line!
Nine-Line!
Nine-Line!

The Spraktes Family, Christmas 1961. From left: Shirley and Emmett Jr., Violet and Barbara, Emmett Sr. and Diane. Dad and Diane perished just over two months later.

Author's Personal Photo Collection

MY FATHER'S LEGACY

"What we do in life echoes in eternity."
Maximus Decimus Meridius

"I believe that what we become depends on what our fathers teach us at odd moments, when they aren't trying to teach us. We are formed by little scraps of wisdom."
Umberto Eco, *Foucault's Pendulum*

Sacramento, California
8 Mar 1962

Harry Blevins[1] chuckled to himself. *They'd never seen anything like me before, that's for sure.*

His heart still racing, he remembered the looks on the girls' faces as he'd dropped his trousers. They were young. Sweet.

I saw the innocence drain from their eyes.

Blevins, twenty-two, drove in circles, not really knowing where to go, or exactly where he was, for that matter. Having recently relocated from Southern California, he was still getting his bearings. He'd drove around downtown for awhile before he came across two girls strolling

---

[1] This is a pseudonym. This account was created from the report in the Sacramento Bee. Harry Blevins denies everything except the accident—and he claims this wasn't his fault either.

along the sidewalk. He'd pulled over, gotten their attention and exposed himself. Their screams were almost pleasurable as he quickly returned to his car and sped off.

Excited by the reaction from the teens, he shifted in his seat and swallowed. His thoughts were sluggish from his time at a nearby bar earlier, but other areas of his body were still very much awake.

It might just be worth another go around...

He pulled his black 1961 Chevy Impala onto 24th Street and headed back. They'd probably run home to their mommas, but he just couldn't help himself. As he finally pulled onto Broadway from 17th, the patrol car caught his eye.

Better slow down. I don't want to attract attention.

Passing by slowly, he peered over and realized the officers were talking to the girls. Surprise marked their faces again—but this time they pointed and the officers jerked their heads his way. They were moving for the cruiser.

Blevins jammed the accelerator, and the chase was on.

Emmett Augustus Spraktes's family had grown. Only six years earlier the house was empty after his wife passed away and her kids moved on. Then he met Violet—a spunky brunette who was a Rosy the Riveter during World War II. She was a single mom with beautiful blue eyes, and that girl had pluck. She grew up on a farm in Wyoming out in the middle of nowhere. Although strong, she still had an innocence about her.

They married, and Violet's teenagers, Neil and Shirley, lived with them. Within a few years, they added two girls of their own, Diane and Barbara Ann, bringing the household to six. Emmett was thrilled to have his home full again.

Emmett was a former Sacramento police officer. He'd spent years on the streets arresting people, going to accidents, and dealing with situations each shift held. At the age of forty-two, he'd turned in his badge and gone to work for the Department of Motor Vehicles as a driver improvement analyst.

About the time Emmett turned fifty-five in 1962, Neil left home for the navy, deploying to the Philippines. Just as one young man left, another was born. Emmett was a father once again, but this time it was to a son, Emmett William.

It was a dream come true, having a son to carry on the family name. Whenever Violet dressed that little man in some blue jeans she'd found at the store, he beamed with pride. He was damn proud of his boy.

Every Thursday evening the Spraktes family packed themselves into their Volkswagen bus and headed to Gunther's for ice cream and a car ride. This Thursday was no different. Two-year-old Barbara Ann and Shirley, thirteen, sat together in the back. Diane, just four years old, stood behind the passenger seat where Violet held the six-month-old in her arms. Diane just couldn't keep her eyes off that baby as she talked with her father about the possibility of men going to the moon.

Emmett drove east on X Street.

"Just think, Diane, there could be a man walking on the moo—"

He saw it in the corner of his eye—a black mass. Instinctively he threw himself forward right, arms out, in front of his wife and infant son.

6 Selfish Prayer

Glass exploded in all directions as the vehicles collided. Metal twisted and upholstery blew apart, and Emmett and his precious family were ejected all over the intersection of 13th and X Streets.

———

Officers Shierts and Johnson slowed slightly at each corner to search the streets. *Where'd that punk go?* When they slowed at X, they saw the mess just a block up.

Oh God...

The scene was horrific. Men had run out of a motorcycle club on the corner when they heard the crash. They were horrified at the carnage. The Volkswagen bus had been shoved into a utility pole—hard. Harry Blevins's Impala rested on its roof. Unconscious little ones were sprawled everywhere, broken and bleeding.

A kind man went to Violet and gently covered her with his coat—her dress had flown over her face as she skidded across the pavement. She had enough clarity to thank him before she slipped into unconsciousness again.

Not far from her was the baby, who flew with her until she landed. He shot out of her arms, rolling over and over on the debris-covered street until he came to rest in the gutter.

Shierts and Johnson found Blevins sitting nearby, smoking a cigarette. His gelled hair was tousled, his pants ripped and soaked with blood. When they asked him about the earlier incident with the girls, he confessed. When asked why he did it, he replied, "I must've been drinking." He was arrested on charges of manslaughter, felony drunk driving, reckless with injury, driving without a license, and lewd conduct.

All the victims were taken to the hospital and treated for their wounds. Violet remained in the hospital for weeks, but Emmett never regained consciousness. He and four-year-old Diane, despite heroic efforts to save them, died in the Sacramento Hospital. They would never see men walk on the moon.

I, Emmett William, was the six-month-old baby. I got away with abrasions and bruises, a concussion, and a nice gash to the head (which might explain some things).

Emmett Augustus Spraktes was a former police officer, an expert on driver safety, a family man, and the dad I never knew.

My father died saving my life.

Spraktes training boat crews on the Sacramento River in June, 2007.
Courtesy of Joe McHugh, Senior Photographer, California Highway Patrol

POLICE OFFICER, PATROLMAN, PARAMEDIC

"What is the use of living, if it be not to strive for noble causes and to make this muddled world a better place to live in after we are gone?"
Winston Churchill

"I have strong feelings about the similarities of police work and military service. I believe soldiers make excellent police officers. They have all the traits necessary to be successful. They work well within an organizational structure. They respect rules and policies. They understand tactics. And most are already adrenaline junkies!"
Kevin Green, Asst. Commissioner CHP, Ret.

Northern California
1986 – 2001

My father left big shoes to fill. I grew up listening to stories and getting to know him through my uncle, my mother, and other family members. I had this larger-than-life image in my head of not only him, but law enforcement in general.

The deep respect I had for my dad translated into a desire to be a police officer. In my early twenties I decided to go for it. I applied everywhere and quickly got a job offer as an intermittent employee for the California Department of Corrections (CDC). I'd heard that if you wanted a job in law enforcement, go to CDC and start out as a permanent intermittent employee. It was relatively easy to promote to full time quickly, because they were expanding like crazy.

Corrections

I accepted a job at the California Medical Facility in Vacaville. Three days later I was offered full-time employment. At the time, Vacaville was California's largest correctional facility. It was then split in two—the medical facility and Solano Prison. There was an intake center, medical facility, a huge AIDS unit, a huge psych unit, administration segregation, lockup, and a large population of aging, hard-core gangsters.

To answer the burning question—no, Manson wasn't there at the time.

The place was full of other notorious people. One night, I was forced to work another eight hours in J2, which was a lifer wing on the second floor. I monitored who went in and out of the wing.

"Excuse me, sir, I'd like to get in the door." The voice directly behind me was polite.

Feeling less of an ultra-aware hallway-ninja, I turned around and found myself staring straight into this inmate's chest. He was huge. I'm guessing six-ten, and weighing into the three hundreds.

It was Ed Kemper—the Coed Killer. He was the one who killed his mother, his grandparents, his mother's friend, and several female hitchhikers in Santa Cruz, California. He hated women. Couldn't get along with them. His claim to fame was that he'd never had sex with a living woman. If you were to meet him on the street, he would be intelligent and extremely polite. This was part of my early education.

You never know who is a serial killer. You never know what's really going on behind people's eyes.

I let Kemper through the door and into his wing with a heightened awareness of my surroundings.

I served in corrections for three and a half years. I was involved in Special Emergency Response Teams (SERT) for three of those years. SERT is like a SWAT team for prisons. I went on several call outs; I was also trained as a rappel master. This prepared me for things to come.

At my two-year mark, I needed to decide to either promote within corrections or go to the streets. I didn't want to spend my life in prison. Eight to sixteen hours a day within prison walls—you get saturated with the culture. You begin to look at life differently. I didn't want that

Police Officer

I again applied everywhere and was hired by the California State Police (CSP). The CSP was founded in 1853 as the California State Rangers, who had banded together to catch a notorious gang leader, Joaquin Murrieta. Although they disbanded after he was captured, in 1887 the legislature authorized two officers to protect the state capitol, a beautiful building that resembled the dome of the White House in Washington, DC. Over the years the CSP expanded into protection of the governor and other state officials, protection of state properties and their employees, and other agencies that didn't have their own police force. Eventually the CSP branched into many areas of law enforcement throughout the state.

I was assigned to the San Francisco field office. It was insanely busy in San Francisco. I loved, loved, loved the work. Some perceived that the CSP just walked around shaking doorknobs. Maybe that was true at the

Selfish Prayer

capitol or other facilities, I didn't know, but in San Francisco it was the Wild West. You couldn't drive down the street without seeing a crime in progress. If you didn't go to jail a couple times a night, you were hiding. Guns, drugs, foot chases—it was dangerous and exhilarating.

My first felony arrest was a rapist. A man raped a woman and then beat her to a pulp. He had already been to California Youth Authority for beating up a district attorney's wife so bad that she was never the same (she suffered a traumatic brain injury in the attack). Responding to the call, I chased him from the scene through the Greyhound bus station, through the streets of San Francisco, and over a pedestrian overpass. I finally caught him when he ran out of steam and stopped running, dropped to his knees and barfed. That's when I realized how big this fucker was—six feet six and 260 pounds. When he stopped, I thought, "Oh, Shit!" I drew my .357 and yelled at him to lay on the ground.

Everyone congratulated me on my first felony arrest. They said it was a job well done. But all I could do is wish that I'd gotten there just fifteen minutes earlier. It was awful.

After a year of fun in San Francisco, I was picked up on a transfer to Sacramento to work the governor's protective detail. This move allowed me to get back to my young family. I was assigned to Governor Pete Wilson's team for a short time. Governor Wilson and his wife were very kind people. His call sign was Bulldog—because he was a former marine. Mrs. Wilson had a beautiful singing voice, so her call sign was Songbird. I remember sitting outside their residence early in the morning, Uzi in hand, waiting for a couple of hours to take him to work. He was notoriously late. He'd get up, exercise in his garage, and then go to work. He stayed long hours—many times we didn't take him home until midnight.

I wasn't ready for protective detail. Very early in my career I was indoctrinated by chasing, arresting, and fighting bad guys. To be a bodyguard, you have to worry about "the protective envelope," "the package," conducting surveys, and planning for events. I just wasn't mature enough in my career to get excited about it.

I transferred back to the streets and worked the same beat my dad had worked with Sacramento Police Department. These were the same streets he had walked. They were the same places he had made arrests. I really enjoyed that.

As I progressed in my career, I was on three different SWAT teams, the bike unit, and the Public/Policing and Problem Solving Program (POPPS). The POPPS program encompassed fifty projects in the south Sacramento area. I met with site managers of commercial areas and asked what crimes were occurring there, what were the quality of life issues, and if there were vagrancy or parking problems. I met with these people a day or two a week, then partnered with other agencies and participated in drug raids and warrant arrests. I often teamed with the Bureau of Narcotics and Enforcement—these were exciting times! I took people down at gunpoint, worked with customs, the Department of Insurance, and the Employment Development Department (EDD)—they always needed uniformed officers to help serve warrants. That was another year of exhilaration and living dangerously.

I had a good friend who took the east Sacramento POPPS program—Rodney Van Bebber. My initial perception of Rodney was that he was a turd because he had volunteered to be in the capitol core. This was a group of officers who were assigned only to the capitol as embassy-types. I thought, why would any self-respecting cop do that when there's so much more fun to be had?

What I learned later was he wanted to be involved in his kids' lives—soccer, baseball, etc. I had to eat crow. He's probably a better person than me because I was much more self-absorbed. I wanted to do the job, not concerning myself too much with home life. One day Rodney came out to meet me and I'd arranged a drug raid. This was a whole new world to him. He was hooked—on fire! From then on, we often teamed up with other agencies and jointly conducted drug raids.

I had an inner mandate to take sexual predators off the street. I worked with parole officers, and they trusted me enough to give me files of sex offender registrants that had not reported into their parole officer. Parole agents were really worried about them but didn't have time to track them down. Under parole, offenders are still under punishment for their crimes, but they had agreed to stay out of trouble in exchange for freedom. That included meeting with their parole officer regularly. They gave me lawful detainers—signed documents that gave the power to return these guys to prison if they broke parole. So, I'd do everything that my job required me to do in a crammed time allotment and then I'd go out hunting. I'd look at the files and call the old numbers, which would lead me to something, which led me to something else, and eventually I'd find the dude and arrest him. I hooked a lot of people that way.

I never targeted anyone, but I kept an eye on specific people. When I was on bike patrol in the downtown Sacramento area, there was a scumbag who was always slinging dope. He was a big dude, dealing drugs out on the K Street mall. Wallace Rowe[2] was his name, and he was a predator. I even had his date of birth memorized for a time. He was bigger, younger, stronger, and faster, and I knew he could kill me. Eventually I caught him with enough packaged marijuana to pop him for possession for sales. I finally arrested him.

The deputy district attorney told me her office loved me. They had been trying to get Rowe because he was suspected of breaking the legs of his girlfriend's child. She was so terrified of him that she wouldn't testify, and without her testimony, they couldn't prove anything. My arrest put him in jail long enough to turn her around. We got him! That fired

---
2 This is a pseudonym.

me up. I wanted to get more predators off the street, because just this simple arrest led to a better quality of life for this woman and her child.

In 1993, California went through a budget crisis. They declared that those with less than eleven years on the job would be laid off. I had a family that depended on me, so as much as I loved it, I started looking. I got picked up by Vacaville Police Department. After six months, the state budget crisis was resolved. As much as I loved community policing, I had more arrests and excitement on the bike patrol in State Police than I did in Vacaville. I was still on fire. I returned to the state.

In 1995, the State Police merged with the California Highway Patrol (CHP). Since its formation in 1929, CHP personnel were known as traffic officers, who worked the freeways and county roads in unincorporated areas. They investigated accidents, worked crimes related to traffic, and wrote tickets. But the merge incorporated dignitary protection, SWAT teams, and officers on horseback and bicycles from the State Police. This move was part of California's plan to merge agencies and save money.

For some, including myself, it was a hostile corporate takeover, and I wasn't happy about it. I didn't want to chase bumpers like a dog; I wanted to chase real bad guys! This was at least our perception of the CHP. They in turn thought we did nothing but shake doorknobs. Both were grossly inaccurate perceptions.

Once the merger was complete, I stayed at the state capitol since I wanted to stay on the SWAT team. That was the deal; to stay on the team you had to work the capitol area. No problem—the capitol was surrounded by sprawling, park-like greenery—absolute beauty. It also attracted freaks and feral humans—right up my alley.

One day Rodney Van Bebber and I were working the street and arrested a dirtbag in an occupied stolen vehicle. We took his sorry ass to jail and then went into the basement report-writing room of the Blue Anchor building. Our locker room and briefing area was located in an asbestos-laden dungeon. It was located near the southwest corner of the state capitol. While there, we talked about the arrest and how we thought the report should read. As Rod and I hashed it out, a youngish, slightly pudgy Hispanic with a sorry-ass mustache walked in.

We had been getting an influx of traditional Highway Patrol guys into the capitol area, which was a traditional State Police area...so there were some personality conflicts. As senior officers we felt protective of the new guys, though they be road dogs and unworthy. I asked him if he was a new guy, assuming he was an officer. He simply said yes and introduced himself as Max Santiago.

Rod and I proceeded to tell this new kid that there had been some rough patches with the merger. We said we would handle it if anyone gave him any shit as long as he was doing his damn job and not hiding and always doing the right thing. We also told him if he was a slug, we would crush him. About that time one of the sergeants walked out of the briefing room and addressed Max Santiago: "Oh hey, Lieutenant. How are you doing?"

Crap! We just told the new lieutenant we would crush him!

Much to Max's credit he took in all that we said, took it for what it was, and, for some reason, had respect for Rod and me. Max was one smart son of a bitch. He had a perfect memory—he could actually see the text as written in his head. Max climbed the CHP ladder to eventually become the deputy commissioner before he retired.

SWAT

After the merger, I stayed at the capitol because the SWAT team asked me to participate. I volunteered my time because they didn't have authority to bring another person in. They wanted my experience and training, but they couldn't pay me. I'd have to do it on my own time. So I did.

After quite a wait, they finally were given permission to allow me to train while on duty. I served on SWAT for about seven years.

In April 1996, CHP SWAT was called up to assist an allied agency in Orland, California. The surrounded murder suspect had apparently "dispatched with great prejudice" his fellow entrepreneur and business partner, likely over a sales, manufacturing, or marketing dispute. He was also wanted in connection with a recent kidnapping; no doubt a strategy in dealing with a competitor in a niche market (the methamphetamine business can be brutal). Our methed-up and sleep-deprived businessman was an HIV-positive three-striker. He claimed he had explosives, many firearms, and would not be taken alive. Sweet! I was going through my first divorce—this seemed like an adequate distraction.

On arrival, his apartment was already surrounded by allied SWAT teams. They had taken turns on the perimeter, and it was exhausting. We were briefed in detail and immediately tasked with relieving the perimeter team, who had been there for hours. I set up behind a Ford Mustang where I could see his front door of the six-plex. Within five minutes, as I stared over my MP5-40, he tossed out a throw phone (used by police negotiators to communicate with bad guys) and shot it a couple times.

I guess negotiations have officially broken down...

Throughout that day and into the night, the suspect periodically fired off errant rounds just to keep us on our toes. The immediate area had been evacuated, but we knew a stray round may clip an "innocent" at any time.

After about thirty hours of this crap, the TOC command decided it was time to go in. We went over the plan and everyone knew his or her role. I was tasked with throwing the initial flash grenade through the rear window as fellow teammates were to shove a bang pole (a pole that had several grenades attached) through the same window and run around to the front to flush him out.

Three-two-one...*green light*!

I rushed in with the guys behind me, pulled the pin, and threw it hard. That damn grenade hit the center of the window with all that I could muster—right square into a metal strip that separated the glass. It ricocheted off the window, bounced onto loose landscape pebbles at the team's feet and exploded. Flash—bang! Shit!

Peppered with rocks and blinded, the team pressed forward and in went the bang pole. I stood there for a second all kinds of pissed off, and then barraged the apartment with flash bangs and tear gas grenades. Smoke billowed out as the suspect began firing in all directions not ten feet from me. All I saw were flashes of gunfire and the suspect's smoky silhouette.

Hell, maybe he'll hit me and the pain of the divorce will go away.

Jim Williams, our team sergeant, ran toward me out of the darkness. "It's time to go, Emmett," he coaxed.

The plan worked. The gas and bangers pushed him out the front door, where the allied team shot him with nonlethal shotgun beanbag rounds. They twisted him up and took him into custody.

I'd thrown so many gas and flash bangs the apartment caught on fire, and then *really* caught on fire. Once the scene was secure with the criminal in handcuffs, the firefighters on standby put the wet stuff on the red stuff, extinguishing the fully engulfed room.

I never lived that one down. I have a nicely framed newspaper picture of the charred apartment labeled, "Designed and decorated by Emmett Spraktes, April 1996" from fellow SWAT team member Van Bebber. It hangs right next to the Division Chief Accommodation I was given for the same incident.

Unbeknownst to me, this was an indication of future grenade shenanigans.

Paramedic

There was an officer named Greg Expolias (we called him Expo) who was one the first officer paramedics in the nation on the SWAT team. He was also a motor[4] in North Sacramento. Because of all the changes in the patrol, we couldn't keep him anymore as the team paramedic. That left us in a bind. The SWAT team had no paramedic, and some of the places we went were remote. We couldn't ask the fire department or private EMTs to go on these calls with us, because there was no policy in place. We had to be self-sufficient. There were several people on the team who were qualified to step forward because of their prior training. No one took it, however, because it was a lot of work. I decided to step up.

---

4 He rode a CHP motorcycle.

20 Selfish Prayer

I didn't know what I was getting into at first, but I ended up loving it. The highway patrol put me through a joint CHP/Sacramento County Fire paramedic program administered through American River College. This was well over a year of my life eating, breathing, sleeping, and shitting nothing but medical.

I went through the first phase in the classroom and was in the upper third of my class. The second phase was the clinical portion in the hospital, assigned to a nurse. The third phase I was assigned to the field with experienced paramedics. I was required to have forty-eight advanced life-support calls but the calls didn't count if you screwed up or had too many of the same type. I worked so many cardiac calls that they declined many of them. I didn't mind; I loved living the fire-department life (cooking, cleaning, La-Z-Boying). After completing the program, I became the assigned SWAT paramedic.

In the meantime, I had seen other agencies with paramedic bicycles that were able to maneuver through crowds and get to people rapidly. I felt that if we incorporated this concept on the grounds of the capitol and adjacent state properties, we could better serve those we were charged with protecting. I took this idea to my division chief, Dave Wilson. He said, "Great idea, Emmett! No fucking way! We just can't do it right now." Bad timing. I respected his honesty.

Three days later, I was on the east side of the capitol when we got a call for service. It was for a longtime lobbyist named Michael Kilbane who was well known and liked. He had a heart attack and was probably dead before he hit the ground. He had facial abrasions as he collapsed face-first. We hurried to his location and were working on him within a minute's time. We were performing CPR when the fire department rolled up. Fire quickly got an endotracheal tube in, and then I went with Kilbane all the way to the hospital.

Fire's response time was five minutes. So there was a gap of four minutes where we could've shocked him if we'd had the equipment; maybe got his heart going again, maybe not.

Chief Wilson and Commissioner Spike Helmick were on the grounds on the opposite side of the capitol. They heard the commotion and tried to call me. Everybody was asking—senators, representatives, and staffers—"What's happening with Michael Kilbane?" In the meantime, I literally had my hands on this guy. They kept calling again and again, but I was working on him with the other paramedics, doctors, and nurses. They pronounced him dead at the hospital after many attempts to revive him.

I returned to the capitol to write up the report. The chief walked up and declared, "Hey, you know the bicycle paramedic thing? We're gonna do that. I told the commissioner we need to have two, so who's gonna be the other paramedic?"

Jesus, three days ago there was no fucking way.

"Well, Chief, I'm the only one. We'd have to send someone else through the paramedic program."

"OK," he agreed. "I need you to make that happen." That's when I called my buddy, Rodney.

Chief Wilson had been an enlisted marine based out of San Diego. He was a big, tall dude, and somewhat obnoxious, but always funny. He was good to me on the patrol. But Chief didn't want to be called Chief. He was Dave, and it bothered him that no one would call him Dave. After a SWAT meeting in which no one spoke up in response to a question, he called me in his office. "Why won't anyone talk to me?" he asked.

I responded, "Chief—it's not you. Everybody likes you. It's not personal. You are a chief in the California Highway Patrol, and we respect that. You can't expect us to turn that off." He got it.

One day an auto tech called me for a favor. Because I was now on the paramedic bicycle and got to places quickly in the congested downtown area, he asked if I could swing by and pick up Chief Wilson's car nearby. Sure! So I biked over, got into the chief's car, adjusted the seat way up (because I'm much shorter than he), and drove it to the office. On the way, I saw a cassette tape hanging out of the stereo, and curiosity got the best of me. I popped it in. I imagined it was Captain and Tennille or the Osmonds. No, it was the Marine Corps hymns.

So, Chief Wilson listened to "From the halls of Montezuma..." every morning on his way to work. Really? Because I was in Navy Specwar as a reservist, I felt it my duty to screw with him.

I parked his car, and rode my bike to the nearest music store and bought him some real music—the Village People. I couldn't resist.

I replaced the Marine Corps hymns with the Village People, fast-forwarding to "In the Navy" and then hid his tape somewhere in the car. Then I waited.

A couple days later, Chief Wilson was in a foul mood. He was furious. He stalked the office hallway accusing people of putting that tape in his car. I just chuckled to myself as he chewed a few sergeants' asses.

Later he spotted me in a lieutenant's office and he yelled, "Goddamn it, Spraktes! I know you put that damn tape in my car!"

Without missing a beat I answered, "Well, Chief, I was as surprised as anyone to learn what kind of music you prefer—"

"Goddamn it! The conflagration of bullshit that comes out of your mouth!" He then stormed out. The lieutenant just looked at me in disbelief.

I smiled. Mission accomplished. I love marines.

A few days later, Chief pulled up in his car, motioned me over, and confessed, "Emmett, no one has ever gotten me that good. Great job!" That was the end of it.

Tanks, Carts and Helicopters

In addition to the EMT bicycle program, I developed the Self-Containing Breathing Apparatus (SCBA) for the state capitol CHP officers. This stemmed from a truck driver who drove into the capitol in a suicide attempt and set it on fire. The SCBA was an air tank, much like a scuba; it had a face mask and a regulator. This air tank allowed the officer to breathe regular air when working within smoky areas. The idea was to use them solely to evacuate the capitol, nothing else. The SCBAs had low-air alarms on them, alerting the user when the air level was low. I put it together, led everyone through the training, and did the testing of the equipment. I also developed, at the request of Assistant Commissioner Kevin Green, a smaller EMT kit to replace the large medical bag that went into the patrol cars.

Then, every other month for a year, I rode in a CHP helicopter that was assigned to the CHP Academy as a flight medic/observer. I could've done it full time, but I didn't think it was fair. I pulled my friend Rodney in, and we switched off so we could both get the experience. We were counterparts once again. After some changes, the helicopter was moved to a small community in the foothills above the valley called Auburn, but I didn't want to go there. Instead, I went back to the capitol and developed an emergency medical technician cart under the direction of Captain Dennis Williams.

It seemed that my life followed in the footsteps of my dad. I was a police officer, but as the years wore on, I moved toward aspects of safety, coming up with products and programs that helped the Highway Patrol save lives more efficiently.

I'm not the guy who just showed up and got his paycheck. I'm also not the knight in shining armor, and I haven't lived the perfect life. I've done some things I'm not proud of. However, I've always had a sense that there are things that are inherently right and things that are inherently wrong. I am blessed to be in the middle to keep things that are right and true and safe in their place and keep the things that aren't away. I'm blessed to be able to arrest the bad guys, to try and change some lives for the better. I'm blessed to be able to help people. I have a passion for it; probably inherited from my parents.

Military

Once my father died in the car accident, my mother's brother, Uncle Bill, was really my only male role model. Uncle Bill was a humble, quiet man. He was kind and giving, yet a man's man. He grew up during the Depression, so at times he had to hunt for food. He worked in the coal mines, which made him a rough-and-tumble guy. He got a lot of pleasure from hunting, four-wheel driving, and camping.

My cousins used to tell a story about when they were camping in the middle of nowhere, and a bear invaded their camp. Uncle Bill immediately grabbed a garbage can lid and a club and started banging the club against the lid, moving aggressively toward the bear. The bear stood up on his hind legs in protest, but Uncle Bill eventually chased him away. I had visions of Uncle Bill posturing himself in between his family and the predator. He didn't hesitate or back down. I never forgot that story.

Uncle Bill had been in the navy on crash boats in World War II. They were tasked to rescue air crews shot down in the ocean. It was hard work. He told us they had recovered bodies, but never survivors. It bothered him that he never rescued an airman alive.

My dad never went into the military but wanted to participate in World War II. He was in law enforcement at the time, and there was talk of releasing him to the military. Because he was older, they kept him stateside. It was one of his few regrets.

I took all of this in and it drove me. Right out of high school, I wanted to go into the military. I wanted to jump out of airplanes and kill people. But when I talked with a recruiter, they wanted me to do something else. I didn't want what they were offering. So I didn't go in as a young man. Instead, I went into law enforcement.

Seven years into my law enforcement career, I recognized I still had a need to serve in the military. Even though I was serving my state and community, I hadn't yet served my country. I remembered my dad's and uncle's regrets, so I became a reservist in the US Navy in 1994, serving with Special Boat Teams[5]. For several years I served in the navy, just like my uncle Bill.

And then, 9/11 hit.

---

5   Special boat teams are part of Navy Special Forces (Specwar).

A NEW MISSION

> "I can hear you, the rest of the world can hear you and the people who knocked these buildings down will hear all of us soon."
> George W. Bush

> "The events of 9-11 set me on a path that I had never intended. Much of who I have become today was determined by images from the other side of the country...black smoke boiling from burning towers over the city skyline...a proud and defiant American flag raised by brave and weary heroes over rubble and devastation. Those images I can never forget..."
> SGT Michael Ferguson

September 11, 2001
Northern California

"Emmett, turn on the TV. You're not going to believe it."

A fellow officer and close friend was on the phone and had interrupted my sleep. It was a beautiful morning in Northern California on September 11, 2001. My wife, Rhonda, and I had just returned from a trip to Colorado. We had plans for the day with the kids—something a highway patrolman does in the middle of the work week. I turned on the television, wiping my eyes to focus.

"What the hell?!"

28 Selfish Prayer

The live feed showed the Twin Towers on fire. Then they replayed a tape that showed an airliner plowing into the second tower. My stomach tightened. I felt heat rising in my neck, and my jaw clenched. Obviously this wasn't an accident.

Who would do such a thing?

Our plans for the day faded away as Rhonda and I sat glued to the television. We watched in horror as the Pentagon was hit and the Towers fell. I knew that many of my law enforcement brothers, military brothers and sisters, and firemen were killed doing what they do.

Doing what *I* do.

Sacramento, California

Early Tuesday morning, Mike Ferguson drove his old, beat-up pickup truck through Sacramento to the fire academy. He rode in silence, his short black hair bending in the cool, open window air. It was Mike's fourth day of classes, and he was excited. He'd gotten a taste of firefighting about seven years earlier, when as a newlywed he and his wife spent time in Oregon with her grandparents. They contracted with the forestry service to fight fires up there. He'd spent that entire vacation on the fire line and knew this was what he wanted to do.

He joined up with his buddy, Rob Walters, and they headed for class. Some of the other guys mentioned something about an aircraft crashing into the World Trade Center. Mike and Rob had thoughts of a small plane sticking out of the burning building. They never imagined it was an airliner.

Class began like normal. They had a guest lecture from Coach Al Baeta, a big name in US Olympic Track and Field and the godfather of firefighter physical fitness in the Sacramento Fire Department. Halfway through the class, the academy drill master interrupted the speaker. He was visibly shaken as he announced that one of the twin towers had fallen, and hundreds of brother firefighters from FDNY had perished.

The entire academy class of recruits was put on notice that they would be sent to Travis Air Force Base to assist with the mobilization of the FEMA Urban Search and Rescue Team (Task Force 7), which was sponsored by the Sacramento Fire Department. The class was given a long break, then tried to proceed with classes for a little while until the drill master returned with the horrible news that the second tower had fallen. He released them for the day to be with their families.

Before they were dismissed, the captain challenged them to reflect on whether or not they wanted to continue in this career in light of the loss of hundreds of firefighters. He advised them that there would be no shame in deciding it wasn't for them.

Every one of those recruits stayed.

Alexandria, Virginia

Captain Jimmy Blackmon was born and raised in Ranger, Georgia. His parents worked at the cotton mill, and his future looked to be much the same. There was never a question about what he would do; the only question was which shift would be the most conducive to his lifestyle when he grew up.

Then a United States Army recruiter came through town and knocked on the door. "How'd you like to be in the army?" he asked. Remembering his dad's wool Eisenhower jacket from Korea hanging in the closet, Jimmy answered in his thick, Georgian drawl, "Well, I'd love to."

Basic training for Jimmy was a Forest Gump-like experience. He obeyed what they told him and he succeeded just fine. He loved boot camp! That was the beginning of Blackmon's army career. He never went back to work in the cotton mill.

On 9/11, Captain Blackmon was working for the Department of the Army Secretariat for Promotion and Selection Boards, located in old town Alexandria, Virginia. He drove into work on the 495 listening to the Jack Diamond morning show. They said a plane had just hit the World Trade Tower. Jimmy had this vision of a small plane stickin' out of a window.

Some idiot has flown his Cessna into the World Trade Center...

Jimmy parked the car and took the elevator to the fifth story. His co-workers had CNN on, and he saw the tower burning and then watched the second plane hit. About that time, they all felt a jolt—a shock wave through the building. Looking wide-eyed at each other, they asked, "What was that?!"

Jimmy went to the window and saw thick, black smoke rising up from the Pentagon.

Uh oh. Life just changed.

Sacramento, California

Al Smoot was acting fire captain at Station 13 in Land Park, Sacramento. He woke up early and put on the coffee. He turned on the TV in the kitchen and saw the World Trade Tower burning. He watched a bit, wondering.

How the fuck do you fight that fire?

About that time, the second tower was hit, and Al knew right then it was a terrorist attack. He knew there were hundreds of firefighters in that building, going up and going to work.

How are they gonna put that out?

Smoot could feel the emotion just below the surface. His training as a fireman and as a flight medic in the California National Guard switched on, and he pushed away the thoughts of fallen brothers with the best way to approach the rescues. He was tough as nails on the outside, but his compassion for people on the inside was sometimes more than he could stomach. Harsh language, a little shock factor, and stern concentration on the task at hand were enough to harness feelings brewing beneath the surface. Still, these thoughts drove him.

I don't want to wake up the crew. Let them have their last moments of peace before they wake up and realize the whole fuckin' world's changed.

After Al had some coffee and watched events unfold, the guys started waking up. He brought them in to see what was going on, and about that time, the Pentagon was hit. They were shocked.

How the hell do you fight those fires?

Al knew that when the planes plowed through the towers, they sheered the standpipes. If there aren't working standpipes, water won't be able to rise above the impact floors. In a building that big there are additional pumps that pump water from the ground and then up the rest of the way. They won't get an adequate amount of water if those pumps don't work. As they were discussing this, Al predicted the building would go down.

"There's no way they're gonna put that fire out. All they're doing is getting people out of there; there's no way to fight that fire! New York has thousands of firemen on duty every day—still they cannot put that fire out. It's either going all the way up, or the building comes down."

A few minutes later, it did just that.

It was a total shock to all except Smoot.

He had attended the Fire Department Instructors Conference (FDIC) in Sacramento with a number of FDNY firefighters. He just knew some of them were in the buildings.

Get everyone else out of the second tower…it's comin' down too.

The city of Alexandria was evacuated. Chaos reigned. Captain Blackmon couldn't make a cell phone call in DC because there was no way to get a signal. His family didn't know where he was. He returned to his car and started home. It took hours. As he drove, he began to think about who was behind this attack.

We'll be headed somewhere soon to get these guys…

As the day unfolded, everyone was responding to help needed on the East Coast. Smoot got a phone call from his National Guard unit and was put on alert. He told the Guard he couldn't leave—Sacramento fire's Urban Search and Rescue (USAR) team was heading out, and they were maximized. Smoot was held at the firehouse until after the USAR team was mobilized, when they found a fireman to relieve him late that night. Rather than going home, he stayed and talked with the guys for hours, when they started to get a real idea of how many firemen were lost.

The next morning Smoot and the others did a "boot drive" to collect money for the victims and families of the fallen. As motorists went by, they slowed down and dropped cash into the boots.

I remember this because I was working downtown. The firemen were standing in traffic on Sacramento's I Street, between 12th and 13th, holding their big rubber boots. As a cop on patrol, I was concerned at the time, thinking they were gonna get clipped by a car, although traffic was moving fairly slow and people seemed eager to help. I didn't know Smoot yet, but I witnessed the boot drive.

As a flight medic with the Guard, Smoot thought they'd be deployed soon, but it turned out to be another year before they were sent. In the year that followed the attack, the Guard started focusing on Afghanistan, modifying the training to include high-altitude combat work. They'd done work in the Sierras before but switched to a different focus. They pushed up the risk assessment, beginning to do hoist missions in the mountains, one- and two-wheel landings, and combat hoisting techniques. They focused in on Sked© work, which was putting people on litters and safely drawing them up to the aircraft.

The Mission: Operation Enduring Freedom 2001-Present

Within a month of the attacks, President Bush committed the nation to pursuing those responsible. They learned it was al-Qaeda, a terrorist organization under the leadership of the infamous Osama bin

Laden, who planned the operation, paid for it, and carried it out. On October 7, 2001, Operation Enduring Freedom was launched with the mission to dismantle al-Qaeda and its base in Afghanistan, remove the terrorist-supporting Taliban regime from power, and create a democratic state in its place.

Along with our Coalition allies, we successfully ousted the Taliban from Kabul in a matter of weeks. We quickly declared victory. In December 2001, the International Security Assistance Force (ISAF) was created to secure the capital, Kabul, and surrounding areas from returning Taliban. The first elections were held in 2005. But before we secured the ability of the Afghans to defend themselves, we focused our attention on Iraq.

And, of course, al-Qaeda didn't go quietly. By 2003, the Taliban regrouped and created an insurgency campaign based out of Pakistan. We realized later that we had both an insurgency and a civil war going on, which complicated things. It was happening right underneath us.

Afghanistan has a long and deep history of battles, typically with the home team coming out on top. Alexander the Great came through and eventually got his ass kicked. The Mongols lost there as well. Even the Russians, in more recent history, could not tame the wildness of the people and terrain in Afghanistan.

The people are different throughout the country. Afghans who live in the cities have a completely different culture than those who live in the country. The religion is the same, but the way of life is completely different between Kabul and Kandahar. In the remote areas, life is largely tribal. Each of the valleys is completely clannish. The differences create conflict out of the smallest issues, and they have fought against each other for centuries.

Once the United States came in and set up shop, the villagers had to survive. Because they are master survivalists, they are not necessarily going to pick a side. They take part in *shuras*, where they sit down in a key leadership engagement and discuss what the village needs. We want intelligence details and information in return, but they don't give us much.

The Afghans are not there to be in confrontation with the rifles; they are there to live their lives in little villages in a remote area of the world. It has been this way for generation after generation in their tribal areas. When someone with a rifle shows up and wants to give them a pump for their well, they'll be gracious about it. It also doesn't mean that they will choose that side from beyond that contact. Because after the Americans leave, there will be another regime, and they have to survive.

The only Afghans who have really chosen to be on our side are those in the Afghan National Army (ANA), Afghan National Police (ANP) and Afghan Border Police (ABP). Those are the guys who are making a choice, especially when they are going from point to point. Once they leave their tribal area, not only are they outsiders, but they are strangers in their country in some respects.

Generally there are three kinds of people who are engaged in battle with the Americans. First, the locals who are paid to fight. They are trying to earn extra money, and they are not emotionally attached to the war. Second, there are mercenaries coming in from Pakistan over Alexander the Great trade routes—again, usually just for the money. Third, there are jihadists, who are emotionally attached to the issue, such as al-Qaeda and the Taliban.

Along with the town issues and tribal areas and the layers of distrust among them, there were also layers of complexities to their simple way of life—as simple as the illegal logging in the Korengal. The Marine

Corps went in and told them to stop, and the locals got angry. Who the hell were we? Not only were we promising them stuff in hope of support and information, now we're telling them not to do something that will support their lifestyle. It would be like telling them not to grow opium or grow corn. That doesn't go over well.

To make matters worse, whenever the jihadists killed someone or ruined something, they blamed the Americans. This angered many of the locals and created a hostile environment for our troops.

We'd been fighting since 2001, with increased violence since 2006. Attacks, IEDs, and battles have taken many lives of American and Coalition soldiers as well as the enemy. Much blood has been spilled. At the time of this writing in early 2013, the American plan is to power down our presence in Afghanistan and let the nationals take over. The idea is to be gone by 2014.

After the initial shock and mourning of 9/11, I thought a lot about what happened, and what my response would be. I was with the US Navy, but I wasn't sure if I would be able to accomplish what I wanted—to get at those who'd done this to us. Those who were responsible had to pay; I had a need for vengeance.

Deployment

I'd been to Central and South America with the US Navy, but this did nothing to fulfill the need for retaliation born on 9/11. At the time, there weren't many boat teams going to Afghanistan—A land of mountains, rocks, and caves.

I'd heard of a medevac program with the California National Guard (CNG) and that they were looking for paramedics. There was a problem, however. I had a prejudice against the Guard. In 1987, I worked with the National Guard Counter Drug people, and they were not a high-caliber group at the time. In fact, they were a bunch of knuckleheads. So I had a deep distrust for the Guard. And, to be fair, the movies I'd watched—like *Rambo*—usually portrayed the Guard as a bunch of buffoons.

As part of Naval Special Warfare (NSW), I'd worked with some high-caliber people. This was a tough transition for me. But I swallowed my pride and met with National Guard medevac personnel anyway. It was then I realized that times had changed, so I talked with a recruiter.

The result was a trial year—this was the shortest amount of time that I could join the CNG. I told the recruiter if I didn't get everything I was promised within that year, I would go back to Special Boat Teams. The recruiter told me that I could fly Search and Rescue (SAR) and medevac missions for the State of California and would likely deploy soon. I agreed.

The recruiter told me that there was a fire captain in downtown Sacramento that I could talk to about Medevac. I visited Fire Station Two and talked with Al Smoot. Struck right away by all of the La-Z-Boys around the television, I entered the station. Al was cooking away, like all good firefighters do, and we hit it off, even though he was a fireman and I was a cop. We had a conversation about Medevac. From there I interviewed with a panel, and they drilled me on patient care. Evidently I did OK, because I was in.

Well, one year turned into three, and I still hadn't deployed. So I jumped ship to a field artillery unit, because I just couldn't take it anymore. I deployed to Iraq as a ground medic and worked in a place that did not exist with people who were not there. I can talk about it in about sixty-eight years—maybe that'll be my next book.

Marriages

In the midst of it all, I blew through two marriages. As you can see, I was not balanced. My passion for being a police officer, a medic, and a military man drove me forward. That passion took me beyond the streets of Northern California to Thailand, Central/South America, Puerto Rico, Kuwait, Iraq, Afghanistan, Peru, and all over the United States, including Alaska.

I don't know if I'm the guy who should've had marriage and family. I got married the first time at nineteen, and in my thirties it just fell apart. We had two children together, William and Kaitlin.

Then I met Rhonda. I was married to her for ten years. On my deployment to South America, I came home on an emergency pass. I met up at the airport with my father-in-law. I said, "Thank God I came home to a home-cooked meal." He says, "Nope, we're going to the hospital. She's in labor."

I made it just in time for the birth of my son, Joseph, but after two weeks I had to return to South America. Rhonda and I never recovered from that. After the birth of our son, she had some complications that put her over the edge, and I wasn't there to help. The damage had been done on both sides. We tried twice to work it out, but it wasn't to be.

I don't blame her. I get it. Deployments are hard on spouses. How many women are wired to put up with that shit? It sounds good, and it looks good in the movies, yet it's such a difficult life to live.

Finally, Afghanistan

While I was in Iraq, I learned Charlie Company was deploying to Afghanistan. I had been in contact with Smoot via phone. I really wanted to deploy with them to Afghanistan in 2008, but Al told me I wasn't going. And kept telling me I wasn't going. I got back from Iraq, and he said I was "on the bench" for deployment but probably still wouldn't go.

After a month off, I returned to my job at the California Highway Patrol Academy where I worked for Captain Brent Newman. I was one of the on-call paramedics for the resident cadets on site. At the time they were ramping up to put through some of the largest classes in the history of the patrol.

I told Smoot that I needed to be honest with Captain Newman and the rest of my CHP unit about being deployed again. He responded with a call one night.

"Hey, Emmett! Do you still really want to go to Afghanistan?"

"Well, yeah…I thought I wasn't going. That's what I've told everyone. What's going on?"

"I have to be honest. Emmett, at this point I have to take you. It's not an option anymore."

I'd only been home a few months from Iraq. I was to be deployed to Afghanistan in a matter of weeks.

A close friend I worked with was vocal about how he felt screwed over and that we would have a giant hole in our unit. He didn't feel good about me leaving again. The only way he could support me was if I were to transfer to another command and/or get a temp to take my place while I was gone. He said if I did that, we wouldn't have any problems emotionally. OK, fine.

Selfish Prayer

I went to Captain Newman. He was very approachable. I didn't tell him about the condition my friend had given me, but I did tell him I didn't feel peaceful about leaving the unit without my position filled. I offered to have him transfer me back to the capitol. He looked at me and said, "No way. Absolutely not gonna happen. I'll get a temp in here; somebody who knows they are a temp, will be a temp, and when you come back, will go away. It'll be great for their career, give them some experience, and when you return, we'll be waiting for you."

I didn't expect that at all. His response came out of left field…in a good way.

I took this back to my friend, and he said we were all warm and fuzzy again. And then two hours later, he blew up at me. There was no making him happy.

The CHP Flag

There were people who were frustrated with me for leaving again so quickly, and there were those who were extraordinarily proud of me. There were those who were willing to suck it up, and those angry about the void. I had this roller coaster of emotions from other people I was dealing with, as well as my own. I had to stand tall and take the high road and be gracious to those who were angry. And I was extremely grateful to those I had in my corner.

Assistant Commissioner Kevin Green was a tall man, and funnier than shit. By way of Assistant Commissioner Max Santiago, he put some heavy responsibility on me at times. I ate it up, was happy to do it, but man, there were some sleepless nights with some of the projects he had me take on. In my mind, Kevin Green was a visionary. He was always looking to expand our duties and serve the people of California well beyond the traditional Highway Patrol role. Green was a tall, somewhat thin man with a presence about him. He, like Max, was articulate and also had a sorry-ass mustache.

At one point, Green needed some CHP boats as soon as possible before a fiscal deadline. Max knew that I had a lot of experience with boats and put me in charge of researching, finding and recommending for purchase two boats in less than seventy-two hours. The Highway Patrol bought off on all my boat recommendations, eventually tasking me with numerous additional related projects.

This project was my first introduction to Commissioner Green. Afterward, I considered Max and Kevin friends. I came to trust both men and have a tremendous respect for their leadership and their support of the military.

Max Santiago had served over twenty-one years in the United States Army Reserves and California Army National Guard as a Military Police Platoon Sergeant and CID Special Agent (Criminal Investigator). During his service, he attained the rank of Sergeant First Class and deployed on missions to Central America, the Republic of Korea, Republic of the Philippines, and the Kingdom of Saudi Arabia. He is a veteran of Operation Desert Shield, Operation Desert Storm, and the Southwest Asia Cease-Fire Campaign.

Kevin was also Military Police. He picked up a secondary MOS of 71 Delta as a legal clerk and was the only military police observer on an OH-58[6]. He left military service in 1981 as an E5 because the CHP had begun hiring large numbers of people after a long slowdown. Green, like me, had always wanted to be a police officer.

Just before I left for Afghanistan, Green came to a little going-away party for me. He handed me a folded California Highway Patrol flag.

---

6 A Kiowa helicopter

"I want you to have this," he said.

"What's the deal?"

"We want you to take this with you. We want you to know that you have a home with us back here. We're family."

Whoa...

"I'll take it, but I'm not going to accept it for myself," I muttered. "I'll accept it for every highway patrol service member, and I'll take it in their honor. I want this thing to have a history."

The flag was specifically designed to fly over the new headquarters building that hadn't broken ground yet. They broke ground while I was gone, and they didn't have that flag. I had it.

It took me awhile to figure out what I wanted to do with it. In Iraq, I'd seen people fly flags on missions and then send them home. That was cool, but they were other people's missions. When I got into country, I took some extra clothing out of my go-to-hell bag[8] and tucked it there. That bag flew with me wherever I went. As a highway patrol officer and service member, this flag would be with me on all missions.

Mike Ferguson, Rob Walters, and Al Smoot were deployed with me in 2008-2009 to Afghanistan as fellow flight medics. Rob and Al were already with the California National Guard when 9/11 occurred. Mike eventually joined, as did I, when we both realized that the branches of military we had joined would not provide the action we craved. We met

---

8 An emergency bag containing extra ammo, water and clothing in case we were shot down

Jimmy Blackmon in 2008 in Afghanistan. He was the Commander of Task Force PaleHorse, a true leader, and eventual friend.

The events of 9/11 changed the course of our country. Just months earlier during the presidential election debates between George W. Bush and Al Gore, terrorism wasn't even a topic to be mentioned. That day awakened a mission within the minds and resolve of Americans everywhere. Thousands joined the Armed Forces, ready to contribute to the new war effort. A patriotism that had long been sleeping came alive, and it needed something to do.

As for me, a California Highway Patrolman, a flight paramedic, and a military reservist, 9/11 set me on a course for the mission I carry forward to this day.

Along the way, I learned of another battle—one that had been going on for years within the US Army itself. I didn't sign on to this battle for vengeance; it was a motivated activism that came from deep within.

RIGHTING WRONGS

"No man in the wrong can stand up to a man in the right who just a keeps on a coming."
Motto of the Texas Rangers

"If we can get 60,000 people all-you-can-eat crab legs once a week into a landlocked third world country, but we can't get 270[10] people (the entire flight medic inventory) to EMT-Paramedic, something is wrong."
MAJ Robert L. Mabry, MD

**El Paso, Texas
December 1989**

On December 9, 1989, the police Mountain Rescue Team from El Paso, Texas, was called to assist a family in the Franklin Mountains. Their nine-year-old daughter, Debra[11], had fallen while hiking, and they suspected a broken ankle. The team arrived at dusk, packaged the girl on a litter, and tried to carry her out on foot. It didn't work, as the terrain was too steep. With darkness closing in and temperatures dropping, they made the decision to call in army assistance from Fort Sam Houston. They were requested to evacuate the patient via a cable line from a hovering medevac helicopter. This is called a hoist extraction.

---

10 This was the number at the time. We are now pushing over 1,000.
11 This is a pseudonym.

Selfish Prayer

A UH-1V Huey helicopter responded and hoisted their medic down fifty feet while the ground rescuers directed them in with flashlights. The active-duty flight medic did a quick check of the litter, attached it to a cable line and sent Debra up.

Immediately the litter started spinning uncontrollably.

"Oh my God! She's spinning! Lower her back down!" the flight medic shouted.

The crew chief flipped the control switch and the litter hesitated and then changed direction, though still spinning. At thirty feet above the ground, those with night vision goggles watched in horror as Debra catapulted feet first out of the litter and crashed against the mountain in the dark.

The medic panicked. "Oh shit! I lost her! Where'd she go?!"

Family and rescuers on the ground began a frantic search with help from the helicopter lights above. They found her crumpled against the mountain, in far worse shape than a broken ankle. The flight medic administered first aid and then firmly secured her to an army Sked litter. The Mountain Rescue Team suggested they use tag lines on both ends of the litter, which is simply rope attached and held by rescuers on the ground to prevent spinning. Soon the child was on her way to William Beaumont Army Medical Center.

Debra spent the next four months in a body cast. She suffered head and internal injuries, a fractured pelvis, and other broken bones.

An investigation revealed there were several reasons this happened. They found several mistakes made by both the Mountain Rescue Team and army Medevac. Among others, reasons included the initial absence of the tag line to prevent spinning, the flight medic's lack of knowledge and training, and the army's lack of guidelines/recommendations for this practice.

Fort Bliss, Texas 1990

A year later, Al Smoot was mobilized to Fort Bliss on the other side of the Franklin Mountains through the California National Guard and provided medevac support to civilians near El Paso. This deployment was a Military Assistance to Safety and Traffic (MAST) mission. He concurrently served with the CNG as an infantry medic and as a civilian-trained paramedic alongside his preceptor[12], Danny Corder. When Smoot arrived at Fort Bliss, he was told of the incident in the mountains. It was a story that haunted Medevac and was fresh on the minds of those who served.

Nothing upset Smoot as much as stupidity and decisions made with the wrong priorities. Especially when others paid the price. He'd learned this at eight years old when he drove the family car home as his father was too drunk to drive. These early circumstances made him a survivor, a rescuer, and cemented a deep-seated mission to do the right thing.

Smoot recognized the problems within Medevac. He saw that the training of flight medics was severely lacking—in their medical training as well as rescue. In Smoot's mind, poorly trained medics were writing checks the patient's ass couldn't cash.

There are three levels of an Emergency Medical Technician. The first is an EMT-Basic, in which the technician is trained in CPR, defibrillation, controlling severe external bleeding (applying tourniquets), preventing

---

12 A paramedic preceptor mentors and evaluates paramedic interns in a field setting.

shock, immobilization of the body to prevent spinal damage, and splinting bone fractures. They are allowed to administer non-prescription drugs, such as aspirin and EpiPens. This level requires 120 hours of training.

The second level is EMT-Intermediate. This includes interventions of the EMT-B but also includes IV therapy, the use of advanced airway devices, and provides for advanced assessment skills. They are trained in techniques such as chest decompressions, endotracheal intubation, and use of cardiac monitors and can administer some medications to control cardiac arrhythmias. This level requires 250-500 hours of training.

The highest level is an EMT-Paramedic. This level includes all of the above but also pharmaceutical administration, fluid resuscitation, cardiac monitoring, obtaining IV access, and other advanced procedures. The hours required for certification are 1,200–1,500.

The army standard for flight medic training was equivalent to an EMT-Basic. In El Paso, Texas, the rescues Medevac was asked to do required a higher-level skill set than this.

While Smoot went through paramedic school, Danny Corder was his partner and later his preceptor. They went on many calls together in Sacramento County. When they were mobilized to El Paso, they were the only two that were licensed and trained to work the calls. The active-duty EMTs were not trained nor did they have the experience to deal with the serious calls they were expected to answer. Consequently there were a few outcomes that weren't good, such as the Franklin Mountain incident. In Smoot's mind, this was unacceptable.

For four months straight, Corder and Smoot responded to calls in remote locations while the others were trained up to an EMT-Intermediate level. It was exhausting.

Danny Corder was a para-rescuer from Vietnam. Short, balding, and a little on the pudgy side, he usually didn't say much about his former deployment. One night, at a dining-in event, some officers noticed his Air Force Cross and asked him about it. He went on to tell them of a rescue in North Vietnam in which while retrieving a pilot who was shot down, his own aircraft was shot down and the entire crew killed. Danny escaped and evaded back into South Vietnam to friendly lines with the surviving pilot in tow. He was considered MIA[14] for two months. After he told the story, those at the table were surprised because he was so unassuming.

Sacramento, California
1991 – 2008

Smoot had the utmost respect for Corder. Danny had trained him right; he would do the same for others as his career progressed. But there were other issues. In addition to the obvious training deficits, Smoot had to fight for needed equipment. The US Army freely spent $100K on a helicopter rotor but wouldn't spend $100 on a tagline rope. After two or three years of active arguments, they finally got their rope—but through funding from the California National Guard, not the US Army.

Then a blow came to the entire program. Shortly after the Gulf War, there was a pairing-down of the military as a whole by the Clinton Administration. One of the programs cut was the MAST mission, thus ending all real-time training for army active-duty flight medics. The only way to obtain real-life experience was on calls.

About the same time there was a mass exodus from the military as they lost a large number of people who had joined for the college money. Smoot took this as an opportunity and became the standardization

---
14 Missing in action

instructor for the unit when that position came open. This allowed him the ability to recruit paramedics. As guys retired or moved on, Al brought in paramedics to replace them. At first, there was push back. He was told, "You can't do that!" His answer? "Well, I just did."

This began to change the face of CNG Medevac—our Sacramento unit's standards were higher for medical training. The CNG as a department then required its own medics to be certified EMT-Basics. This was a full fifteen years ahead of its army active-duty counterparts.

When the CNG was called up to Bosnia in 1998, Al's unit was better than 50 percent paramedic. They were the first aviation medical unit mobilized since Vietnam. While in Bosnia, they introduced themselves to the doctors and were allowed to do more as trust was placed in their abilities. About that time they started receiving more advanced medical equipment. Under Al's leadership, the entire unit was maintaining an overall standard of EMT–Intermediate care.

California was not the only place this occurred. Oregon did this as well and currently has 70 percent paramedics in their program. But big army did not support this movement. Al realized it was very important to start educating people—because decision makers had no idea what Medevac was doing.

Smoot ran his mouth. Medevac was responsible for en route care, sometimes for up to an hour. If the flight medic didn't know how to care for the patient, the patient grew worse and could even die. When there was an initial injury, medics on the ground and in the air could stop the bleeding, get a basic airway, and give them oxygen. That wasn't the problem. If the patient needed intubation, medicines, and advanced care right away, but the flight medic didn't have this knowledge or training, the patient could die in the helicopter. When patients came out of surgery and then needed to be transported to a hospital, it was these same medics who went with them. Ninety percent of what these patients needed was above and beyond the abilities of an EMT-Basic. If anything changed, which was often the case, the EMT-Basic medic was in over his or her head. That's when people died.

By 1998, training for EMT-Basic was mandated by the army, but by this time Al had already guided our Sacramento unit well beyond that standard. The Guard had already started recruiting civilian paramedics, who were of better quality because they already had the training and ongoing experience. As reservists, typically the Guard doesn't have a lot of time to train.

In 2003, Smoot and Walters were deployed to Afghanistan. This was crucial. Unit Commander Major Bruce Balzano took a stand that he would not take anybody but paramedics. When the 126th assumed control of the mission, Smoot and Walters found the active-duty flight medics they were relieving were very inexperienced, even though they'd been there a year. There were ventilators in the aircraft, but no training on how to use them. The prior medevac had been picking up patients but couldn't fully manage their care. This was troubling, as patients were a lot sicker than those in Kosovo. They were also under fire in Afghanistan, and transport times were much longer.

The Problem Defined

Medevac is an area of specialty that army leaders did not understand. The statistics for soldier mortality in Iraq and Afghanistan were the same as in Vietnam. The difference is that we're forty years smarter—advanced medical training is available to us that was not developed until after Vietnam. The attitude of mediocrity was killing our soldiers.

There was a gap within medevac transport. On one side of that gap is the FST. Before that gap is the combat medic in the field. The combat medic can put a tourniquet on, pack a wound, decompress a chest, maybe put in a nasal-pharyngeal airway (NPA), and he's pretty much wrapped the whole thing up as long as Medevac can get to him within a reasonable amount of time. An hour-long critical care transport to and from surgery is where the gap is. Everything that surrounds the patient's care, from the field medic to the FST, is great. The crucial exception is the movement piece. But it's significance is huge.

Those who oversee us think a patient simply moves from point A to point B when they call Medevac for transport. They don't understand why patients die en route or show up in horrible condition. They readily acknowledge patients have shown up hypothermic, hypoxic, and hypovolemic, yet don't understand why they don't survive. It seems they assume Medevac puts them inside a vacuum tube, and they immediately arrive with no additional deficits.

In reality it is an extremely intensive hour. Flight medics give blood, maintain paralysis, maintain temperature, maintain oxygenation status, and many other life-sustaining procedures. About half the time, we've juggled another patient lying next to him, needing care much the same.

Our Turn
2008

Learning from the deployment in 2003, we set up for our 2008 deployment. Walters and Smoot had been to Afghanistan and saw what was needed, and they started putting together a team and a plan. Among other paramedics, they brought in Ferguson, myself and Ruben Higgins.

We began our training several months before heading out. We did hoist missions and practiced medical care in the back of the helicopters. Any time Al heard the pilots were doing a training mission, he put medics and crew chiefs in the back to train. We continued our medical training for the mountains of Afghanistan well into our time at Fort Sill, Oklahoma, which geographically was as flat as a pancake.

Then we underwent what we called the draft. Based on experience and abilities, Al and senior enlisted and officers placed us where we were best suited. I was one of those strategically placed medics. Because I had key contacts from Iraq, I had decided Bagram would be the best place for me. I felt I could get my hands on meds and gear we may need in country, and Bagram was where ordering took place. But then Al came to me and said Jalalabad was where he needed me to go.

"That's where the hoisting is," he said. "I need you to do hoists in the mountains. You have the most stateside mission experience."

Hoisting happens when the terrain or circumstances are such that the aircraft can't land. We swoop in to where the wounded are, and the medic is lowered down on a cable to render medical aid. The medic then packages up the patients, sends them up the cable, and hooks on, and then we fly off to the closest FST. I had done this with the Guard many times. My abilities placed me in Jalalabad, lovingly referred to as Jbad. I was joined by medics Marc Dragony, Nate Whorton and Smoot.

For Rob, Mike, and Ben, long-transport critical care was their specialty. We planned who went where. Our commanders listened. The right people went to the right places. Bagram was the best place for them.

Arrival in Afghanistan
December 2008

Jalalabad fell under Task Force PaleHorse, which fell underneath Task Force Thunder in Bagram. We were with the 7th Squadron 17th Cavalry Regiment of the 159th Combat Aviation Brigade, 101st Airborne Division.

There is such a rich history within the 101st Airborne. Although I'm really a city boy, I like to think I'm a cowboy from rural Northern California, so this was very appealing. These guys wore Stetsons and spurs and had a whole culture surrounding what scouts were from the old days. Nowadays they fly Kiowas—small attack helicopters—and essentially are scouts. They go in ahead of everyone with guns, engage enemy, and report back. They do crazy things like fly low and slow and get it on with the bad guys.

Task Force PaleHorse included the Pale Element, which was the Kiowa UH-58s. We had Apaches (AH-64s), otherwise known as Blue Max and the Black Widows, which were Black Hawk escorts (UH-60s). These helicopters were the gunships and rained hell on the enemy. We had CH-47s (Chinooks) that did transports and were armed as well. DUSTOFF, or Medevac, flew UH-60 helicopters and were unarmed according to Geneva Convention restrictions.

PaleHorse also included the Pathfinders, who were infantry soldiers responsible for setting up impromptu runways in the midst of combat, recovering downed aircraft, and clearing hot zones so helicopters can land.

Leadership

We arrived at Bagram Air Field in Afghanistan. We completed a RIPTOA, which stands for Relief in Place; Transfer of Authority. Once that was complete, we were waiting on the flight line at the airfield in Bagram to fly out to Jalalabad. This is where we met LTC Jimmy Blackmon, the incoming task force commander.

That boy just walked up and said, "I'm Jimmy Blackmon. I am the PaleHorse CO. You're the Medevac guys, right?"

We responded that we were indeed Medevac and were glad to meet him. He was very friendly, very approachable. Almost like a human being, even though he was an officer. It gave me immediate comfort, because he seemed very grounded. This is important when you go into things you don't know about. We found later that he was willing to lead instead of allowing us to fail first and then give direction. In Afghanistan, failing could be death.

Smoot was the platoon sergeant (E-7), so he was in charge of all the enlisted there in Jbad. I was in charge of the medics. I was an E-6. Although I worked for him because he was the NCOIC (non-commissioned officer in charge), he worked for me because I was the lead medic. So we had this unique dynamic. He would step into areas that were mine as an E-7, and I would tell him knock it off, get back in your lane. He would get mad, and then he'd realize that I was right and we'd both get over it and move on. We had our moments, but overall we had a great working relationship.

Al Smoot is a guy who wants to have his fingers on the pulse of it. He's the guy who promoted because it was the right thing to do for Medevac, but it didn't give him personal satisfaction. He didn't want to be the guy who had to do the bullshit paperwork; he'd rather go out and fly missions and save people. That's what he really wanted, so he did. Sometimes he'd step on my toes. I understood who Al was but had to tell him, diplomatically, "That was my spot. These are my medics."

Captain David Lovett was the OIC[16] of Medevac. We had our pilot core. We had medics, crew chiefs, and maintenance mechanics, who did all the maintenance when the aircraft was on the ground. We had operations personnel that took all the radio calls and were in charge of communications. Together, we made up DUSTOFF.

---

16 Officer in charge

The RIP

We did our right seat-left seat ride, which is basically the procedure for taking over a mission from those who'd been there the last year. It's referred to as the RIP. I immediately discovered they did things differently. But during a right seat-left seat ride, my attitude was that these guys had been here for a year, so see what's right about it, what's not right about it, and adjust. They showed us the compound, where the food was, where the store was, etc. They showed us FOB Fenty (forward operating base) – the place we would live and function in for the next year. Then they flew us to the training area, which was outside the FOB but was a relatively safe area to train as a flight crew. They showed us the routes, land areas and rivers, other FOBs, and FSTs. We looked around, observed what they did, who was there, and how they ran things.

On the very first medevac I did, I worked with the medic I was to replace. He was a great guy and received a Silver Star for the work he did there, which was uncommon. I learned then that they didn't have any pain medications on board with them. I couldn't believe it. When we landed in Jbad, I hopped off the aircraft to go with the patient. The pilot who was with the prior group asked our pilot, Jason Penrod, "Where's he goin'?"

Jason answered, "He's going in to do a patient care report."

"We don't do that!" the pilot scolded.

"Yeah, yeah we do."

These medics were not following the patients in to communicate with the FST. The FSTs had no baseline or trending vitals, no information regarding what interventions had been made, what they had observed, medications given, or even what their injuries were. They basically dumped patients, then left to reset the aircraft.

This is so out of standard for emergency medical services in the States. You would lose your license if you did that in a civilian emergency room (ER). The civilian standard is not "drop and run." Even in theater, we usually had time to do good patient care and a good patient turnover report. Here's where army active-duty pilots had a basic misunderstanding. They expected the medic to stay in the aircraft and clean up the helicopter without giving patient care turnover reports, which is critical to quality patient care. The turnover was first. If we had time, we would many times assist with care, and then we returned to the aircraft for cleanup and reset.

Stepping in we saw there were huge differences. We'd go to FOBs and FSTs and give them a patient report—at first they didn't know what to do with us. Stateside, they're used to that. They're board-certified; they're expected to run the program above the level of the civilian counterpart. But they had gotten used to the flight medic dropping patients and running, so when we came in and gave reports, they didn't know what to think. But because the personnel in FSTs are rock stars, they very quickly recognized that we were different. The dysfunction went away. It was a huge relief.

How we did our tactics was different as well. Typically the army worries about training because they don't want training accidents. If someone gets hurt when you're in charge, it counts against you. So the thought is, "We're not going to risk this on a stateside mission—it's not worth it." People get hurt in training—we're in the fucking army! You don't do it unnecessarily, but you gotta train to be ready in real time.

What I witnessed in the RIP was the manifestation of dysfunctional army training.

When I went through my flight medic training in Fort Rucker, Alabama, they talked about the hoist, and we practiced on a tower. We were hoisted up, hoisted down, and then we got to run the hoist controls. Hoist somebody up, hoist somebody down. Then they used an old piece-of-crap Huey to hover forty feet above the ground. We had to run over, hook in to the hoist and they'd raise us up and then lower us down. Thus, our "real" hoisting experience was complete.

That was it. Any additional hoist training fell to whatever medevac unit medics were assigned to. It was whoever's training program that dictated what experience we received. Thank God my experience was with the CNG—they ran an extraordinarily aggressive and realistic hoisting program. Hoisting is dangerous if you don't have adequate training.

The people we put together in Jbad were well-rounded and experienced, and the ones that lacked experience were very grounded and humble and eager. All the right ingredients. These guys had their human frailties, but all of them at their core, with few exceptions, were givers. They were willing to give everything time and time again.

Doc Kavanagh cares for an Afghan child struck by a vehicle.
Courtesy of Sebastian Rich, Photojournalist

WE'RE NOT IN AMERICA ANYMORE

"And that, ...is the story of our country, one invasion after another... Macedonians. Saddanians. Arabs. Mongols. Now the Soviets. But we're like those walls up there. Battered, and nothing pretty to look at, but still standing."
Khaled Hosseini, A Thousand Splendid Suns

"Our approach was a cooperative mission with lots of support for the local populace with life-saving medical care... We tried to win the Afghans and not just defeat them outright. It made me feel like I was on the right side of history...But it is going to be very difficult to change thousands of years of culture in a decade..."
SSG Rob Walters

Bagram, Afghanistan
December 2008

Mike Ferguson, Rob Walters and Ruben (Ben) Higgins along with Stephen Solum were the flight medics stationed out of Bagram, a large base in northwestern Afghanistan, about sixty kilometers north of Kabul. It is located on an ancient trade route from the Mediterranean to China along the Silk Road. Bagram Airfield, founded by the Americans in 1976, was home to old Russian hangars left from their occupation in the 1980s. This was headquarters. We called it the Flagpole.

Heathe Craig Army Hospital sat right next to the airfield and was the medical hub of the country. It was the last stop before patients were sent home for recovery, usually via Germany. Surrounding areas were largely flat, with the exception of the mountains to the west. Weather from India such as monsoons and thunderstorms made their stay quite interesting.

It is told that when Medevac moved into the hangar at Bagram in 2003, some guys found pictures of hundreds of executed Russians hanging from the rafters after the Taliban came through. It was somewhat disconcerting to look at the place in the photos and know it was directly over the sleeping quarters. Rob Walters, who was there in 2003, heard the story but didn't actually see the pictures because they were confiscated right after they were found. But as he looked at one beam that supported the roof, it was clearly deformed and warped from heat. This led him to believe the Russians were not only hung, but burned. He'd listened to an audio book on the history of Afghanistan so had some insight on the attempted escape and abandonment of the Russians. They were on the run and got slaughtered like so many others on Afghan soil. For Rob, it brought a sense of realism and seriousness to the war at hand. These were very hard people.

Rob and the others were chosen during the draft to go to Bagram because of their medical knowledge. Ben Higgins had been an army medic in the late 1970s-early 1980s in the 82nd Airborne before going to work as a fireman and paramedic in the civilian sector. He became a flight paramedic for a trauma hospital and eventually for the army and took many years of experience with him to Bagram. Quiet and soft-spoken, Ben was always thinking. The brain underneath that salt-and-pepper hair worked well, and a lot of the time he was quite serious. Except for the times when he wasn't. His specialty was settling into the care of a patient in the helicopter for long transports.

The first few weeks in Bagram were for settling in. They did their right seat, left seat, RIP—where the guys who'd been there the past year oriented them to the living quarters, operating procedures, and where the Green Beans coffee and Dairy Queen were located. After they left, the Bagram guys unpacked their stuff, restocked the medical supplies for the new way we were to do things, and wrote new medical protocols.

During the first couple weeks they'd been weathered in a lot. Ferguson didn't even know how close the mountains were, because he'd been unable to see them yet. The smog was thick from the burning the Afghans did to keep warm in the winter. When he finally saw the mountains, he was surprised to see they were right on top of Bagram.

One of the first medevac calls in Bagram was to a New Zealand military FOB to pick up a patient with "female problems." It turned out they transported a fourteen-year-old Afghan girl who had been given a hasty and traumatic cesarean and was showing signs of sepsis.

Eventually the real story was told. This poor girl had been raped and became pregnant as a result. About the time she was beginning to show, her mother and brother took her out to the barn and cut the fetus out. Once the abortion was done, they sewed her up with baling twine. Three days later, when she wasn't doing well, her father took her to the FOB for help.

Higgins picked her up at Bamian, about seventy miles west of Bagram, and transported her back to Heathe Craig Hospital. The transport was uneventful, as she was only in the earliest stages of sepsis and remained stable. At Heathe Craig, she was given powerful antibiotics to fight the developing infection. It was only early recognition, transport, and intervention that allowed her to physically recover after an extended hospital stay. But those at the hospital were reluctant to send her home, afraid that she would be stoned to death for "getting herself into the position of being raped." It became a social and legal issue and got very complicated for those involved.

In the meantime, the brother and mother were arrested, not for what they did to this young girl, but because they had performed an illegal abortion. The rapist was also arrested but then professed his undying love for the girl and agreed to take her as his wife.

Beyond the language and cultural differences, the girl remained distant as she'd been through intense trauma. She had been brutalized already, but that wasn't the end of it. She was actually sent back to wed her attacker, because this evidently was how the family honor was appeased. They now live happily ever after…yeah, right.

This situation gave us the feeling that things were not quite the same here in Afghanistan, to understate it. This just wasn't American and went well outside the realm of a paramedic's experience. It was hard to comprehend.

Women don't have a voice in Afghanistan—even men who were moderates felt this way. It's an ugly thing to be a woman in Afghanistan, especially in remote areas. We saw a woman with nine bullet wounds because two Taliban leaders were sweet on her. Instead of being men and fighting it out between them, they shot her!

Over the coming weeks, we began to understand the blatant differences of human value in this place. In America, we value our children above all else. But this is not the case in Afghanistan. We worked on several children over the course of our deployment who were sent out to dig up mines so that the family could sell the explosives and bring in money. We worked on children who were burnt and shot by being in the vicinity of explosives and battles. We watched some of them die, and the parents walked away with simply a shrug or a comment that the child was lazy.

Later on in our deployment, I came in as second-up on a mass casualty call. It was a gruesome, chaotic scene. The injuries were caused by an

RPG fragment, which rains hell on people. I ran to the scene and asked the first-up medic, Marc Dragony, which patient he wanted me to take. I thought I would take the bulk of the other patients to help him out—there were a lot of them.

"Take the baby!" he barked.

Marc Dragony was a six-five, 250-pound hotshot on a fire in Santa Barbara County when he caught a ride on a CNG troop mover. It was a Black Hawk Medevac helicopter. He took one look at the big red cross on the side of the aircraft and decided, "I want to do that!" Following up on it, he eventually met Al Smoot, who asked him if he was a paramedic. Marc said no. Smoot didn't want anyone but paramedics, but Rob Walters took him under his mentorship anyway. Rob was able to bring Marc up to progression, building on what he'd known as a medic with the fire department in El Dorado Hills and going through Advanced Individual Training (AIT) with the army. Smoot added him to the rotation on its way to Afghanistan, first as an alternate, similar to my situation. We continued to train him, even after we arrived in theater. Dragony was a sponge, taking in everything he could learn, surrounded by paramedics who were experienced and sharp. Even with the extra training, he was still inexperienced with children.

I, on the other hand, had more medical knowledge to deal with pediatrics. Babies were difficult patients. It made sense for me to take the baby.

This baby had been eviscerated. His abdominal contents had been opened up by an RPG fragment, and the intestines were spilling out. Those who were there originally covered it with a dry Israeli bandage, which was not good. The baby's vitals were deranged and he was slow to respond.

He was a beautiful child. Dark hair, beautiful eyes. Perfect skin. I had this little perfect creature barely alive with his intestines hanging out. We scrambled into the back of the aircraft and flew to Bostic. I put oxygen on him but did not intubate. I had to start an IV, but there was no vascular access, and this baby was really sick. So I drilled a hole into his bone to start an intra-osseous infusion (IO), which is a needle placed directly into the marrow of a bone to provide a non-collapsible entry point. The procedure is to flush it and then introduce fluids and medicines. The level of response came up a little bit and he responded to the pain.

Good.

The vitals were within reason for a significant injury, but my IO failed. It didn't flush. When the FST finally got him, they did an IO, and it failed too. I think there was another circumstance, perhaps malnutrition, that had complicated his anatomical development. Eventually they got a third IO to take.

The boy died in the operating room.

Later, there was another child who was carried into the Bostic FST while we were on Medevac standby. He looked very similar to the eviscerated child but had a single penetrating shrapnel wound to the head. It was an obvious brain injury. He died right there, too.

We were learning that Afghanistan was a very backward place. Hell, even some of the Hadji toilets were mounted backward to make it easier to move their robes out of the way.

This was to be home for many months. We'd have to make the best of it.

Mike Ferguson and Ruben Higgins prepping for the next mission in an HH-60 helicopter

STUDY AT BAGRAM

"Truth will ultimately prevail where there are pains to bring it to light."
George Washington

"I believe the documentation we produce will help to shine more light on the activities of Medevac missions, so that future changes and enhancements can be made. As a result, more lives will be saved...We are doing our best to bring the army kicking and screaming into the twenty-first century of medicine."
SGT Michael Ferguson

Reno, Nevada
2008-2009

Jason Penrod was born and raised in Reno, Nevada. His father was a surgeon, and he planned on going into medicine as well. After high school, he completed his undergrad work and then joined the Nevada National Guard in response to a childhood dream of flying helicopters. He went in as an enlisted flight medic with aspirations of going to flight school. He had experience working as a medic with a local civilian air ambulance in Reno when he went into the Guard.

What Penrod found as a flight medic was a vast difference in skill sets and focuses. Guard flight medics were given little if any time to train medical skills; they were required to be focused on the mechanical workings of the helicopter more than the treatment of patients. Penrod and other civilian air ambulance personnel that had come and gone were trained to be patient-centric. Other medics working as civilian paramedics saw the futility of trying to change a broken system and left.

Penrod eventually went to flight school, came back, and went for his doctorate in pharmacology.

In 2008, Penrod was deployed to Afghanistan. Originally he was supposed to go with Nevada to southern Afghanistan, but ended up in Jalalabad with us from California. The entire experience was to be what he calls the Super Bowl of his military career.

He and Al Smoot had something in common. They both had seen firsthand the shortcomings in the training and experience of active-duty flight medics; and the army's reluctance to do something about it. In the course of preparatory e-mails with Smoot for the deployment to Afghanistan, Jason decided he would conduct a study in theater.

The driving force behind the study was the unwillingness of the Army School of Aviation Medicine and the Medevac Proponency Directorate to acknowledge the lacking training and proficiency of the army flight medic course. Jason felt strongly the only way to induce necessary change was to force it upon them by conducting a study that highlighted the differences in care between a critical-care trained paramedic and the typical army flight medic. He, Smoot, and others had tried every other professional means to get flight medics the training they desperately needed. The court of public opinion was the last venue to convince the army to change.

The study was something he had talked about long before the deployment. With the level of paramedic training we had collectively, we knew that this was an excellent opportunity, and it was a big one.

Seeing Is Believing

Medevac is a specialty. Even if you experience an injury on the battlefield, you have only a glimmer of an idea of what we do; very few see us with clarity. In Bagram, there was a Task Force Commander and Sergeant Major who were very concerned about their wounded soldiers. They were often present at the offloading of their own. They witnessed our level of care and attention, and immediately recognized the stark differences in how we approached patient care as opposed to active duty. Thereafter, we had 100 percent of their support.

There are many layers (filters) between what we do and the decision makers. These filters affect the decisions made. It's certainly different to look at an impersonal computer to check survivability rates, as opposed to looking in the back of the helicopter after the wounded are pulled out. The computer screen doesn't show a deck covered in blood, piss, vomit, bandaging, vials, and packaging everywhere in a mangled mishmash—sometimes with shell casings scattered about.

Rarely do leaders get to see flight medics and crew chiefs in action—shooting at the enemy while simultaneously caring for the wounded, hoisting in under fire, and thinking about the tactical considerations of an ever-fluid environment like hoisting in under goggles in hot zones.

Only conceptually do some of our leaders understand how many plates are spinning to do what needs to be done. It requires commitment, courage, and training, not just from the crews, but from leadership as well. They are the ones that read the reports and make decisions.

We knew change needed to be driven by us. We knew we could improve—those at the top had no idea what we were doing, let alone what was needed to do it better. They saw the numbers from Vietnam, calculated we were at 86 percent survivability, and called it good! But leaders didn't operate in our environment and didn't seek input, yet they made decisions on how we did our jobs.

Patient Tracking
Fort Sill, Oklahoma

Jason's intent was to write a study and compare our data with other rotations. He wasn't sure of the method at first, but working with Mike Ferguson on the patient care reports (PCRs), they captured all the data points into a computer document where it was easily extractable.

Mike was instrumental in allowing us to capture consistent, readily extractable, quality data. Rob Walters, Al Smoot, and the leadership that founded the original 126th Air Ambulance provided the vision that made the study possible. Their insistence of paramedic-level care aboard our unit's aircraft was the key to providing the necessary standard of care to which we could compare all others.

Initially Jason's plan was to have all the PCRs uploaded to Mike in Bagram from each team. These PCRs would be stored until we returned home. He really had no idea how he was going to capture the data from the other rotations, as he knew their documentation would be poor at best given there was no standardized PCR in army Medevac.

The Schoolhouse's original care report was too simplistic to capture any pertinent data or to document paramedic-level medical care. Most medevac units did PCRs that never made it to the soldier's medical file and didn't work for the army's new medical system, Medical Communications for Combat Casualty Care (MC4). The computer system they fielded to us was made for doctors to diagnose patients. This was of no use to us. It was a system that revolved around doctors, not medics, and was designed to require a doctor's signature before it could be transmitted into the system. This was fine for an aid station or combat hospital, but Medevac doesn't have any organic doctors. We don't diagnose; we document injuries. So Ferguson took a trauma nursing note that was a Word document file and cut and pasted it together. He then modified it, sought our input, and after several revisions, it became our new Medevac PCR. This was done at Fort Sill, Oklahoma – burning the midnight oil in his room after hours during our pre-mobilization training.

Once the care report was constructed, he then spent many late nights testing and determining how to upload the PCRs into the MC4 system. Since it was not designed to upload documents and it didn't support any other format, additions had to be pasted in as bitmap image files.

Once in country, Penrod spoke to the in-theater MC4 team about patient tracking software. They explained that a patient database did exist. It was known as the Joint Theater Trauma Registry (JTTR). Armed with this information, he planned to coordinate with them and seek approval for a formal study once we returned home.

The study was a retrospective analysis, meaning we were looking at what had already occurred and set parameters by which to measure outcomes. The forty-eight-hour, post-injury mark was used as prehospital care has a significant effect on patient morbidity and mortality.

The doctor who was ripping out before we got there had done some tracking of patient care. We were able to use that data. Once we were in theater, it was maintained through our flight surgeon, Dr. Mark Kavanagh[18], using the new PCR that Ferguson put together.

---

18 This is a pseudonym.

Push Back

Midway through our tour, there was a change. During the second half of our rotation, the country was cut in half. Another combat aviation brigade and their Medevac took over the care for southern Afghanistan. We were eastern. JTTR was happy with our documentation and so asked the new southern Medevac to send up their PCRs. When they did, they weren't actually the full PCRs. Southern Medevac utilized field ground tags, which are fine for ground medics that don't carry advanced equipment but are wholly inadequate for the first stage of definitive prehospital care. These documents consisted mostly of stating the injury and noting if morphine was given. There were no significant vitals trending, no documentation of treatment, no assessment of injuries or neurologic capacity, no oxygen saturation data, no data on the efficacy or patient response to advanced airway procedures or medications administered—nothing. Many report narrative sections were written as "Patient 1—gunshot wound to chest; Patient 2—gunshot wound to left arm."

The PCR is the lynchpin for professionalism—the documentation for what was done. Without an accurate accounting of what was done and the response, it is impossible to determine where improvement is needed. You can't possibly fix something you don't know is broken. The PCR is not driven by the people on the ground—it's for those who are making decisions. The PCRs contain the information needed to make those decisions, and without them there is no objective way to decide whether success or failure occurs. There is no other way to find out if patients are living because of flight medics, or in spite of flight medics.

When we asked those in southern Afghanistan to fill out our new PCRs, there was massive resistance from the commanders. They argued they didn't want Medevac to do this, claiming the crews had too much to do. But Major Biever with the JTTR went to bat. She needed the information to follow the patients from point of injury to Germany and home to see whether or not the medical system was working.

She was told by other commanders that they didn't want medics to know how the patients fared. As a medical provider herself, she asked Ferguson, "Why would they *not* want to know their patient's outcome?" Ferguson replied, "Because many probably don't want to know who died. Most flight medics have not been trained to an adequate level. They are being asked to work way beyond their capabilities. If I were in that position, I wouldn't want to know who lived or died because I wouldn't want to feel responsible."

With the few reports she had been able to gain from the other units, Major Biever already had some significant concerns if the en route care given was adequate for the patients' needs. She opined, "I'm afraid to lift the lid off this box for fear of what I'll find." Ferguson challenged her. "You've got to! Nothing will change unless you do."

The turnover rate has been astronomical for active-duty flight medics. Typically after four years and numerous combat deployments, they get out of the army and are gone. They were asked to shoulder the burden of tremendous stress, yet they were not adequately prepared for what they faced. Many do amazing work in terrible situations without the consolation that the army has given them enough advanced training to make a difference. It's been a travesty.

Medevac Meetings
Bagram, Afghanistan

As the medic in charge of patient care reporting, Ferguson was invited by Brigade Surgeon Major Laura Kaster to take part in Medevac doctrine meetings held at Bagram. He'd created the PCR and was heavily involved in tracking all the data. He was the only enlisted member in a room full of medical command staff nearly all of whom were majors or greater. In spite of this, he became the most vocal person in the room.

We'd been in the Afghan war for ten years, yet there was no data collection until recently. They wanted the data—Mike gave it to them. He also gave it to them straight.

In one particular meeting he told a full bird Colonel in a medical command for Afghanistan, "The army is not training the medics to the level they need to be. If I did my job on the civilian side like the army does it here, I'd not only lose my license…I'd go to jail! It is criminal incompetence. It's not the medic in the aircraft's fault. The army hasn't taught him what he needs to know to do his job!"

The Colonel was a little taken aback.

"Why does the army think it's a great idea to supply a helicopter with all of this whiz-bang advanced-level equipment and then not train the guy in the back to use it properly?" Mike added. No one in the room had an answer.

Meeting with the Surgeon General
Jalalabad, Afghanistan

We were overloaded with patients during the killing season, and it was crazy. We were tasked with a visit from the Surgeon General. It came at a time when none of us were sleeping, especially our flight surgeon, Mark Kavanagh. We were told when the Surgeon General arrived, this would be the proper format to discuss how Medevac works and some of the deficits and training needs. We would have an hour and a half to spend with him, showing him Medevac, the aircraft and the FSTs and talking about some of our calls. We saw it as an opportunity to share our findings, our solutions, and our passion.

So Doc Kavanagh went to task. He compiled data and prepared a PowerPoint, talking points, and pages of information that went with the PowerPoint. He spent hours working on this and did an incredible job. But after he put it together, he decided it would be better if one of us medics actually presented the information with his support. He asked me to speak on behalf of Medevac. I felt guilty about this. Doc did the work, but I would get the credit. I reluctantly agreed. No good deed goes unpunished!

The day came. As we were waiting for the Surgeon General to come, we started receiving messages that he would be delayed, and for several minutes we were scrambling to figure out how we were going to do the presentation within the diminishing timeframe. It was ultimately reduced to a fifteen-minute meet and greet. Doc and I raced to the FST to meet with him—without the PowerPoint, but with a copy of it in hand. I was pissed. After all Doc had done to prepare, this was to be the result. He had no time for us in the middle of the killing season.

It turned out to be a room full of VIPs. I'm not sure exactly who all of them were, but I later learned that some of them were congressmen, one was the Surgeon General of the Navy, and there was a senator present. With Captain Kavanagh behind me and facing the Surgeon General eye to eye, I read from the pages before me. I was direct. The Surgeon General was kind and patient with me but kept interrupting to say that our information needed to be forwarded to the army center for lessons learned. I took that as, "Go away, kid, you bother me." I got angry but kept it polite. He'd already taken away the time allotted for our presentation; why not give us the courtesy of listening? But I pushed forward—he needed to hear what I had to say, because frankly, soldiers were dying. I had to drive the point home.

I gave two examples. First I looked to the senator and presented a scenario. "Say a neighboring state had a major natural disaster and they request mutual aid. You send all your experienced paramedics there, and all you had left are EMT-Basics—would you be willing to put them on helicopters and have them do critical-care transport for your own people?" He didn't say a word. But he smiled and shook his head no.

The second example wasn't original; I'd stolen it from Smoot and Walters. "Sir, a homeless drunk slips on the street, falls down, and hits his head. He is unconscious. Someone calls 911, and the fire engine responds. At least one but more likely two of those who arrive on the scene are experienced paramedics. When the ambulance arrives, it has at least one but probably two or more paramedic-level trained personnel, all to work on this drunk in the street. When our soldiers step into combat and they get hit, the army responds with Medevac that has an EMT-Basic with little to no experience. Our soldiers deserve better."

I knew this was provocative. I knew this would get a reaction, but I didn't care. I was an E-6 Guard dude; send me home if you don't like what I say.

The Surgeon General's face went red. I gotta hand it to him—he was polite, professional, and didn't crush me. But it was evident he wasn't happy. He walked away, not even taking the printed information that Doc had worked his ass off for. As he left, the Navy Surgeon General stopped, smiled, and asked if he could have it. I replied, "Sir, I don't care who does Medevac, as long as it's done right." I gave him the information.

Funny, I was never asked to do another high-level presentation after that.

I'm sure Doc caught a lot of shit for this. He seemed to manage it well, but I'm sure it affected his career to some degree. I got flak as well.

Smoot came to me and told me the Major in charge of the FST and the enlisted were livid about the presentation. What? Why? I went to the Jbad FST and found the Major.

"Sir, I've been told you're angry with me. What's the deal?"

"You said that our EMT-Basics are not good enough," he replied. "They're not happy with you."

"I don't know what to say. I didn't say anything negative about them. They do a fantastic job." They do. They're like fuckin' machines in there. They're better than any trauma room or ER I've ever been to. So this bothered me.

"You said our EMT medics are undertrained."

I clarified. "Whoa, that's not what I said. I said army flight medics are not getting the support they deserve. I said throwing an EMT-Basic into a dynamic environment with blood products, drips, paralytics, vents, and all these medications they're not trained on is a recipe for disaster. This has nothing to do with your FST. This has nothing to do with their training or abilities. You were there. You heard what I said."

The Major stepped back and was quiet for a moment. I gotta hand it to him. He said, "OK. I'll take care of it."

I offered to apologize and explain. But he said he'd deal with it. And he did.

Our Air Force Ally

Colonel Warren Dorlac with the US Air Force was the Joint Trauma Theater consultant and a well-published trauma-neurosurgeon. He was very interested in how we conducted our business as EMT-P flight medics. He was aware of the significant problems with Medevac and was a critical link in the chain.

He showed up on our doorstep in country because the mortality rates were improving in theater. Our numbers were better than all other theaters that were operating across the board. He had questions, namely: is this real? Why are your numbers so low during a time of war that is a kinetic mess? Penrod and he met for just a few moments. Dorlac listened to his ideas for the initial paper he was writing, and the study we were gathering data for.

A little later, Penrod wrote a document out of frustration with the Medevac Proponency Directorate and their unwillingness to acknowledge the problems plaguing Medevac. This paper primarily focused on the flight medic but also addressed everything from other crew member training to the aircraft itself. He sent this document to Colonel Dorlac.

Dorlac forwarded this to several people, including Major Bob Mabry, a former 18 Delta Silver Star recipient who was in Mogadishu. He was the real deal, and a physician. He was also very passionate about care on the battlefield. This set into motion the connection key to the study. Penrod had all the paramedic data. Mabry had access to the JTTR (whose job was to track patients from point of injury to final care in the States) and the Army Institute for Surgical Research center at Fort Sam Houston. Once the data was in, it was the new partnership of Jason Penrod and Bob Mabry that produced the results.

We had a special purpose to our mission. We brought our expertise. We knew what we were up against. We had trained beyond the normal standards. We'd planned and prepared, and once we were in theater, it was time to engage. But we were just a few who had to work with many to accomplish what we had gone there to do. It was imperative to develop good working relationships with those around us. And that's not always easy.

SSG Spraktes performs a combat hoist at night under goggles. He picked up two army scouts injured in close quarters battle with insurgents. Image taken from an Apache gunship.
Courtesy of CW4 Gary Heyne's Helmet Cam

SSG Spraktes hoisting out of Kala Gush. IED wreaks havoc on Humvee (story in chapter fifteen).
Courtesy of CPT Luis Arriola, 2-77 FA BN S6

COMBAT HOISTS

"I learned that courage was not the absence of fear, but the triumph over it. The brave man is not he who does not feel afraid, but he who conquers that fear."
Nelson Mandela

"The willingness to die for another person is a form of love that even religions fail to inspire, and the experience of it changes a person profoundly."
Sebastian Junger, War

Restrepo
December 2008

When Medevac picks up the wounded, the best-case scenario is to land the helicopter, hop off onto land, run over and fetch the wounded, and then return to the aircraft with the patients. We then load and go. But in the mountains of Afghanistan, this is sometimes impossible. Battles happen everywhere, in all types of terrain, and in all types of environments, day and night.

If we're not able to land, we have to do a hoist. A regular hoist means we fly in slow, stop, the medic goes down the hook, disconnects, and then the aircraft flies away. If there is enemy nearby, we're on station too long, our signature is too big, and we're a stationary target. It's dangerous.

To minimize the risk to the crew and aircraft, we performed combat hoists. This is where we fly in at high level, making us more difficult to shoot at. As the aircraft flies in, the crew chief lowers the medic down as the aircraft moves forward toward the target. Once he's on the ground and on target, the medic disconnects and then signals to the crew chief he's disconnected. The crew chief immediately brings up the hoist. When the cable is clear enough, the aircraft peels off.

When I did hoists, I told my guys not to slow down too much. I got to the point where I could grab the dirt with my feet and jog while unhooking so the aircraft didn't have to cease forward movement. Because the crew is important, we need to get them out of there so they're not used for target practice by the hadjis. I needed them to come back!

Active-duty crews don't do combat hoists. They prefer to be stationary. It's dangerous for the crew, the aircraft, and the people on the ground. But as low as they fly sometimes—if something goes wrong, they can crash right on top of the people they're trying to rescue! If they're seventy feet or more up, they can peel off and go crash somewhere else. There's a difference between four dead people and fourteen dead people. That sounds harsh, but it's the reality.

On December 23, 2008, we did our first combat hoist. We got a nine-line call for several patients in the Valley of Death, about a click away from Restrepo. Coming in over a village, Smoot's team got there first. As they were making the approach, our guys had just dropped mortars into the area and were providing suppressive fire. As Smoot was heading down the hoist, the escort Apaches started shooting rockets directly over his head.

Whoa!

Smoot unclipped and hit the ground disoriented, but he recovered and ran over to assess the first patient. The terrain was very steep, about a forty-five-degree angle, and he struggled to keep his footing.

The first patient had taken a round in the back. There were also two patients who were ambulatory, which means wounded but able to walk. He directed a couple of soldiers to move the gunshot-wound patient up to where he was to be hoisted out. Man, it was noisy—gunfire, bombs exploding, the helicopter rotors, and the radio was just going nuts. They had to yell at each other on the ground to communicate.

In the meantime, our aircraft came in. I stayed in the seat because I was told to. We were still doing our RIP with the previous team, and the flight medic I was replacing wanted to show me how it was done. Really?! He hoisted down to join Smoot.

"What do you got?" the medic asked.

Smoot answered, a little out of breath. "That guy gets Sked'd,[20] and I need to get these two out."

We sent down the Sked and peeled off to make room for first-up DUSTOFF. As our medic unrolled it and packaged up the first patient, Smoot hooked up the two ambulatory soldiers. He clipped on all their gear so those on the ground didn't have to carry it out, and then he clipped them on to the hoist. They were brought up, unclipped, and then the hoist was sent back down for Smoot.

As Smoot was heading up on the cable, he slowed at twenty-five feet. He felt like he was dangling out there forever; he looked at the houses and the hills from where he thought the fire had come from. He noticed that hadjis had come out to watch.

---

20 Put on the Sked stretcher to be hoisted out

This is my third mission, and I'm not going to make it through this fucking tour! I don't know where it's gonna come from, I don't know how long I'm gonna be on the ground for, but one of these times I'm not gonna make it. I'm going to die.

The hoist continued up, and Smoot climbed in. As he worked on the patients, his thoughts went back to that hoist. He'd done one combat hoist in 2003. This time he not only did a combat hoist his first week in, but he had rockets shooting over his head and mortars landing as he was lowered.

What the hell did I get into this time?

Our turn. The aircraft came around and let down the hoist. Our crew chief hoisted the gunshot casualty up into the aircraft. The patient was screaming so loud that I could hear him over the rotors. I jumped in and started to strip him and flip him, which means I exposed him to examine for wounds. I started an IV and checked his blood pressure and other vitals. The medic was hoisted back up and joined me on the deck. I was ready to do pain management but I didn't have any medicines yet on the aircraft, as we were still in the RIPTOA.

"We need to get him some pain meds," I directed.

"I don't have any."

"What?!" I blurted out. "What do you mean?"

"I don't have any."

"What the fuck am I supposed to do for this poor bastard?"

The medic looked at me and shrugged.

I couldn't believe it. He was obviously going into surgery. He was likely going to have a laparotomy. They were gonna open him up and run the bowel and see the trajectory. He needed pain management. Now.

We landed, and I was absolutely stunned that he didn't have any medications. What did they have on board? What if we needed to sedate him? What did we have? What if we needed to paralyze him, to control his airway?

But nothing was available.

We took the patient to the FST. After we did our patient care turnover, we reset the aircraft. Then Smoot and I went in to check on the patients. Our gunshot patient had been x-rayed, and we were able to see where the bullet stopped. It hadn't gone very far. It must've come from a long distance, as it had just enough power to penetrate. It just sat there in the abdomen.

I thought about the active-duty medic on board with me, who'd been there almost a year. No meds. No ability to treat the patient effectively with the meds he had on board, as he'd only been trained to an EMT-Intermediate level. Just enough knowledge and training from the army to get on board the helicopter, but not enough knowledge, training and medications to be powerful and effect change. Kind of like that bullet in the soldier's belly—just sitting there.

I have much compassion for active-duty flight medics. They are given just enough training and skill set to earn the title of flight medic, but not enough to treat really sick, critical-care transport patients effectively. We as civilian-trained paramedics are not any smarter; we can't run any faster; we are not better-looking. We are the same as our active-duty counterparts in most ways. The difference is our training and experience in the civilian sector. We are exactly the same people. But the system did not support them for what they were asked to do.

Unfortunately many who are in this system don't know what they don't know. They are strictly a product of army training with little or no outside experience. Others don't wish to acknowledge the shortcomings, because they have pride. They are proud, and they should be proud. But sometimes an ego develops, and this inhibits their ability to see that they need more.

As our journey progressed, we saw more of this.

Asadabad
February 2009

Donald Baker[22] referred to himself as a gun-toting mechanic, which is pretty accurate. He was actually a crew chief. His primary duties as crew chief in our medevac unit were to fix the aircraft, protect the medic, and help in the back. He was a practiced combat lifesaver.

A little shorter than he'd like and a little rounder than he'd like, Donald was hysterical. He talked in short, quick bursts, and by the time the mind registers what he said as funny, he was on to the next joke. I found myself all smiles whenever my buddy Donald was around.

Donald was responsible for the safety of the medic, himself, and the others that come on his deck in the back of the aircraft. Hoisting was always a big safety concern. We had internal hoists, so the crew chief would reel out a little cable, hook it up to the medic's vest, and unhook the medic's tail[24]. The medic would then check Donald's tail to make

---
22 This is a pseudonym.
24 A tail connects the crew member's vest to a secure point in the helicopter.

sure it was secure, because if Donald fell off the aircraft while the medic was dangling, that would not be good. It was time to open the door.

Once the door was open, Donald leaned out with the cable in one hand, the controller in another, and his foot on the moving cable. He leaned forward and guided the pilots verbally. As the pilots come in, they can't see sometimes, so it's Donald's job to look left, look right, look up, and look down, so that the aircraft on station (stationary) doesn't drift or spin into something. He said slide right or slide left, do a reverse count, hold hover…he directed the pilots to go where they needed to go.

While he was multi-tasking, the challenge, especially under night goggles, is depth perception. They have to bring the cable in and drop that medic in a specific spot. Timing is crucial. It takes years of practice. When you're talking a couple hundred feet, the depth perception is so difficult. It's also hard on the neck.

Now add a temperature of 110 degrees, even at night. It's hot as hell in Afghanistan. And people may be shooting at the aircraft. It adds a whole new dimension to what these guys do. Donald tends to downplay his role, but the safety of the entire aircraft was in his hands.

Baker and Marc Dragony were up at Asadabad towards the end of winter, maybe February. Up to that point, Baker hadn't even done a hoist mission yet. It never failed—he'd picked up the pregnant girl, or the broken finger, nothing exciting or challenging, even though everyone else had had their first and even second hoists. They had been there all night sleeping in the helicopter, when finally, about four o'clock in the morning, Donald got his first hoist mission.

They flew up into the hills facing east. Nobody was shooting at the moment, but he and Dragony still had to pull out four casualties.

Donald had essentially been up all night and was tired. He was running on pure adrenaline at that point. Because of the terrain, the aircraft was not able to land at all.

When Donald looked down, it was dark. He had to have his night goggles on to see the ground from about 125 feet above the trees. When he looked up, he saw the sunrise. It was so bright he had to take off his goggles. The pilots flew without goggles, but Donald had to put them on to see down through the trees. That was the first difficulty—seeing.

The second difficulty was hearing. The rotors on the aircraft were loud. Then there were the Apaches, who were flying around watching for bad guys, ready to rain down trouble should anyone get the idea to shoot down the air ambulance. There were also five radios going at once—the two pilots in the front, the ground guys, SatCom, and the medic.

Donald was in charge. If anything went wrong, it was his fault. The DUSTOFF pilots couldn't see; they were flying partially blind because of how close they were to the trees. They also couldn't see behind them—there is no rear view mirror, so to speak. It was Donald's communication they had to rely on—he directed them while simultaneously watching the Apaches, the medic, and operating the hoist while the aircraft was moving. It was pure concentration to manage everything safely and effectively.

Donald fastened the hook on Dragony's vest and put him out the door about a hundred yards before the target. Donald called this maneuver the Superman: they run him out so his feet aren't in the trees—much— and keep lowering him down as they grow closer to the target. When the aircraft stops, he's down. The helicopter keeps going. The idea is to limit the hover as much as possible so they don't get shot out of the sky.

Donald lowered Dragony down 125 feet; he unhooked, gave the signal, and then Donald brought the hook up. As the hook cleared the trees, they flew away.

Dragony did what he does best on the ground, which was to package up the patients. Donald listened for his communication. Dragony gave them the situation and directed them to what he needed. The aircraft came back, and he sent up two patients. Donald unhooked the patients and took their weapons.

Donald was a safety nut about confiscating weapons in the helicopter. His fear was that these guys would start shooting in the aircraft when they woke up wounded and disoriented. It was his practice to pile all of the guns at the front—that way there were no surprises or mishaps.

Donald sent down the hoist again, and Dragony hooked up two more patients. Donald brought them up and released them. The hoist was sent back down for the last time. Dragony hooked on, and they brought him up. The medic is always the last to come out.

Once the medic was on board, Baker shut the door, gave the pilots their signal, and then helped Dragony render aid to the patients.

These stories were some of the first hoists in country. We went on to do many hoists over the course of the year, some amid fire and others amid the threat of fire.

We'd been given a lively welcome in those early months, even despite the cold weather. We learned how it worked with the active-duty medics and implemented our experience and training to make it better. That was why we had come—to improve things.

Donald Baker aboard Medevac helicopter with Apache escort near Asadabad, Afghanistan.

Courtesy of Elizabeth Kimbrough

BUILDING TRUST

"A mysterious bond of brotherhood makes all men one."
Thomas Carlyle

"The unique thing about that Task Force is I knew [Medevac] would come get me...everybody would've laid it on the line for each other. And I don't always feel that way. We used to pass by your porch everyday on the way to chow. And you put the little Cav symbol on the tail of your helicopter. That was like saying you were family."
CW3 Gary Parsons, Kiowa Pilot

**Afghanistan
2008-2009**

We were in Afghanistan at a time when things were really escalating. The second election was that summer. Insurgents wanted to prevent or influence the vote, and they certainly didn't want women voting. Our own election in the United States dictated a shift in our mission in the Afghan war, as while we were deployed, our country elected a new president. The paradigm that drove this new president was very different than the previous administration, and our commanders were asking the philosophical questions of why, how, when, and where.

LTC Blackmon was one of those asking the questions. He was aware that things had changed over the years. In fact, every deployment to Afghanistan was different—places, names, conflicts, and therefore mission—all at the mercy of those who made decisions and the intensity of the enemy. The war had ebbed and flowed as both sides increased or decreased their fervor. Caught in the middle were our troops.

The new leadership in theater had some goals they wanted to accomplish that year. The initial strategic perspective was to question why we were occupying some of the more remote outposts. Early on in the war, Tenth Mountain had established these places, but it was an entirely different war then. They were driving pickup trucks up there and not getting shot at. They had planned to make a highway all the way to Barge Matal. We could drive all the way down to the Kunar Valley, trade goods, and have a route to civilization, first to Asadabad and then down to Jalalabad. At one point, that was a real expectation. But as things changed and became more kinetic, those outposts became very isolated and therefore were at risk. The commanders questioned Keating and Bostic. They questioned the Korengal—the bloodiest piece of turf in the country. Could we just leave it after those sacrifices? It was also considered the birthplace of the 9/11 attacks. All of the planning and training for those attacks were done in the Korengal—could we just shut down and leave?

Up in the Kamdesh, they were considering the purpose as well. There was no reconciliation of the people—only 4 percent of the Afghan population lived there. Their lives consisted of the events that went on in that valley. They had no concept of anything else. Kabul was another country to them. Were the lives of America's sons and daughters worth the risk?

Amid the rethinking, the questions and the new direction of the war by our commanders, Medevac pushed forth our own mission. This was to do everything in our power to not only bring home the wounded of that year alive, but to affect change in the care of the wounded after we were gone. A small task in the midst of a complex situation, but it was the most important mission in our view of the war.

We were blessed in that it seemed like everything lined up. We were surrounded by people who cared, who were flexible, and who were driven by the right motivations. Because we were older, prepared, and had more life experience and professional experience, we were able to get others on board with what we were trying to do.

Medical Personnel

When I met the doctors and nurses in the FST, I introduced myself as Emmett. We were in the medical field together. I understand the ranking system within the army, but Emmett has to tell a Lieutenant Colonel (LTC) what he's bringing him. And Emmett must do it at a human level to let the LTC know that Emmett gives a shit about who he's handing off. Emmett also knows that he has to come back to the LTC and pick up this guy for transport who's been opened up, sedated, paralyzed, put on pain management, on blood products, sometimes vasopressors, fully catheterized, on multiple drips, on an EKG, with a Pro Pack, and he has to go to the LTC and ask, "What do you have?"

"Well, Emmett, this is what I have"—it's a conversation that has absolutely nothing to do with rank. The acid baseline was trust. The medical personnel needed to trust us when we dictated what needed to be disconnected or altered to reflect the circumstances on the aircraft. When we explained situations to them, there was a new awareness and comfort level. They came to trust us, befriend us. We even shared a cigar or two with the radios close by.

Captain Mark Kavanagh was assigned to Jalalabad as our flight surgeon. We called him Doc. Doc came from an Irish Catholic military family. His father was a flight surgeon in the US Air Force before he became a cardiologist. Both of his grandfathers were in World War II—one in the US Navy, the other an army air force pilot. He was drawn to medicine in high school and college. He also played football during this time, until a back injury ended his football career. When it came time to apply for military scholarships for medical school, this injury caused some difficulties, but the army was happy to take him. He served in the reserves while attending medical school in Chicago, and then did an internship in San Antonio, Texas.

After he married in 2007, Doc asked himself what was the best course for his new family. The answer was to go to Fort Rucker, Alabama, and become a flight surgeon. He was then assigned to Fort Campbell, Kentucky, with the 101st Airborne and thus was to be deployed with Task Force PaleHorse.

The responsibilities of a flight surgeon are to keep the active-duty unit healthy and to be the medical director that oversees medics.

Smoot and Kavanagh were introduced by e-mail before they got to Afghanistan. Smoot told him about our unit, that we were civilian-trained paramedics. Doc felt a bit better about this—we were far more qualified than what he expected.

Because of the severity of the injuries and the inabilities of the EMT-Basic flight medics, the prior task force required a doctor to be on board the helicopter. This was pretty intimidating for Kavanagh, who was a new doctor. Medicine in war was messy, and these were American soldiers.

Once in theater, Doc found out quickly that we didn't require a medical director, supervision, or training from a brand-new physician. We didn't need Doc on board the aircraft like the previous rotation. Essentially, we needed a doctor to do rectal exams, which was troubling in that Doc had been a football player and had big hands.

According to Doc, we were intimidating at first, especially Smoot. But I saw something in Kavanagh. It was hard for me to believe he was an officer and a physician yet had no ego. He was hungry to learn and eager to help. It was all about the patients. I respected him tremendously. Our relationship allowed things to progress. At first the other medics were reluctant to have him fly with us and assist with care. We were there to treat patients, gather data, and hopefully prove a point to the army—and his presence on the helicopter could've interfered with both. So Smoot asked him to draft a letter that said as medics, we had the final say in who could be in the back of the aircraft. The letter was rescinded for the relieving active-duty Medevac when our rotation ended.

Doc's first flight with Smoot broke the ice. After he'd proved himself a bit, Smoot eased up. And Doc learned a lot from us. He recognized after a very short period of time he didn't know what he needed to know. He went through a complete readiness level of progression to be able to function in the back of the aircraft. Even basic things, seemingly intuitive, were counter to what he was used to.

Smoot's second mission in theater, which was while they were still in the RIP stage, was picking up four patients at Lowell. One particular patient caught the eye of Doc and the flight surgeon from the outgoing task force, who was an emergency physician in the States. They decided to do an ultrasound in the aircraft to evaluate the lungs for pneumothorax. Some doctors, especially ER docs, see the value in using ultrasound technology in a field environment.

Smoot took the other three patients and an aid bag for the return flight on another aircraft. Ten minutes later, Smoot emerged covered in blood as he'd been managing the care of three patients, which included decompressing a chest. He was livid. He pulled Doc aside and told him never to pull that shit in his aircraft again. That wasn't the place or the time for ultrasound technology. There were three other patients to care for.

Smoot will never be a diplomat.

On another flight, Doc and I had a patient who had a fractured femur. I told him the vibration would cause him more pain as the transport progressed and we needed to give him Fentanyl to get ahead of it for proper pain management. Doc assessed the patient, saw that the femur was immobilized pretty well and that the soldier's pain severity was only about a two out of ten, so he wanted to withhold the Fentanyl. I let him. Several minutes later, as the vibration of the aircraft drove the patient's pain level to an eight, Doc understood. Things are different in the back of a helicopter. I gave Fentanyl.

After a few months of intensive work, Doc was competent enough to take care of sick patients in the aircraft. By the end of his rotation, he'd responded with the medics on 80 percent of all DUSTOFF missions flown. Towards the end of his time in theater, Dragony even let him perform a couple of hoist missions. I was so angry about this. I felt that Doc was the advocate we needed for our mission. He was a medical doctor who saw what we were trying to do, and I didn't want to lose a flight surgeon on a dangerous hoist mission. That would be devastating. But, luckily, nothing happened.

The reason Doc was able to do all of this was that he worked with a seasoned physician's assistant, Major Roger Ball. Ball had been there, done that, and was content to hold sick call and keep the flight physicals current. So Doc was free to fly with us. He told me later that the experience made him a better doctor. I told him it sure beat doing Smoot's rectal exam.

Blue Max

Medevac aircraft fly without weapons. We are there to pick up our wounded, not necessarily to fight. Crew chiefs and medics carry sidearms and automatic rifles, but that's it. In theory, the rule in war is that you don't shoot at aircraft with a red cross. But terrorists don't give two mangy camels who you are or what aircraft you're in, and they don't care that you're unarmed. They'll take out anyone, anywhere, no matter what's painted on the side or whom it holds. So we must fly with escorts. The Apaches were our escorts in high-risk areas; they always flew in pairs.

We were co-located with Blue Max and so shared the communication center, office space, and the planning room, and our housing was side by side. By proximity we became close friends.

Blue Max took us into the aggressive areas because of their weapons capabilities. They understood we were going into battle with no weapons and no way to defend ourselves, so they promised they'd take care of us. That was their job.

After seeing some of the crazy shit we did, they developed a deep appreciation for us. They saw we were willing to risk our lives for others we didn't know. Time and time again, we flew into these outrageous calls, Apaches overhead. They fired off rockets, shot their guns and placed themselves in between us and the enemy. Their job was to protect us by killing bad guys, and they were very effective. But they put themselves in danger all the time. Blue Max was like a big brother. They were bonded to us like family, and we felt the same. After calls, we'd all talk shop together, gaining one another's perspective and learning.

I think they were used to the active-duty medevac's attitude. They might put themselves in harm's way, but there was a divisiveness in the active-duty medevac culture. A lot of it stemmed from poor air crew coordination. The crew mix—separation between officers and enlisted—often didn't allow those in the back to have a voice. In contrast, even though we were enlisted, we were always able to give our opinions as part of the crew. The ruling attitude was what was best for the patient.

The trust was there.

Fragging Scottie

One area I was not able to get *anyone* to trust me was with grenades.

I fragged an officer—Scottie St. Aubin. I'm sure there are now many an enlisted soldier who will buy me a beer for having fragged an officer. Nothing like a good fragging, right?

Scott was one of our medevac pilots, and a good buddy I hung out with on the porch. One day we were with Special Forces training on an approved range. During the training, I threw a grenade as far as anybody else had—it had good trajectory and direction. But for whatever reason, it bounced up and blew fragments back at us. I saw Scottie catch a fragment in the left arm. He sure squawked a lot, but I was damn glad he was alive. It could've been horrible.

I fragged him and then worked on him. We then flew him back to Jbad, where he was down for awhile. During his recovery, Scottie had me do this and that for him—*Can you pick up my laundry, Emmett? Can you shave my face, Emmett? Can you change my bleeding bandage, Emmett?* Prick! Slight exaggeration here. Actually I didn't mind at all. Scottie was a close friend; I owed him and was happy he was alive.

I knew the incident would come back to haunt me. The crew ended up in LTC Blackmon's office. I felt awful. I also felt like I was in the vice principal's office again after getting into yet another fight at school. To this day I'm stunned that Blackmon didn't scream or throw items adorning his desk. He was very clear about his feelings, but still a gentleman.

I did refrain from telling Blackmon that we had thrown a few on a prior training day. I certainly never surfaced that I helped recover an unexploded one. Someone wasn't instructed on the secondary safety pin... Yes, the culprit's name rhymes with Demmett Cactus.

I'm not sure what it is with me and grenades.

Flight Crews

Putting together pilots, crew chiefs, and medics on an aircraft can have it's challenges. The attitudes and behavior of the pilots can range from prima donna-like expectations to a genuine interest and care. We saw it all.

During our first day in Afghanistan, flight medics Mike Ferguson and Dave Cornell, a civilian flight nurse with years of experience, were called up to fly to Good Army Airfield in Gardez. They were to pick up a post-surgical patient injured by an IED and take him back to Bagram. Because of the weather, it was decided to fly two helicopters from two different places and meet at a midway point. We call this a tail to tail.

Gardez is a little FST that sits at 6,500 feet altitude. In the middle of the winter, the cobblestone landing zone (LZ) was covered with snow.

The patient, a critically injured Air Force Master Sergeant, was on a ventilator. He was chemically sedated, paralyzed, and hooked up to several drips. He was basically an ICU patient. There were two other ambulatory patients on the trip as well.

Mike and Cornell were on the receiving end. They got a short report from the other medic.

They stopped the drip and picked up the stretcher. The patient was evidently very tall, and his head wasn't properly supported. So when they began carefully pulling him out, his head suddenly snapped back.

"Oh, shit!" Mike cursed.

Mike grabbed the patient's head and held it steady. He wrapped gauze around the litter handles so the patient would have his head supported. They then stumbled across the LZ—about five hundred feet—to the awaiting aircraft. They situated him into the waiting helicopter feet first, and Mike jumped in to hook him up to the monitor. They had a flatline on the ZOL. He realized the endotracheal tube was extubated, meaning the patient couldn't breathe on his own.

"Cornell, we need to re-intubate him, and right now! He's not breathing." He grabbed the kit and handed it to Cornell.

So, on the side of the aircraft, Cornell got a tube into his throat.

Mike and Cornell then were able to get a good CO_2 on him and stabilize him. They then placed him in the aircraft. Mike and Cornell just saved his life.

The pilot who had been waiting in the warm aircraft while this was taking place called back, "What took so long?! We can't take this long!"

Mike was furious, but he didn't say anything. He was new to this, after all. But the irony was there.

After that, training PowerPoints were put together to help pilots understand what we do in the back of the helicopter. It's Medevac;

therefore the mission revolves around the needs of the patients. Some pilots came in with the attitude that their role was more important than others, and conducted themselves as such. Ego took precedence over patient care, and this was a struggle in some places. I occasionally dealt with this on tail to tail missions, and in one instance blew up at a pilot because I didn't like his attitude.

Luckily, our Guard pilots in Jalalabad had an attitude that reflected more of a collective crew effort; even our one active-duty pilot was all about the patient. We all had our roles. We worked together to do whatever the patient needed.

Eventually through education, training, and experience, we were able to impart our perspective to other pilots as well. With careful communication and respect, we were able to show that Medevac is not about individual performance or ego, but a joint effort to serve the guys on the ground. It was all about the patients and their needs. But that took some time to implement.

Other "Solutions"

In some ways the Army has acknowledged that active-duty Medevac needs help. They've acknowledged this in the simple fact that they've brought in doctors and nurses to fly with them. This seems on its face to be a good solution, but it's not.

I've already mentioned a few struggles Doc went through to be proficient in the aircraft. The same goes for nurses. But among the many other problems with augmenting nurses is that the army is already short. There are not enough nurses in the FSTs, so if you put a nurse on an aircraft, you've shut down the team on the ground. Those nurses need to be where they can be most effective. If you take them out, you rob the next patient who comes in and decrease the outcome across the board. It's extremely chaotic if people aren't where they're supposed to be. All the parts of the system need to work together to succeed. It really takes years to be able to function well in the world of sensory deprivation patient assessment and treatment in Medevac. It also takes years and constant training to become a proficient crew member.

One of the other challenges we faced was outside allied agency interference. Air Force General to Army General, there were requests that Air Force Para-rescue (PJs) be involved in Medevac. This was and is a huge mistake. This is an army issue for allowing it, not an Air Force issue. Para-jumpers are Special Forces. They have some of the best training in the world. They are generalists. I say this because their job is combat search and rescue; they train for everything. They train jumping out of airplanes, HALO, scuba, and of course aircraft and personnel recovery—all the "cool guy" stuff. PJs are initially trained at a paramedic level and take a two-week refresher course every year. But they don't do patient care on a regular basis to maintain perishable medical skills. In this respect, because they are generalists and not specialists, their medical care is lacking. To be frank, it's poor.

On the other hand, civilian-trained paramedic army flight medics are specialists. Everything we do is to take care of the guys in the back. We don't do combat search and rescue, we don't train the high-speed (operator level) skills. We do combat hoisting and fight back when we have to, but we have a very specific job.

For years, the army's thinking was that you could throw anybody with minimal medical training at this mission and have it be successful. The numbers clearly don't crunch.

If I gave a fully trained California Highway Patrol officer the keys to the prisons and said, "You've got the general idea; go for it," they would sink in a heartbeat. Until you know what you're doing, you don't know what you're doing. It takes time and training. PJs are ill-prepared to do this job because they don't get to train it enough; that's why they're more likely to cut a hole in a patient's neck, shove an ET tube in and then high-five each other after it's all said and done. What they should've done was suction the poor bastard's airway, drop in an NPA and bag 'em.

PJs have the paramedic book knowledge, but as a whole, not the experiential training to be effective. In addition, they also carry every bit of their equipment with them, so the weight requirements severely limited their ability to do rescues at altitude without putting everyone at risk. For them to do Medevac effectively and safely, they would need to change many of their current procedures and training focuses.

In our experience, they interfered. Every rotation it was the same thing. We would finally get them to understand these principles, and then in a few months they left and another team came in wanting to do Medevac because there were no regular search and rescue missions. We'd have to start all over again. We saw three different rotations while in theater. They kept jumping calls on us, perhaps to try to prove themselves. I've also been told that the PJs had the medevac mission forced upon them to help justify a very expensive CSAR budget. Either way, that kind of thinking kills people.

When we interject civilian-trained paramedics into the Medevac mission, the mortality rate drops significantly. The army was slow to recognize this, and extraordinarily resistant to this change. The army model was that you must be an EMT-Basic (68-Whiskey). It was not required to go through any additional training other than readiness level[26]. As a result, they were not able to deal effectively with the major injuries they were faced with. Our study would later prove that.

---

26 Readiness level training required to be aircrew

Working and cultivating an understanding with the different components of the Task Force was essential to our success in theater. It was really about taking the time to share our mission and the reasons we were doing things differently than they had seen before. We were human. We ate together, joked together, and shared our lives with each other. This was extremely important. We all wanted to do the right thing; but often you must have people's trust to show them what the right thing looks like.

As we moved on through our deployment, we saw just how vital this trust was.

Marc Dragony works on multiple patients in the back of a Medevac helicopter. The patient on the left was just hoisted in.

Courtesy of Sebastian Rich, Photojournalist

AFGHAN POLICE OFFICER

"They die in assaults on lonely mountain checkpoints and in group beheadings captured on hand-held video cameras. They are engulfed by flaming car bombs and are shot at point-blank range by men who often dress up in the same plain gray uniform as theirs. Forever maligned as corrupt, incompetent and drug-addled, Afghan National Police officers have sacrificed unlike any force in the country...taking casualties at a rate far higher than Afghan soldiers..."
Joshua Partlow, Washington Post, August 30, 2011

Khogyani
9 Feb 2009

I really don't like watching people die.

By the time I got to Afghanistan, I'd been a paramedic for quite some time. I'd seen a few people die along the way, and some of them still haunt me. At this point, I'd been in Afghanistan for about seven weeks, and had had some serious calls. But so far nobody had died on me.

We got a call to Khogyani, in between Jalalabad and the Tora Boras. Lovett was flying, and Penrod was pilot in command. I hopped on with Marc Dragony as the lead medic. SGT Mike Gorham was on board as crew chief.

An IED ripped apart a truck that several Afghan National Police (ANP) officers were riding in. Three died instantly. The vehicle was a smoking hole in the ground. One officer had an isolated eye injury, and two guys were seriously fucked up. Their lower extremities were completely thrashed; they were peppered with shrapnel all over their bodies.

We took two Afghan police officers on board. One was completely unconscious—Dragony worked on him; I worked on the other. My guy was full of metal from the waist down. He started to fight because he was in an altered level of consciousness.

As we took off, this officer was fighting me and bleeding everywhere. I started cutting his clothes off, which usually is easy, but he had on several thick layers of clothing. I threw a tourniquet on and tightened it up. I put another on his other leg; it, too, was bleeding out. These guys were in trouble—they had more holes in them than the California state budget.

"Penrod, we're in deep shit back here! Step on it!"

"Roger that."

He radioed to our Apache escorts. "We need to hurry, so we're gonna put the hammer down. We'll catch you later."

He fuckin' stepped on it. The vibration increased, and we felt the thrust. Our escorts were left in the dust. Our aircraft could outfly the Apaches—we had more power.

Dragony was working on his officer, first cutting away his clothes. The patient had a very thick wool coat on. As Dragony cut, he felt vials of glass within the uniform break.

Very strange.

The airway seemed protected, but Dragony was concerned about possible hemorrhage and the need to start fluid resuscitation. His extremities were so buried in his clothes that immediate peripheral access was not an option. Dragony went for an IO, called a Fast One, to the sternum. This was supposed to be inserted straight into the marrow of the bone. But the damn thing snapped! At that point, I suggested he just confirm the airway.

I was working on my patient, struggling because he was thrashing about. I needed to see the severity of his injuries. While he was thrashing about, Gorham was trying to get oxygen on him. Gorham called out to Dragony, "Help me out here!"

"Leave him, alone, Gorham," I answered. "He's in his own hell right now."

As I worked on my patient, I saw that he was bleeding out. Blood was all over us. I struggled to cut away the layers of clothing to see his injuries. I was wrestling to put tourniquets on both legs because blood is slippery, and he wasn't being still for me. I got them on, fastened the Velcro and tightened them up. Next was the airway.

All of a sudden Dragony's patient locked his jaw and went stiff. This was not a good sign. He couldn't get a basic airway, so he had to do one of two things—either a rapid sequence intubation (RSI), then open up his airway or do a surge crike.

Two minutes to landing.

"Bag past his airway through his nasal passages and see if you can get compliance. We don't have a lot of time until we offload. To do a crike would be tough," I suggested.

He agreed and was able to get some compliance.

These were Afghan police officers. Cops like me. I didn't want to lose them.

We landed and piled into the FST where Doc Kavanagh joined us. Dragony's patient was time-sensitive. We lost his pulse so we started CPR. Kavanagh put in a chest tube and intubated him. The surgical team opened up his chest and started direct cardiac massage. I walked around the bed and offered to take over. This freed up the surgeon.

I reached into the chest of the police officer and put my hand around his heart.

"How many beats do you want me to give him per minute?" I asked.

The surgeon replied, "About eighty." *OK.*

I squeezed his heart. And again. Again. And every once in a while, there would be an inherent beat. But not enough—only about three beats a minute.

After a time, the surgeon whispered, "Take your hand out of his chest. There's nothing we can do for him."

We had reached a point where it wasn't practical anymore. The Afghan police officer was gone.

This was a hard loss for me. My first patient ended up losing a leg. The second patient was my first death in theater. I had his blood all over my boots, but I couldn't bring myself to clean them. I wore those boots until they nearly rotted off because I didn't want to forget him. I didn't want to forget his sacrifice.

Now and then, I look at my right hand and I can still feel his heartbeat.

Ground crews and Medevac members offloading a critical care patient from a Medevac aircraft.

Courtesy of SSG Angela Brennan, Medevac CE

CRITICAL CARE TRANSPORT

"What most people don't realize is that a huge percentage of Medevac flights entail the transfer of wounded troops from one level medical treatment facility (MTF) to another. These patients often are hooked up to various types of medical/life sustaining equipment which the typical flight medic is not trained on or certified to use. As a result there is a substantial risk to many patients during the transfer flight that their condition may seriously deteriorate."
Administrator Post, www.medevacmatters.org, May 16, 2012

"I see the fear on the faces of my medics when they are handed off multiple sick patients from the FSTs in the area, when they realized how far in over their head they are. I think that both our medics being charged with this mission, and the patients for which they are responsible, deserve better."
CPT Mark Kavanagh

Salerno, Afghanistan

Not all of our casualties are from battles or IEDs set by hostiles. Sometimes bad things happen wherever you are, whatever you're doing. For this Air Force Master Sergeant, this was the case. He'd been in the country for perhaps a half hour. He was standing in a building that had a sandbag roof. It was shoddy construction, and thousands of pounds of sand were resting on top of the plywood. This guy just happened to be underneath when it gave way. He was medevac'd, operated on, and ready to be transported to Bagram.

Ben Higgins picked him up way down south, near Salerno. Initially, the Salerno-based flight medics were asked to take him halfway to Bagram for a tail to tail transfer, but they intervened when they recognized the degree of instability of the patient. They also knew through previous discussions that all of the Bagram flight medics preferred to conduct the entire transport for such patients. Ben was an advocate for improved continuity of care for critical patients. He knew unstable patients were at higher risk when care was relinquished under adverse conditions with risks associated with tail to tail transfers. Ben readily accepted the flight because it was faster and safer for the patient, and he preferred to fly all the way down to Salerno. Generally, the longer the flight was, the better he was able to apply his finest skills. These were the benefits of his civilian flight paramedic experience.

The patient had a disrupted vertebrae impinging on the spinal cord without severing it. This was the most profound case of neurogenic shock Ben had ever seen, and probably ever will see. Neurogenic shock is the result of a spinal cord injury that decreases innervation below the injury level. This is a serious injury that results in an increase of the vascular system capacity without an increase in the blood volume. It has a similar effect to losing a significant amount of blood without the normal ability of the body to compensate for the loss. This patient was sick and at real risk for dying and had reached the limit of the FST's capabilities.

This Master Sergeant was post-surgical, as the surgeons just completed a stabilization of his cervical spine while also managing his perfusion deficits. He received a halo device to externally stabilize his neck, relieve pressure on the cord, and prevent further injury.

Ben arrived at the Salerno FST to receive the patient report and prepare him for transport. The patient report was provided by the attending surgeon, a Colonel, who described an immediate post-surgical patient requiring blood pressure support for the transport. "This patient isn't transportable," Ben asserted. "He's not stable enough for transport."

There was a sudden revelation to the referring medical providers that the patient wasn't quite ready for transport. As the patient's advocate, it was Ben's responsibility to ensure that the patient was adequately prepared, and he was compelled to do what was necessary for the patient's welfare. Ben quickly developed a plan of care for the transport based on the surgeon's report and a physical assessment. Understanding the needs of the situation, the Salerno flight medics jumped in and started a Dopamine drip using an intravenous pump with good results. With the drip and Neosynephrine intravenous boluses, the patient's blood pressure stabilized sufficiently for management during transport.

Preparing a patient for transport is an involved process typically called patient packaging. It is an effort to make the patient and all ongoing treatment portable without causing any negative effects to the patient's condition. This patient was sedated, chemically paralyzed, and pain managed with narcotics through intravenous catheters. He was intubated and mechanically ventilated. An arterial catheter was used for invasive blood pressure monitoring for increased accuracy. The effectiveness of mechanical ventilation as well as the placement of the endotracheal tube were both monitored with End Tidal CO_2. The patient's oxygenation was continually assessed with pulse-oximetry. Supplemental oxygen was provided using the ventilator and mixed with ambient air measured as a fraction of the inspired air. On the long transport, Ben used a lot of oxygen on this guy.

They got him situated in the aircraft, and Ben managed him—he'd done it many times before. But it was tricky. Taking a patient out of a relatively stable FST environment and placing him into a helicopter for transport has its own inherent risks. The helicopter environment introduces variables such as temperature, pressure, and instability from gravitational forces and vibration. These environmental factors generally have negative effects on the patient. Of course, there are always the risks associated with flying. If those risks were not enough, this mission was accomplished in a combat zone.

There were several life threats on this guy. His blood pressure was pretty low with the potential for irreversible shock. His cervical spine was fractured with at least an impingement of the central cord and the potential for permanent deficits. He was also sedated and chemically paralyzed to ensure adequate ventilation which carries its own degree of risk if not managed correctly.

So Ben managed his pressure, pumped him with Neosynephrine, got his Dopamine going and titrated it to effectively get fluids going, and ventilated him.

One thing we don't want to do with a patient who's got a diminished return of blood to the vascular system is to increase the pressure within the chest. High volumes of air result in higher intra-thoracic pressure that can impede blood return to the heart and, in turn, decrease the amount of blood distributed out to the tissues. Close monitoring and critical thinking throughout the transport are necessary to effectively manage these patients. Ventilation for a patient with low blood pressure is also tricky. Too little or too much volume can lead to a bad outcome.

These procedures alone are challenging, even for a paramedic with several years of experience. And Ben was doing well with him.

Then all of a sudden, DUSTOFF flew into a developing dust storm. First it closed around the front of them. The pilot, Major Daniel Anderson, began a turn toward clear weather, and the storm closed in behind them. They were socked in. It was time to land and figure out Option B!

By some form of good fortune, there happened to be a FOB right in front of them. The pilots landed there to wait for the storm to pass.

The FST surgeon came out to the helipad to see if they had a patient. The surgeon stood outside the helicopter and communicated over an intercom headset under the turning rotors. Ben informed him of the situation and requested an exchange of oxygen cylinders to replace his diminishing supply. With adverse weather, a critical patient, and the weather delay, it was important to take advantage of the resources available. He opted to remain in the helicopter with the patient and wait for the weather to clear. He knew that a transfer would be risky for the patient, and the transfer would only be temporary, requiring another transfer later on. It was better to wait for the storm to clear than to subject the patient to two transfers. The patient was well "dialed in," and the FST could not offer anything more for the patient than Ben was already doing.

Ben kept him going, titrating the supplemental oxygen flow to the patient's condition by monitoring the pulse-oximetry and heart rate. He had to decrease the amount of oxygen use to a level that met the patient's physiologic needs but without any waste. Critical-care transports are a balance of the resources available with needs of the patient (or patients in many cases) in a relatively dynamic, adverse, and austere environment. We only use what we need because of limited resources. In the combat environment, we never know what will happen next, and the Medevac helicopter is a limited resource.

Decision time coincided with a clearing of the weather sufficient to allow lift-off and continuation of the transport. Ultimately they were grounded about a half hour without any deterioration of the patient's condition. Ben was comfortable managing the patient because of the degree of control he maintained with the electronic monitoring, ventilation, and medications on hand. He sat with the patient, managing him, the helicopter running, and the weather crappy. It was just another transport well within his capabilities.

Critical-care transport within a combat theater is challenging. There are many considerations we don't find in the civilian sector. The injury patterns alone are well outside those of the civilian flight paramedics' normal experience. On the other hand, civilian flight paramedics see more of the non-traumatic patient such as the cardiac or medical critical-care patient that present different challenges. In either situation, critical-care transport is demanding. There are many considerations that range from armed security of the helicopter on an unsecured landing zone to determining the cause and effect of decreasing the tidal volume on a neurogenic shock patient at an elevation of seven thousand feet.

Critical-care transport is like trying to keep many plates spinning. He had the altitude plate, the titrate plate, the weather plate, and the temperature plate. Those are just the regular plates. And if one plate wobbles and crashes, you must get it back up and spinning immediately, otherwise the patient crashes.

We have some of the best equipment available for medical transport. We have the capability to effectively monitor critical-care patients and the chemicals to manage them. The most difficult aspect of such an endeavor is the environment. All tasks and efforts are many times more difficult in the aviation environment, related to the environmental factors of temperature, pressure, and stability. In addition to the factors previously described, there are also the limitations imposed by tactical conditions such as lighting restrictions, the numbers of patients onboard, and access to those patients. Although we fly mostly night missions using night-vision devices, we don't normally attempt to manage patients with them. Night-vision devices are for scanning outside the helicopter when performing crew tasks. A small amount of blue/green light is best for attending to the patient inside the aircraft. There is also the elevated ambient noise in the helicopter, which is both a distraction for the flight medic, a source of stress for the patient, and a hindrance to assessment.

Complete understanding of the equipment is important. A typical transport requires close monitoring of the heart rate and rhythm, the pulse-oximetry that tells us how well the patient's lungs are oxygenating, and end-tidal CO_2 indicates how well the lungs are ventilating. The blood pressure can be monitored non-invasively or invasively using an arterial catheter. The patient's core body temperature is always a concern and can be monitored as well. More than simply monitoring the cardiac rhythm, we can also obtain a twelve-lead electrocardiogram. We can intubate patients with or without the use of sedatives and temporary chemical paralysis, known as Rapid Sequence Intubation (RSI). Patients can be mechanically ventilated with waveform end-tidal CO_2 monitoring for assessing the placement of the endotracheal tube and the effectiveness of ventilation. Chest tubes can be placed and monitored in order to evacuate air and/or blood from the lung cavities. Access to the central circulation can be achieved with an intravenous catheter or an intraosseous needle. Medications can be infused with controlled dosing using an intravenous pump. Army flight medics carry a well-stocked drug box with ACLS drugs, sedative/hypnotics, narcotics, paralytics, vasopressors, steroids, and others. Blood products are available for initiation as needed and are commonplace for the post-surgical patient transport. The one common element that incorporates assessment, treatment, and monitoring variables is critical thinking.

I shudder to think of the Master Sergeant in the hands of a twenty-year-old EMT-Basic. It may have been a different kind of ride.

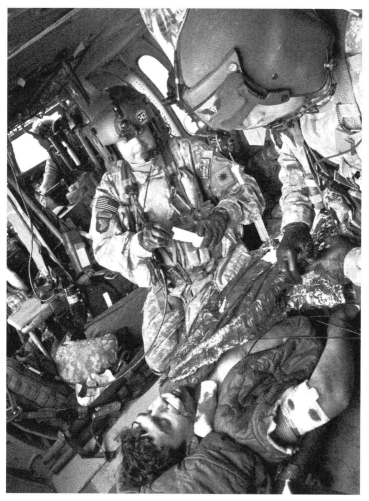

SFC Al Smoot and Doc Kavanagh working on a patient with multiple gunshot wounds. Smoot's helmet bears the 343 insignia honoring the firefighters who died in the World Trade Center on 9/11.

Courtesy of Sebastian Rich, Photojournalist

SEVEN MINUTES IN HELL

"You may have to fight a battle more than once to win it."
Margaret Thatcher

"You can't tell a man who's scared to death that he has only a few minutes to live. You have to force a smile and give them as much comfort as you can. Later this moment will haunt you. It will haunt you that you lied, and you will wish that you could somehow have made those words true."
Michael Bailey, *The Madness of the Combat Medic*

Kot, Afghanistan
15 Mar 2009

Nine-line! Nine-line! Nine-line!

The call came in as an IED versus Humvee with two serious casualties. The explosion had already taken two other lives. Two of our DUSTOFF birds responded. The plan was for each helicopter to take a patient and bring him back to Jbad.

I was not present for this call. I had taken an early leave so that I would be present for the busiest time of our deployment, the killing season.

Al Smoot was second-up. It was about a ten-minute ride from Jalalabad to the kill zone in Kot. Donald Baker was crew chief, and together they checked equipment and then watched the terrain pass by, mentally preparing for what lay ahead. The area was flat, barren, and seemingly one boring color—bland tan. Occasionally there was a patch of agriculture that gave the valley a pop of green, or perhaps a leafless tree here and there. Even the sky seemed a little hazy in the light March sun. But still, it was a beautiful morning for Afghanistan.

Cole Gould was at the controls. He brought in the aircraft near a village road, and Smoot and Baker took note of the smoldering debris nearby. As they lowered, Baker noticed body parts strewn about near the road. The Humvee was blown to bits, pieces all over the field. He noticed a huge piece of metal sitting on top of another Humvee about a hundred yards away. *Damn.*

First-up was in the lead, but at the last minute, the pilot pulled out and circled around. He didn't like something he'd seen, perhaps waiting for the Kiowas. But Smoot's aircraft lowered down onto a patch of tall grass swaying from the wash of the rotors. It was a dark contrasting green next to the surrounding dirt. The rotors kicked up dust—more brown.

Baker jumped off with his rifle. There were three mud huts right there, and about forty villagers came out of them—males and females of all ages. They seemed agitated and kept pushing up toward the aircraft. One of the ground officers was throwing smoke their way to keep them back, as they thought the smoke was tear gas.

This is never good when civilians do this. They may be curious, but they also might be ready to ambush, even women and children. We knew they could be just as deadly as the men. There was no aircraft above, because the kill zone was within a ten-mile radius of Jalalabad—considered the safety zone. But because of the situation, the Kiowas were on their way.

Baker came up with his weapon. He noticed a wire from one of the huts rolled out toward the kill zone—so these people may have been responsible for the explosion. It was a stressful situation—Baker was convinced they could be ambushed. About that time, the Kiowas came in, swooping low, and the villagers retreated. They didn't mess with the gunships.

As the aircraft doors opened, six fully armored soldiers approached the aircraft, carrying a stretcher. Smoot had barely stepped out of the chopper when the men passed him by, loading patient number one onto the deck. Smoot noticed the soldier's legs were missing at the knees, his thighs bloodied and duct-taped to the litter. His huge arms were raised straight up in the air, leaning against the female soldier who helped carry him. Burnt skin and small remnants of his uniform wafted in the wind. He was badly burnt. He was screaming, but Smoot barely heard him above the noise of the helicopter. They slid him in, and Smoot noticed blood dripping on the deck, despite the tourniquets.

Before he could wrap his brain around the extent of injuries to this soldier, a second soldier came up on Smoot's right. His buddies were carrying him on a Sked litter, and rapidly approaching. He was white as a sheet, eyes closed, his head flopping forward.

There goes his airway...OK, it seems we're taking two.

First-up landed about forty yards from Smoot's aircraft. Doc was several yards from the patients, so he jumped out into the deep grass, hoping to give Smoot a hand. Seeing the second patient loaded onto their aircraft, Doc began to sprint toward Smoot's aircraft.

"Doc! Hold on a sec!" someone warned.

The COMS cable attached to his helmet went tight, tugged a bit, and then snapped. *Oops.*

Doc arrived at the open door of Smoot's bird and prepared to jump in to help. But then he stopped cold.

It was horrific.

Two young soldiers, covered in blood and charred uniforms. Missing legs...

Doc's head began to spin as he went through mentally what could be done to stabilize them before they took off.

Where do I start?

Smoot hopped in, and bellowed out, "Close the door!"

He looked to his right where a young female soldier stood at the door, probably the ground medic, standing there without a helmet. Her face was in resigned sadness at the gruesome display before her—this was goodbye. Crinkling her nose to raise her glasses, she tossed a boot on the stretcher. "Here's his foot," she yelled. "He'll be needing that."

Smoot thought to himself, *No he won't.*

Doc was just standing there at the door. Smoot yelled, "Shut the fucking door! Let's get these guys outta here!"

Doc climbed in between the patients, and Baker backed in, finger still on the trigger.

"Goddamn it! Shut the door!" Smoot shouted again.

Baker stepped over the conscious soldier and slid the door shut. They lifted off.

As soon as the door closed, the pungent smell of burnt flesh and blood filled his nostrils.

On the deck, Smoot drew his attention to the unconscious soldier. He took a cursory glance—he was fairly intact but was unresponsive. He had a deep gash on his cheek that didn't seem to be bleeding much. Likely shrapnel. He suspected internal injuries, but first he had to open that airway.

Marc Dragony was in first-up DUSTOFF. The moment they landed, Doc had run off to join Smoot's aircraft and left him alone with Tom Gifford as crew chief. Dragony jumped out of the aircraft, which was about a hundred yards from the kill zone, and just about tripped over the door of the blown-up Humvee.

Damn, this is catastrophic.

He jogged over to Smoot's bird and caught a glimpse of the patients in the back. One of them was screaming so loud he could hear him over the rotors.

Holy shit.

Baker tucked his weapon away safely and took in the patient before him. There was a pile of boots, bones, and bloody stumps with tourniquets on them, and this guy was big, awake, and combative. He was trying to sit up, grabbing at the tubes and wires hanging over him. Shocked by his condition, Baker blanked.

What was he supposed to do?

The awake soldier called out, his arms still raised upward...Baker heard him over the high-pitched hum. Baker inched closer, knelt over him and told him he was OK, but he wasn't OK. He was struggling to breathe, he was burnt and mangled, and any medical knowledge Baker had acquired in his years of experience flew right out the window.

Kneeling between the patients, Doc fumbled with the equipment.

We don't want to lose these guys...

The awake soldier grabbed the IV tube and yanked. Baker responded and wrestled to get it out of his hand. He called out, but Doc couldn't make out the words over the helicopter noise.

He retrieved the bag valve mask (BVM) and handed it to Smoot who placed it over the unconscious soldier's face. Air...

Next, Doc got out the finger monitor and popped it in place, and then waited for Smoot to read the monitor. Smoot's expletive informed him.

There was a heartbeat, but very weak.

Doc turned to the awake soldier and checked the tourniquets. They were tight. He checked his vitals and then muscled the IV out of the patient's hand. *Geez, he's big.*

Once second-up was on its way, Dragony went back to the kill zone. There were two heroes (soldiers killed) to retrieve. He was shown where the first hero was located, wrapped in a blue tarp not far away. His body was broken apart, and he had to be carried in the tarp and then placed carefully into a body bag. The next hero was worse.

While Dragony worked respectfully with the bodies, he noticed the Lieutenant Commander in charge of the PRTs standing there watching him. As they met eyes, the officer hung his head and broke down, sobbing.

Dragony loaded their bodies onto the helicopter and transported them back to Jalalabad.

Doc switched to Smoot's unconscious patient to assist. He took a look at his blood- and soot-covered uniform and decided to expose him to evaluate the rest of his body. He slid his shears up his uniform pants and shirt, cutting them off. Once the shirt was off, he noticed an IV in the patient's arm, with a severed line that was leaking blood.

Smoot grabbed the intubation pack, pulled out one tube, and tossed it aside. He pulled out another and quickly glanced at the IV.

What the fuck?

The line was red. *Shit!*

He grabbed the tube and tossed it toward Doc.

"You fucking cut the line – try to fix it!"

Doc fumbled to secure the IV site and insert a new line of tubing, but the aircraft vibration made it difficult. The awake soldier's screams were actually audible over the sound of the engines, when usually it is impossible to hear much of anything other than radio transmissions over COMS. It was distracting.

Doc's attempt to replace the tubing should've taken only a few seconds, but given these factors, it actually took much longer. Easy procedures he'd done a hundred times were complicated by the environment in the helicopter. He couldn't seem to get his hands to move fast enough.

Baker quickly handed Doc a new IV.

"I can't breathe!" screamed the soldier, over and over.

Baker grabbed the tubes and wrestled them out of his hands again and again.

"Al!" he shouted.

Smoot didn't hear him. It was time to intubate. Several minutes had gone by, and this kid didn't even have an open airway.

Why is this so hard?

Doc straddled the patient. He placed electrodes on the unconscious soldier's chest and turned on the monitor.

Baker grabbed the awake Soldier's arm to control him—he was getting more and more combative.

"Al! What do I do? He says he can't breathe!"

Smoot retorted, "Give him oxygen!"

It finally clicked in. Baker reached for the BVM.

"I can't breathe!"

Smoot heard it clearly that time. He turned his head and saw the soldier flailing his arms, his torn shirt and burnt skin moving with the wind. Baker was trying to gain control.

Doc noticed too, and he leaned over and took hold of one arm, holding it against him firmly. He moved into him so Baker could get the oxygen going. In response the patient grasped Doc's other hand as they finally got the oxygen going. That quieted him...somewhat.

Smoot turned back to his patient. He noticed a small thigh-high wound he hadn't seen before.

Suddenly they touched down. *Wow, that was fast.*

Jason Penrod was assigned to third-up Medevac. The other two birds were already on this call. He was preflighting the aircraft with Nate Whorton, getting equipment ready in case they were needed. He heard the aircraft coming in, looked up, and saw DUSTOFF haulin' ass coming in. Gould did a tail stand on the ramp—something wasn't right.

He and Nate quickly moved their direction. Penrod caught a look at Gould—his visor was down, jaw tight. He saw the angst on his face. He motioned Jason over. This wasn't good.

Penrod reached the aircraft, slid open the door, and was instantly jolted by a bloody pile of body parts.

Holy shit.

He was amazed the soldier was conscious. He was gasping for air even though they had a mask on him. He was trying to take it off because he couldn't catch his breath. His abdomen was distended, and there was an unnatural movement of his chest.

Litter bearers arrived, faces turning grim. They retrieved the awake soldier first, leaving a thick trail of blood where the edges of the litter were. Penrod grabbed a side and they all moved toward the FLA.

Next up was Smoot's patient. Doc unhooked him, and the litter bearers pulled him out. Smoot got one more squeeze of air and then backed out of the aircraft, meeting them on the other side. The FLA was just ahead.

Smoot had been counting the seconds. "Put him down! Put him down! I gotta breathe for him!" he called out. They stopped, and Al gave him a few breaths with the BVM. They resumed the quick walk to the FLA.

They climbed into the dark truck, and Smoot sat facing his patient on the bottom bunk. Doc and Penrod were on the other side with the awake soldier.

Penrod's compassion took over despite the desperate helplessness that crept in. He knew how this would end; he'd seen it before. Deep breath. "How old are ya, brother?" he asked.

The soldier answered with a muffled, "Twenty-four," then tried to prop himself up.

"Twenty-four. OK, can you help me, guy? You gotta lay flat for me, OK? Lay flat." His voice sounded confident, professional. But it wasn't how he was feeling.

The soldier tried to comply. "Can't breathe..."

"Say again?"

"Can't breathe..."

"OK, we got oxygen on ya; you're doin' all right. Hang in there, OK?" Penrod comforted.

Smoot spoke up from the other side. "Check his lungs, Doc! He may have a pneumothorax!"

Doc answered, "He's got a dart bilaterally."

Smoot struggled with the intubation on his soldier. It was dark in the FLA. There wasn't enough room to maneuver. He could see this guy slipping away, and nothing was going right for either of them.

"Hey! We got lights in here?! Please—I need them!"

The lights came on.

Smoot leaned in to give the intubation another shot, but the FLA took a hard bump. Smoot hit his head on the bunk. "Fuck!"

Doc called out to the drivers, "Slow down over the bumps, please!"

Doc and Penrod continued to calm their patient. "Can't breathe…"

"You're doin' great. You're doin' awesome," Doc lied.

Penrod added, "We're almost to the hospital, and they'll put you to sleep, OK?"

Smoot tried to intubate within the space, but the top bunk was too close.

"Goddamn it! Shit! Hey, Doc—I'm not gonna get a tube in him. There's just no fuckin' way in here."

Doc replied, "Wait 'till we get there. It's OK—just bag him."

"You're doin' good, brother. We're almost there…almost there," said Penrod. The soldier was settling down.

The truck stopped, and immediately the doors flew open.

Doc swung into action. "We got a twenty-four-year-old male bilateral lung decompression. He's awake and oriented. Got a radial pulse! I don't have any other vitals."

The FST medics pulled out Doc's patient, and he disappeared into the FST with Penrod by his side.

The FST doctor came out to meet Smoot. Smoot started a breathless turnover report: "Hyperventilate this guy. He's gonna need a tube. I've got ventilatory effort from probably about ten a minute. No other response. Totally unresponsive. Only thing I see is a wound to his cheek. IV line cut—no IV line right now."

They walked him in, Smoot's despair tainting the edge of his voice. "I would've tubed him in flight, but he was clenched. And then we cut the IV, and then everything got fucked up..."

They pressed into the FST, and the teams went to work, quickly prepping the two American soldiers for surgery.

Smoot stood there, shell-shocked. *What just happened?*

He looked up to see a squad of Afghan soldiers staring his way. The chaos was now on the other side of the unpainted wooden door. He was done for now. People were running in and out, working fervently to save our soldiers.

Someone asked him if there were more patients. "I'm not sure. I took two. I know they were supposed to have another litter. They threw two on my aircraft and fucked up our whole game plan."

"Is there another aircraft on its way there?" he asked again.

"Im not sure if they had another patient. I'll give a call."

Smoot let out a deep sigh.

Once inside the FST's trauma bay, Doc observed that the team now had two critical patients requiring immediate surgery. One surgeon took his patient to the OR with most of the surgical team, leaving Doc with Smoot's patient, a surgeon, and a medic.

The surgeon worked on the right side of Smoot's patient, placing a chest tube and a central line, and yelled at Doc to place a chest tube in the left chest. He barely had a pulse. Once in place, both chest tubes immediately began flowing a steady stream of blood, and then they lost his pulse. Doc assisted the surgeon in performing a thoracotomy, which is opening the chest to evaluate the heart for a repairable injury. But when they got in, they found the heart was empty. Smoot's soldier, despite the fact that he looked relatively uninjured, had sustained massive internal injuries from the blast. He was dead.

Doc hurried into the other OR, but the soldier with the amputated legs had just been declared dead as well. The team had done what it could, but he had died in surgery.

Wanting to learn from the extent of the injuries, Doc examined the hero. Doc saw a blood-saturated trauma dressing within a deep shrapnel wound in his perineum (between his buttocks). He hadn't seen this wound in the aircraft.

The surgeon told Doc that both of these guys had sustained catastrophic wounds that were not survivable. Doc then did what we all do: he second-guessed himself. He thought that if he'd had more experience, if he'd been more composed and worked faster, he might've seen it. If he wasn't trying to fix the IV line that he'd cut, maybe he would've been able to identify that wound, pack it, and slow the bleeding.

If...

Penrod knew they would get Doc's soldier on the operating table and he wouldn't make it. He'd seen too many like this. As he spent his last moments with him, he acted out what he would want if he were in this soldier's place. What could he do for this kid?

He'd asked his name but couldn't make it out under the mask. He'd asked if there was anybody he wanted to talk to. Was there someone he wanted to get a message to? Was there something he wanted to say? But there was no answer. He couldn't breathe. He was distracted, just trying to take a breath.

Doc had been absolutely overwhelmed in the chaos and sensory deprivation of the helicopter. It was unlike anything he'd ever seen. They had picked up two unstable patients who required intubation, but there wasn't room in the helicopter to get this done. He couldn't hear because of the rotor noise, he didn't have much room to do anything, the movement of the helicopter made moving about difficult, and there wasn't time to do what he wanted. Tubes were everywhere, getting tangled in the rush. He felt overwhelmed, not effective. It was the most difficult environment in which to practice medicine that he'd experienced thus far.

He was a medical doctor, yet he felt inadequate.

Smoot was exhausted. It was seven minutes from the kill zone to Jbad: the worst seven minutes he'd ever experienced. The plan to take only one patient per aircraft failed. The IV was cut. He couldn't get his soldier intubated despite numerous tries. Doc and Baker were disoriented and struggled under the circumstances. And then both soldiers died. A very bad day.

One that still haunts him now.

Baker stayed with the aircraft. This was where he was most comfortable. Let the medics handle the wounded; he was the gun-toting mechanic. That didn't change the feelings he knew were there.

He and the pilots pressure-washed the aircraft. They had to clean it up right away—especially the deck. Blood puddles and leaks into the cracks in the floor. Blood is corrosive and will eventually damage any electrical wiring in its path. As they watched the pink mist spray from the deck, they decided they needed a cigar. They lit up, knowing full well that it was forbidden to smoke near the aircraft.

About that time an officer walked by, noticed the cigars, and turned sharply to reprimand them. As he approached, he saw the blood dripping from the deck, debris, and the looks on their faces. He turned away, silent. He knew they were coping. He'd let them cope.

Baker was glad that at least the soldiers died with us, and not out there with the enemy. They were surrounded by their own who had cared for them and fought to keep them alive. It was some consolation.

Later that night, Baker and Dragony were called out to the same area. As they landed, they were handed a red bag.

"What's this?" asked Dragony.

"The rest of them," the soldier answered.

When the mortuary brought all four heroes out, half of the FOB showed up to pay their respects.

It would be something that they would do more and more of as the killing season progressed.

PART TWO
The Killing Season

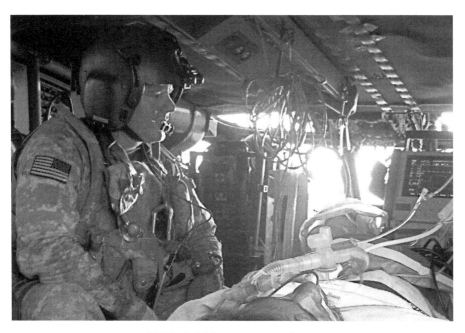

SSG Rob Walters spinning plates.

Courtesy of SSG Angela Brennan, Medevac CE

SPINNING PLATES

"Those who expect to reap the blessings of freedom must, like men, undergo the fatigue of supporting it."
Thomas Paine

"I was deployed to Konar in 2005 with Special Forces and had the same experiences passing off intubated, poly-trauma patients to regular flight medics. On several occasions, I had to board the aircraft myself and fly to Bagram with seriously ill patients, leaving a very dangerous and remote FOB without a Doc until I could make my way back."
MAJ Robert L. Mabry, MD

Bagram to Jalalabad

Rob Walters had been with the Guard since his early days in college, going into the flight medic program as an EMT. Then he'd gone through a civilian paramedic course to help his chances at being a fireman. He found he really enjoyed prehospital medicine. He was able to apply it in the US Army—although very little. He went to Egypt and flew four calls all year long. Then he transferred to Fort Irwin, California, to get some experience, and because he was a paramedic, they put him in charge as the lead trainer. He'd gone to Afghanistan with Al Smoot in 2003. By that time Rob had done three years in the back of an ambulance and had become a firefighter.

Now back in Afghanistan five years later, Rob had much experience with critical-care patients, but it still required a lot of him. Based out of Bagram, he was to pick up a patient from Jalalabad.

He did a tail to tail with Nate Whorton. The patient had been burned and exposed to a fire-suppression chemical from the inside of a burning vehicle. It was called FM 200. It created hydrofluoric acid when heated, and if inhaled just a few times, it was entirely destructive to the respiratory system. We'd seen people walking and talking and within the next forty-eight hours after they were exposed to FM 200, they were dead. Young, healthy people seemingly took just a few breaths of this poison and were wiped out.

This was the second or third patient like this that the guys at Bagram had seen. They identified it immediately. He had facial burns, airway burns, and hydrofluoric acid inhalation burns. He had respiratory issues that were potentially extreme. A burned airway is a huge deal. There are a lot of problems that go with it.

The FST had intubated the patient immediately to help protect his airway. For a patient that is awake, it is necessary to provide sedation, pain management, and chemical paralysis to place a breathing tube into the patient's trachea. This is a common standard of care. Sometimes when we completely sedate and paralyze a patient, a patient's heart rate slows down. As long as the blood pressure and other vital signs remain within acceptable parameters, this is not a problem. During the course of this patient's care, the anesthesia provider decided to partially reverse some of the patient's paralytic medicine to bring his heart rate back up. This was later problematic, because when we block a paralytic, we block it for a long time…which means we block future paralytics for some time as well. Bottom line, it was impossible to paralyze this guy for a while and even harder because Rob didn't know this had happened.

The anesthesia provider had mentioned the name of the medication to Nate only to tell him that he had given the medicine. Evidently there was some sort of tactical rush associated with picking up this patient, and a thorough questioning of this medication was therefore precluded, especially when the pilot-in-command was a pharmacist.

Whorton asked Penrod, "What is this medication?"

"I've heard of it, but I can't remember what it is," he answered, a little busy at the moment. Both were task-saturated with the ongoing tactical situation. Coming up with obscure pharmacology trivia was pretty low on the list of priorities. With things seemingly under control, there probably wasn't much concern about it.

They flew him to Jbad, where another team was waiting to take him to Bagram. Rob did the transfer of care.

Nate explained, "Dude, the anesthesiologist gave him this medicine, but none of us remember what it was or what it does. I know it's important, but I'm not really sure why."

"OK, we'll figure it out," Rob answered.

During that time frame, we had been using so many paralytics that there was no Vecuronium available to us in the entire country. We'd used it all. Between us and the surgeries, there was a high demand for it. So we had to go with our second-favorite paralytic, which is Rocuronium. It had a very similar effect but didn't last as long. It had a shorter onset than Vecuronium.

We finished the patient transfer and got him into the back of the aircraft. We did a cold onload, which means we'd powered down the aircraft and our flight gear wasn't being worn, so it would've been a nice, easy, quiet transfer of care. Rob could listen to lung sounds, perform a complete assessment and packaging, and take a verbal report with much less distraction and noise. He took the report from Nate. Major Dan Anderson was in the back with us to watch the transfer of care and to talk with the crew. As a pilot, he didn't even have medical gloves on—it wasn't necessary.

As soon as they got him loaded into the aircraft, the patient started thrashing around.

Rob was extremely concerned he'd extubate himself, which, with a burned airway, is the absolute worst thing that could happen. If this occurred, there would be a high risk of fatality. This is because the airway is swollen and difficult, and they can't control his breathing. Getting him reintubated may be impossible. There is a high likelihood of having to cut the neck (performing a surgical cricothyrotomy). This is a big, big deal.

Rob moved into action. "Sir, hold his head still. I don't care if you break his neck, you have to hold his head still so we don't lose that tube."

This patient was literally thrashing about; his face was all burned, and Major Anderson's ungloved hands were touching his burned face.

Rob drew up more paralytics to knock this guy back down to get him to stop moving. He gave him 50 mg of Rocuronium. It was an underdose, but that was how the drug was packaged and drawn. He just needed to get something going. It didn't work. He drew up another 50 mg. Didn't work. Another 50 mg. He slowed down a little. Finally Rob gave him 4 mg to 5 mg Versed on top of that. The problem with Versed is it tends to drop blood pressure, especially when slammed like he'd done. Finally, the patient settled down.

Rob realized this was a dangerous situation. It shouldn't have taken this much to get him down. So he decided to really snow (heavily sedate) him to keep him down.

"OK, I think we've got it," Rob said to Major Anderson. "Let's secure his head. Make sure the capnography is right. We're good. Get dressed— let's go."

Hot on the pad, Rob's aircraft was getting ready to taxi out. Smoot ran up and asked if we could take another patient.

"I don't really want to, but I suppose we can."

Smoot explained it would be ideal to take the second patient with them.

"What kind of patient is it?" asked Rob.

"I'm not sure. FST asked me to ask you," he replied.

"Oh, well, it must not be that big of a deal. Go ahead. We'll take it."

They loaded the second patient in with no turnover report. Rob saw that he was intubated but not ventilated, with a gunshot wound through the head. There was a single small-gauge IV placed and absolutely no monitoring. It was as if this patient had come right from the battlefield! Knowing the original patient had a complex need for extremely close monitoring and care, Rob knew he was already way behind with only one patient.

"You're kidding me, right?!" argued Rob.

"There was no report. I had to find it," answered Smoot as he produced a field medical card hidden between the patient's legs. The only thing written on the card was "GSW to head." This wasn't helpful.

"He's intubated! This is a little different than what I agreed to!"

"Dude, then pull him off."

Rob sighed. "He's loaded. It's thirty minutes. I'll figure it out."

Rob immediately set up the safety net for this patient and completed an assessment. He rapidly verified the correct placement of the breathing tube by setting up capnography. He put the patient on cardiac monitoring as well as monitoring pulse oximetry. Prior to sedating and paralyzing the patient, he conducted a brief neuro exam and found the patient was completely unresponsive. This might've been due to the injury itself or perhaps from previous sedation and paralysis. He had no way of knowing or a way to find out. Rob did note the patient had a dangerously low blood pressure (especially with a major head injury) and needed immediate management. This included securing his airway by anchoring the breathing tube and placing a cervical collar on him. Next, he administered slight sedation and paralysis to make sure the patient didn't move during the flight. With all of this completed, he optimized the ventilation settings for his specific situation, being sure to avoid over-pressurization and under-ventilation. He gained a second site of vascular access with an intraosseous line. While giving some IV fluid, he added Dopamine in an infusion to bring up his blood pressure to minimal acceptable levels. He wanted to make sure his brain was getting enough blood to survive.

While all this was going on, the first patient began bucking again. This was way too soon for him to start moving at all, given the massive amount of paralytics he received maybe ten to fifteen minutes prior. Rob gave the last 150 mg of Roc that he had on board the aircraft.

Between the two patients, he had used all of the paralytics he was carrying at the time for this predicted thirty-minute flight. From then on, Rob was going to have to manage the placement of the tube with only Fentanyl, morphine, and Versed. This could be dangerous, since there was no true paralysis, only sedation. To make matters worse, these drugs could impact his patient in ways he didn't want, like dropping his blood pressure too low. Rob was starting to get low on the Fentanyl, Versed, and morphine too. It had been a busy day even before this call. He had no choice.

The patients needed Rob's attention the entire way. It was very difficult to keep up. "Please fly fast," he called up to the pilots. "Are we almost there?"

As they came into Bagram, both of the patients were stable. At least they weren't changing their vital signs and actively trying to die…but they were still both critical and needed immediate intervention from a definitive care facility. They both had a long way to go.

They performed a rapid but cold offload to ensure none of the lines were pulled out or extubated by an excited litter team. If possible, it was usually best to conduct a slow offload under controlled circumstances as long as immediate intervention wasn't necessary. Rob walked alongside the patients into Heathe Craig and gave a report to the trauma team. He transferred care and immediately went back to restock the aircraft for the next mission.

Penrod called Rob later. "Dude, that drug was to reverse paralytics."

No shit. "No wonder I couldn't keep that guy down."

The doses Rob gave were triple what the patient should've needed. That was the only way he could keep him completely paralyzed and thus keep the airway clear.

That was Rob's last flight for the day because he had ERF'd[28] out. This means that based on the types and hours of flight performed that day, he would be taken down for a minimum of ten hours' mandatory rest before the next mission. It was common to ERF out during the summer. In Rob's last three days flying in country, he flew over twenty-seven hours of missions and ERF'd out three times…all while training, evaluating and teaching patient care to one of the new guys.

---

28 Environmental Risk Factors

CHAPADERA

"Poor boy! I never knew you, Yet I think I could not refuse this moment to die for you, if that would save you."
Walt Whitman, Drum Taps

"Scouts are like the neighbor kid who spies on you and plays dirty tricks on you. And the Apache guy is the bruiser. He's the big brother who beat the hell out of you. Black Hawk guys are the cool dudes— white neckerchiefs and sunglasses. Chinook guys are like truck drivers. They just want to haul shit—big shit—the biggest shit out there. But Medevac—you're your own breed out there. I'm a scout, so if I get mad, I just go shoot at 'em. I try to make them make a mistake; con 'em into something. But you guys—balls to the wall in there, balls to the wall out; smellin' that [blood] all the way back. And you can't fight back. Kudos to you…
I love you guys."
CW3 Gary Parsons, Kiowa Pilot

Chapadera District
9 Jun 2009

It was quite a night. The moon was so bright that when I looked up with my goggles on, the reflection blinded me.

I did three separate hoists in a twenty-four hour period. The first was an extraordinarily technical rescue. A soldier broke his leg, and we went in to retrieve him. They signaled us to let us know where they were—which was right on the face of the mountain. This was tricky—the pilots had to get close enough to hoist me in, but not so close that the rotor blades scraped the mountain and wrecked the aircraft. There wasn't much room to work with, as the mountain was steep and huge boulders dotted the terrain.

They carefully hoisted me in. The boulders were as big as a hotel room, with crevices in between. I landed in one of these crevices upside down with my feet up! Because of all my gear, it was difficult to move. "Son of a bitch, I'm gonna be stuck in here," I said to no one in particular. I was literally upside down, but somehow I was able to maneuver myself out of it.

Next, I didn't think I was going to be able to get to these guys; they had to come to me. I radioed it in. Because it was a noncombat situation, they were able to get the patient to me, and we hooked him up on the jungle penetrator. I hooked in with him, and they brought us up. We got up and peeled off out of there. That was the first hoist of the night.

A few hours later, we got another nine-line. There was a lot of confusion at first as to what we were dealing with, but eventually we learned a US soldier was shot in the leg in the Chapadera District. There was an active firefight in progress, so the commanders delayed us a bit at FOB Blessing to secure two AH-64D Longbow Apaches. After a short wait, we got an urgent call to go in immediately. The patient was shot high in the left thigh and was bleeding out.

Mike Gorham was the crew chief on duty. Mike was a towhead and super skinny. He had a large Adam's apple and glasses, kind of like a short Ichabod Crane. Smart as a whip. He and I had a running joke that he had tried to kill me in several different ways during hoists. He slammed me against a boulder during training and got an award for it! He hoisted me down over a campfire. Another time he swung me around so that I kicked a Special Forces guy in the face with my boot.

He swung me so close to the water I thought I would drown. I never complained, though. He gave 100 percent, but sometimes things just get shitty.

On my first hoist in theater, Gorham got me spinning so hard that the centrifugal force brought my rifle out away from my body. This particular hoist was taped by the Apaches. When we watched it later, we heard the pilots on the tape describing it.

"These guys are outta their minds."

"Yup," replied the other pilot.

"That would make me throw up."

"Yup."

On this occasion in Chapadera, I was hooked up, and we were performing a combat hoist. As they lowered me, the aircraft kept moving forward so that we were less of a stationary target. The troops were engaged in a firefight, actively shooting, giving us cover fire. The Apaches were offset a little bit, shooting rockets and hellfires. It was really aggressive.

I told Mike to just get me on the ground. I could see where the patient was; I could navigate the terrain. But Mike was so fixated on getting me in the exact spot that instead of coming forward and dropping me, he stopped. I started to swing a little bit.

Goddamn it, just get me on the ground!

Mike sees a couple of guys in a foxhole. One of them is injured and reclining on his back. There's a medic covering him. He lowers me down right there. My heels hit first on the ground like normal, and then I roll back like in a chair.

"Aaauuuugggghhh!"

I landed in the injured soldier's lap, nuts to butt. His mouth was right next to my ear, so his cry was really loud. But, instead of recoiling, I took in the information he just gave me. He had responded to pain. He had a good airway. He could scream, so he had a good heart rate. Three vitals in an instant!

I unhooked and rolled off of him, apologizing.

"Sorry, dude."

"Oh, God!" he sighs.

Good one, Gorham. Way to stick the landing...

I took a look at his thigh and saw that the blood was still coming. This is common. We are in combat alongside our buddies, fighting shoulder to shoulder, and we love each other like brothers. Then somebody is wounded. Our first instinct is to try to not cause them more pain. We don't want to hurt them, but we have to put on a tourniquet. Tourniquets are fucking painful. In training, we talk about tourniquets, how to put them on, etc., but what we don't say is that it's gonna hurt like hell. We have to stop the bleeding. But oftentimes I found the tourniquets applied in the field were not tight enough to stop the bleeding.

I didn't mess with the tourniquet already there. I put another one on, just barely above it, and cranked it down to stop the bleeding. Then I called in DUSTOFF 24.

While this was going on, I made a conscious decision. We were hunkered down in a shallow foxhole, and I could hear a lot of gunfire. I put my back to where the enemy was, in between enemy fire and this soldier. I felt kind of safe because I had a machine gun crew right there and an M-4 nearby. I knew they were covering us. Overhead, the Apaches were tearing everything up. I had a small amount of cover I could go to if I had to. But not everybody could fit into the foxhole. So I worked on him with my back turned, got him hooked up, and hoisted up with him.

Coincidentally, I had a young ground medic named Culver riding with me. He wanted to do ride-alongs. He had aspirations to be a physician's assistant, so I was eager to get him some experience. Culver was in the aircraft and helped me pile this guy in and shut the door. At that point, the pilot said, "Emmett, we've got another one that's just a click away."

"Oh, shit. OK, let me get back out."

I hooked back up to the cable, and Mike opened the door. I was leaning out because we were that close. We were advised of enemy in the area. Culver and I were hooked up to the intercom. As I'm hanging outside of the helicopter ready for my next hoist, I instructed Culver how to treat the patient we just brought up.

"Assess that tourniquet again. I need a rapid set of vitals. See if you can get some oxygen on him, an IV, and if he's got a good blood pressure, I need some pain meds on him. Get as much as you can done before I get back up, because it's gonna get busy back here!"

"Roger that, Staff Sergeant!"

I'm calling medical treatment while my boots are on the edge of the door. We're moving forward, my gun at the ready.

That moment will forever be the coolest, sexiest piece for me. I felt like I was really on my game. I felt a little pride on that one. I trusted Culver, I had good pilots in the front (Scott St. Aubin and Gary Heyne), and Gorham on the hoist—I was with my dudes. I had the Apaches, ground cover. And I called medical treatment while going into a firefight. I couldn't have scripted that. Practicing medicine in that environment was a high.

Gorham hoisted me down for the third combat hoist of our shift. Talk about night and day—the first hoist was like a desert scenario landscape. This call had ultra-tall grass and tiered terrain. They called me over, popped smoke so I could see them. It was an ANA soldier who was shot in the face. I did a quick assessment of him. The bullet took out his left orbit. It didn't penetrate into the cranium, but there was significant facial damage. He was conscious but altered. Part of his face was missing, but I still had a good airway. He wasn't bleeding into his trachea. Still, we didn't have time to screw around. I prepped him for the hoist. He had no other holes he wasn't born with.

Leaning on my tactical medical training, I thought he (we) would get lead poisoning from the flying bullets if I decided to stay and play, and worry about a possible spinal injury. If there was damage, it had already been done. The ground guys had muscled him around this far, so I thought we were pretty safe on the spinal injury. Lead poisoning was a sure thing if we kept fuckin' around on the ground too long. It was time to go.

I put a strap over the patient to secure him. I called in DUSTOFF 24, and they came back around. I hooked up the patient and myself, and then we hoisted up together, on the move.

As we were hoisting up and they're peeling off, the patient starts to struggle. *Oh man, here we go.* He was altered as he should be, but I'm gonna be a dope on a rope fighting this guy. We spill into the aircraft; I lay him out and shut the door. I unhooked from the cable, then hooked onto my tail to be secure, we got out of there.

Culver and I start cutting clothes and exposing the ANA soldier. I was worried about this guy's airway, so I put him on his back and then positioned him to see what was going on.

The first patient was in a lot of pain. I looked at Culver. "What was his blood pressure?"

"Really good, Staff Sergeant."

I grabbed my auto-injector of morphine and stabbed him in the leg with it, right through his clothes. Culver watched wide-eyed, as it was very aggressive. I let it inject, pulled it out, threw it down, and said to the American, "You'll be OK in a moment."

"Awww, thank you! I love you!" he crooned.

"Culver! Recheck his vitals."

Suddenly the ANA patient with the shot-off-face started to struggle. We tried to get some oxygen on him. Struggle, struggle. We tried to get some vitals. Struggle, struggle. We tried to stabilize him, made sure his airway was really good. All the while, we're wrestling to keep him still.

We didn't have a long flight time, so we didn't get a whole lot done. They immediately knocked him down at Asadabad.

After we got back and reset the aircraft, Culver left. I went to Doc Kavanagh and said, "Doc, we were under fire on that one. If I write it up, would you be willing to submit Culver for a combat medical badge?" For a medic, this is important. I felt like a big brother, and he did a great job. He deserved it.

Doc was thrilled to do so. And evidently they decided I needed one, too. We were both awarded Combat Medical Badges for this rescue.

STETSONS AND SPURS

"Grant stood by me when I was crazy, and I stood by him when he was drunk, and now we stand by each other."
William T. Sherman

"It is in the shelter of each other that the people live."
Irish proverb

**Jalalabad
Summer 2009**

Those of us in Jalalabad were joined with the 101st Airborne Cavalry unit. We were the Cavalry, and we embraced its historical significance and its traditions. Of the many traditions, two we adopted were the gold spurs and the Stetsons.

The tradition of the Order of the Spur goes way back to almost the beginning of the Cavalry. New soldiers were given horses that had a shaved tail. They had to go through much training, especially in wielding a sword on horseback. The horses that had no tails were given more room in which to work, because they were amateurs. The soldiers were not to wear spurs on their boots. They had to prove their swordsmanship abilities before they were given spurs.

The modern translation of this is that there are two kinds of spurs—silver and gold. The silver spurs are earned by a Spur Ride—a weeklong event in garrison, which is back in the States. It was an initiation that included physical and mental tests that soldiers were required to complete for the award of the silver spurs.

The golden spurs were earned by a wartime induction Spur Ride— having served during combat.

Our golden spurs were made from brass collected from the range at Jalalabad. They melted down brass shell casings and gave them to a local Hadji craftsman. He made a bunch of gold spurs for us. I thought this was cool, because our spurs had some history to them.

At first I didn't know what a spur ride looked like, so I tried to talk my pilot buddy, Ross Lewallen, into taking me for a ride on his Apache. Our air warrior vests have a harness that supports the whole vest. We have straps that keep us locked into the vest so that if we were ever lifted up, which I was often, our arms and legs wouldn't slip through. We had one internal harness inherent within the vest that could be clipped onto the outside of the Apache aircraft to lift us up and out of there. I tried to get Ross to hook me up to the outside of his aircraft, because Apaches have hook points for external emergency extraction of personnel. There isn't room to ride inside the aircraft. It's all engines, guns, and fuel in the back. They are flying bombs—there's no room for anyone but the pilots. But if an emergency dictated a rescue, they had the capability.

I told Ross, "Come on, dude, let me hook up and you can take me for a little spin." He just blew me off; didn't think I was serious. But then I asked him again, and he declined. I think that if the higher-ups would've let him, he would've for sure. But he would've gotten into a lot of trouble, and I didn't want that. I was ready, though!

I wasn't allowed to take my spur ride on the outside of the Apache. But we'd been there so long and had done so many hoists and rescues that they decided we'd earned our spurs. So, the ceremony was set for July 17th to represent the 7-17th Cav, and they gave us our golden spurs.

We also took part in a Stetson ceremony. Traditionally, inductees into the Cav unit can get a Stetson by buying it, receiving it as a gift, or by being sponsored by other members of the unit. But it is forbidden to wear one at a unit function until it is properly broken in. When members of the Cavalry rode horses, the hats were made with waterproof liners so as to keep the rain off their faces, but also to water their horses. Soldiers over the years have done a spin-off of that old practice in the breaking-in ceremony. The new soldier holds his hat upside down while the more senior guys pour a mixture of different alcohols into the hat. The newbie is then required to drink it.

In early summer, we had our Stetson ceremony. In the States, they put in all kinds of alcohol and gunpowder. All of this horrible, horrible stuff…even horse shit! But it's not gonna kill you; it just tastes like death. After they mix it up, soldiers have to drink it out of their Stetsons. But, of course, after a couple of big gulps into it, they come by and slap the hat so that the drink goes all over the inductees' faces. That means they've officially broken in their hats. It smells bad. It's awful.

So we did our version of it. There's no alcohol in Hadji-land, so we didn't use alcohol. We couldn't anyway, because we were Medevac—we had to be ready at any time to pick up the wounded. Even our down days were not down days. They mixed together sports drinks, Tabasco sauce, V-8 juice, O'Doul's non-alcoholic beer, and any number of other nasty liquids we had on hand. And yes, we drank it. When they slapped our Stetsons, the hot sauce burned our eyes. And we loved it.

I am proud of my Stetson. I still wear it every July 17th.

Medevac Gurkha designed by SSG Spraktes. Trademark pending.
Courtesy of Scott Wachs

After extricating the patient from the Humvee IED explosion, convoy members help SSG Spraktes package critically injured soldier for hoisting on the Sked.
Courtesy of CPT Luis Arriola, 2-77 FA BN S6

TEN MILES FROM JBAD

> *"A pint of sweat will save a gallon of blood."*
> General George Patton Jr.

> *"Truth is, there is not a soldier, marine, airman or sailor out there that isn't eternally grateful that their Medics and Corpsmen will risk their lives and come running when they give the cry."*
> Michael Bailey, *The Madness of the Combat Medic*

Kala Gush
25 Jun 2009

The vehicles followed each other along the road that wound up and around as the convoy climbed its way toward FOB Kala Gush. This was a multi-agency task force, and a Navy Lieutenant Commander was in charge. The lead vehicle was a Hummer, and the gunner kept his eyes peeled for any danger lurking nearby. It was a nice, cool day at 110 degrees.

Boom!

Steel hurled upward as the front end of the Humvee blew off, flipping it up, over, and down. It came to a hard forty-five degree landing on its side and the gun turret. Dirt, rock, and shrapnel exploded everywhere, as the bomb was blown out of the ground. When the dust settled, it was discovered the Humvee was resting on top of the gunner's destroyed leg.

The convoy came to a halt, one vehicle at a time.

But several hundred yards back, around and down the bend, a truck pulled a little to the right.

Boom!

Nine-line! Nine-line! Nine-line!

Smoot was first-up. They got the Black Hawk in the air; and were on their way.

"Mass casualty incident near FOB Kala Gush...IED...no LZ."

Donald Baker and I grabbed our gear and jogged out to the aircraft.

The radio crackled, and Smoot came on. "We're gonna need extrication gear, so grab the tools."

We were told that there was an entrapment—we were gonna have to do an extrication. That was something that was a little bit different. We brought our own extrication tools, because several of our people were firefighters and they knew the importance of them. Active-duty doesn't really focus on that piece. They rely on Pathfinders who cut through twisted metal on the aircraft or vehicle.

We also heard there were a lot of people injured. So first-up went, and second-up was Baker and me. Doc hopped on board with us.

We don't usually carry the extrication gear with us. The Jaws of Life and gas can are way too heavy, and they take up a lot of space.

We radioed for someone to grab the tools as we fired up the aircraft. They ran them out to us. We lifted out and were in the air.

Along the way, Baker looked for D-rings[30] everywhere. He was pulling them off of vests and other equipment, and he hooked them together to make a chain that was about two feet long. This was to hoist in the extrication gear.

Baker hoisted me down where Smoot was working on the rear security vehicle that was hit. There were five wounded soldiers surrounding him.

"There's a Humvee upside down and somebody's trapped underneath," he barked.

"Well, you can go get him," I suggested.

Al, you're the extrication guru—you do this all the time at home. You're the one who taught me—you're the one who's qualified. I'm not doing myself a favor by trying to take on five patients.

"Nope, you go."

"OK, where is it?"

"It's up there," he said, pointing up the grade.

You dirty bastard, Al...

---

30 Otherwise known as an oval carabiner. Used by mountain climbers, rescue personnel and others, it's a quick and strong temporary tie in. We all have one or two on our vests and hook them to tie downs throughout the aircraft.

I went huffing and puffing up the road, grabbing the extrication gear that Baker hoisted down. There was a Humvee resting on its side and the turret. In between the ground and the turret is this soldier's lower right leg. I know this because the tibia and fibula are sticking out on both sides. He's bleeding. He's alert, slow but still oriented.

Radio chatter said there could be possibly be more IEDs in place. I sized up the situation and realized it wouldn't take much to tip that thing over and crush him. The good news was that nobody was shooting at us yet, as was sometimes the case.

There were soldiers under the Humvee trying to work him out. I ran up and looked underneath.

"Holy shit, everybody out, now! This thing isn't stable at all! Go get bracing—I don't care what you have or what it is, I want bracing. I don't want anybody crushed under this thing."

They braced it with anything they could find. I crawled under there and soon was talking to the kid. He's talking to me too, so I knew he had a good airway. I felt his wrist. He had a rapid heart rate, but I could feel his pulse. I looked down to check the bones and saw a puddle of blood. He had a tourniquet on.

Crap.

"Get me outta here," the gunner says.

Time to get another tourniquet on him.

I found the skinniest kid around and told him to take off his gear. I needed him to crawl under there and put another tourniquet on the gunner's leg.

"I will hold you. If this thing tips over, I'll pull you out." Holding up the tourniquet, I instructed, "But you need to put this thing on. Do you know how?"

"Yes, Staff Sergeant."

"Tight—so it hurts?"

"Yes, Staff Sergeant."

"Everyone else, stay out of the way. If anyone else goes underneath there, have someone hold onto their belt so you can pull him out if it starts to roll." Roger that.

This kid goes under, puts the other tourniquet on, and tightens it up.

"Ahhh!" the patient groans.

I get Skinny out of there. My turn. I peer in, check it, and it's good.

Now, to get him out.

I crawled underneath the Humvee and started digging. The ground was pure concrete. It was the hardest crap you can imagine.

This isn't good. This guy's vitals are not great, and I'm gonna start losing him.

The radio squawked. "We've had reports that there are more IEDs planted nearby. Be advised there is a possibility of an ambush." *It just keeps getting better and better.*

I'm focused but notice the whine of the Apaches above. *They're looking for the bad guys...*

"Get me outta here! Oh God," the gunner bellowed.

"OK. This is what I want you to do," I decided. "Soldiers, keep digging at it. I'm gonna start an IV in case I have to give him some pain management or snow him."

If we take fire, we're leaving his lower leg. The bones are already broken and sticking out; I'll just need to cut through the flesh.

They started digging.

I was weighing my options. If I had to cut this poor bastard's leg off, I'd better get that IV started first. It was better if I didn't snow him yet because his vitals were shitty. I gave him some Fentanyl—it usually doesn't have the side effects of respiratory depression and blood pressure derangement, which were typical of other opiates. But his vitals were still not good, and I was worried about it.

I looked at the Lt. Commander and said, "He's probably gonna have to lose that leg."

Meaning we're gonna have to cut it off.

"Really?" he questioned. "You think you may have to do that?"

"Yeah, I think we may have to. Sir, his vitals are failing; he's trapped. The Humvee could roll and crush him at any moment. I gotta do what I gotta do."

We met eye to eye, and I could see that he understood. He took it calmly.

My thoughts went to this young man. He survived a horrific blast. He'd been trapped under this vehicle for God knows how long. They can't get him out. He's in excruciating pain. And I might have to take his leg off. *And he's gonna be right there watching me.*

"Please, get me outta here!" His pleas grew more desperate.

I was figuring how to do what I didn't want to do. I was preparing to snow him good, although I was hesitant because his blood pressure was so low.

About that time, DUSTOFF spun back around to pick up Smoot's patients. Sand and dust were stirred up by the aircraft as the hoist was brought down around the corner. I struggled to see.

I used the Jaws of Life to cut away parts of the Humvee around him.

Slowly, the others started to gain some ground digging around him.

Maybe...

The final clod of dirt gave way. The ground released. And we pulled him the hell out.

Baker hoisted down the Sked, and we packaged him. I put him on the hoist and sent him up.

I hoisted him up to Kavanagh, who began working on him right away. They sent the line down, put me on the hoist, and we got out of there.

We learned later they found more IEDs up the road. It could've been worse.

We also got back all of our extrication gear, which surprised us. We had left it in haste to get the patients to the FST. When we returned the next day, every single piece was still there.

While I was working on the gunner, I'd been dusted about three times. It was hotter than hell, and I'd been sweating the entire time. Each time the helicopter stirred up the dust around us, it was like being in a sandstorm. Each time they dusted me, I had a layer of Afghan soil that stuck to my skin and clothes. I was covered in dirt, to the point that my uniform wasn't recognizable.

I also had an M-9 pistol on me and my M-4 rifle. They, too, were covered in dirt.

After we dropped off the gunner at Jbad for the eventual tail to tail to Bagram, we went back to the TOC to reset the helicopter. On the way there, pilots Gary Heyne and Gary Parsons took one look at me and couldn't believe how filthy I was.

Parsons said to me, "Give me your guns."

I answered, "Naw, they're my guns. I'll clean 'em."

Parsons shook his head and said, "No, give them to me."

Heyne didn't say a word, just reached out his hand to take one.

Incredible.

I handed them my guns.

I went into the TOC to get the information I needed, and grabbed some water because I was absolutely parched. I sat there a moment to rehydrate, and then I went and reset the helicopter.

Doc and I talked with the trauma surgeon when I went back to Jalalabad. What if I was in that situation again? I'd not been taught how to disarticulate a joint or cut through the flesh. I didn't have the tools to cut through the bone. The surgeon agreed without committing. "You gotta do what you gotta do."

Thus began a serious discussion on what we could and could not do as flight medics. Were we authorized to cut off a limb to save a soldier?

I didn't want to go to Leavenworth, but I gotta do what I gotta do to save these guys. Life with one limb is better than no life at all.

We ordered bone saws through Bagram.

They sent four or five bone saws up with a little note attached: "You sick fucks!"

Fortunately we never had to use them. I thank God I didn't have to break out a scalpel that day. I developed a knife with a saw on the back and called it the Medevac Gurkha. I had five of them made for my flight medics and Doc. Everything on it had something to do with medical except for the blade, which was to defend ourselves.

I still carry a bone saw with me in my med-pack. I could never use it here in the States, but it's just something I can't let go of.

Maybe I am a sick fuck.

LOSS AT BARGE MATAL

"Fallen heroes represent the character of a nation who has a long history of patriotism and honor—and a nation who has fought many battles to keep our country free from threats of terror."
Michael N. Castle

"I treasure my remark to a grandson who asked, 'Grandpa, were you a hero in the war?' 'No,' I answered, 'but I served in a company of heroes.'"
Richard D. Winters

Barge Matal
12 Jul 2009

Bostic had a field surgical team at the northeast part of Afghanistan, very close to the border of Pakistan. If you go a couple miles to the right, you'd be in Pakistani air space. I'm sure there were times when we touched Pakistan airspace as we were getting out of places near there.

Nearby was a town called Barge Matal. Barge Matal was a heavily contested area located along ancient trade routes. These are routes that Alexander the Great used, places tribes and tradesmen have used for centuries. But it's very rugged, high-altitude, difficult terrain. The Taliban, al-Qaeda, and paid mercenaries moved across these pathways. They were trading goods and weapons and moving fighters there.

In summer 2009, the people of Afghanistan were voting for the country's president. This was only the second vote in the history of the country, the first just four years earlier. A free election was a big deal, and women were to vote as well. This was such an agitation to Muslim extremists that they really pushed to disrupt this process. They were either intimidating them to vote a certain way or trying to stop the election process as much as possible.

Our response was to send in Special Forces. They would go in and work with the Afghan National Army, Afghan Border Patrol, and the Afghan National Police to engage the hostiles. There were often aggressive firefights. Our guys were getting shot, people were dying, and Medevac flew in constantly. During the day, under fire. At night, under fire.

We were forward deployed at Bostic on standby during the height of these battles. Several times we flew in over buildings on fire. It was surreal. Our guys were getting sniped, and they were engaged in gun battles. There were many casualties.

This particular time we asked to go in because we'd heard that one of our soldiers, Special Forces, had been hit high in the thigh and he was bleeding bad. We knew that it was a nightmare situation, similar to a *Black Hawk Down* scenario, where a soldier was bleeding out. This was graphic and horrible to witness.

We kept asking the TOC, "Let's go in. Let's go in."

They told us no. It was too dangerous.

The pilots went into the decision makers a couple times but could not change their minds. And we can't just lift off. We wanted to, but there's a whole battle plan going on. We didn't want to become a problem. We had to trust them; we had no choice.

Then we heard that CPR was in progress. Secondary to trauma, that's never a good sign. There's rarely a good outcome. We were stressed out because a lot of people were injured, and this soldier was dying. We anguished all day, until they finally allowed us to go in after dark. But for this soldier, it was too late. He had become a hero while we strained at the leash.

Finally we flew in and landed. We knew we had the SF hero, but several breathing casualties were also waiting for transport. Out of the dark, a Special Forces team came running to me with a body bag and asked if we could take their dead comrade.

"No, we can't take the hero now. We have several others that need immediate medical attention. We'll come back and get him later."

I didn't wait for an answer. I jogged around the aircraft and opened up the door on the other side. As I opened the door, my crew chief, Tom Gifford, falls out on his ass at my feet. He had hold of a body bag as he fell. I looked into the aircraft just in time to see the men set the other end of the body bag down, then turn and disappear into the darkness.

The hero...

Immediately patients started arriving. A villager who was shot through the chest, a Lieutenant who had shrapnel wounds in his left leg and side, and a variety of other penetrating wounds were among those we were to Medevac out. We had five patients in all, two who were critical, and the crew chief, Doc, and I all on board. We packed in like fucking cordwood, and I had a dead American soldier on the deck.

He was mine now. I had to honor this hero.

Doc and I instantly unzipped the body bag to check the hero. We wanted to be absolutely certain there was no hope. Sadly, there was nothing we could do. Here was a man in his thirties wrapped in what looked like a diaper. His comrades had packed his wound high in the thigh and bandaged him up. His clothes were cut away and still present, but, for the most part, you could see everything. I looked at him and thought, I'm going to have to straddle him, step over him, and sit on him all the way back. *This is so disrespectful…shit.*

What's worse, I couldn't get the zipper back up. I straddled his dead, mostly naked body, leaning over and working on other people. Doc and I worked in this symphony of coordinated chaos in carnage.

After starting an IV on the Lieutenant, a wounded soldier sitting up against the back end of the helicopter reached over and pointed insistently at the hero. We didn't understand what he wanted at first; it took a moment.

Oh, I get it. We ripped the Velcro nameplate off the hero's shirt because his buddy wanted it. He tucked it into his pocket.

I felt my guts churn.

As we flew to Bostic, we heard radio chatter that one of our Apache escorts, Ross Lewallen, was having trouble. Ross's helicopter evidently shit an engine.

We landed at Bostic. As Doc and I began the offload, the pilots were calling Ross repeatedly. Penrod couldn't get ahold of him. Finally Ross called back. He is a pretty animated guy anyway, but you could hear the anxiety in his voice. He uttered, "I got a real problem here. One of my engines just came apart on me."

I heard Ross over the radio. "I gotta keep going. I need a runway. I'm gonna try to make it to Jalalabad." We were planning on getting fuel in

Bostic because of the duration of this operation. So we were marginal at best for fuel—getting close to bingo[32].

So Penrod says to me, "A couple of minutes, and we're leaving with or without the patients."

I hopped out with the patients. I burst into the FST and called out in a very loud voice, "Hey, listen! We have brought an MCI to you. I need you to stabilize as many as possible in five minutes. We have an Apache escort that's trying to break an engine and become a smoking hole in the ground. I need it done *now!*"

There were no arguments. The FST worked their magic.

A few minutes later I reappeared with more patients; we secured them onboard and were off. Later Penrod heard the story about a sergeant who stormed into the FST and told a bunch of Colonels to get their shit together. It wasn't true but sounded good, so I didn't say anything about the story.

We had to catch up with Ross a little ways down the valley, but not too much further. Everybody on board was very concerned about our fuel situation, because we were really low. We hooked up with Ross, who was flying a lot slower. He finally got close enough to Jbad for Penrod to feel comfortable leaving him. He was in contact with the tower.

We ended up making it to Jalalabad; we parked, and they brought us fuel.

---

32 Dangerously low on fuel

I was initially torqued at the Special Forces guys because they put the hero on board when I told them not to. Two days later, an unshaven E-7 stopped me. He was tabbed out.[33]

"Hey, man. You're a Medevac guy, right?" He recognized me because I wore extra medical gear on my legs, along with a sidearm.

"Yeah."

"Were you working the other night at Barge Matal?"

I instantly knew who he was. He was there. I didn't recognize him because I didn't see his face that night, but knew he was the man in the dark.

"Yeah. I was in Barge Matal. That was me," I said.

There was a pause, as neither of us knew how to continue the conversation.

I finally broke the silence. "You understand the reason I told you not to put him on board was because I had other patients that were critical. Every amount of space needed to work on them was taken. I had to sit on your friend the whole way back, which was something I didn't want to do. Listen, I know why you did it. I understand why you did it, but I need you to understand why I told you no."

"I understand," he replied.

He clearly hadn't walked up to kick my ass. He didn't have that tone or body language. It was a "sorry we had to throw him on board" look. They needed him to go. It was a psychological blow to fight with a dead buddy next to them—someone they've known for a couple years.

---

[33] He had several rockers that showed he'd been through many special courses.

Someone they lived with and loved like a brother. It was devastating, and they needed him out of there.

We stood looking at each other for a moment, understanding the other man's pain. We simply nodded and quietly went our own ways.

That hero was one that made me drink a lot when I came home. I was alone one night at my computer, and I punched in "Barge Matal" and came upon a memoriam to this hero/soldier. I saw his family and kids and felt something well up inside me. I thought I was going to throw up. It felt like an entity of black, oily evil boiling within, which I had to get out.

Pain. Regret. Sorrow. Anger. Frustration.

A profound sense of loss for this man and his family.

And then, several months later, I learned he was a former police officer.

He was my last hero mission.

CW2 Elizabeth Kimbrough in her Apache helicopter.

Courtesy of Sebastian Rich, Photojournalist

WALMART AND OTHER MORALE BUILDERS

"Lieutenant Welsh remembered walking around among the sleeping men, and thinking to himself that they had looked at and smelled death all around them all day but never even dreamed of applying the term to themselves. They hadn't come here to fear. They hadn't come to die. They had come to win."
Stephen E. Ambrose, *Band of Brothers*

"Yesterday I transported a little 8-year-old boy who had been hit by a truck...I gave him your Combat Duck...he was very happy to have it and didn't let go of it the entire flight. I got a smile out of the little shit that made us all very happy. So I guess I owe you one Combat Duck."
SSG Emmett Spraktes, in an e-mail to SSG Angela Nolan in January 2009

Jalalabad
2008-2009

Donald Baker knew how to *acquire* stuff.

Shortly after we arrived in Bagram, the DUSTOFF crews leaving for home asked Baker if he'd like to coordinate the cigar giveaway program. This was a huge stash of cigars that were sent from Cigar Asylum, a group of cigar enthusiasts in the United States, for the soldiers in the field to enjoy. Did Baker want to take over?

I couldn't think of anyone better for the job.

Shortly thereafter Donald received a collection of cigars stored in a Conex box, and it just grew from there. He contacted people back home—in particular the Blue Star Moms of Chico, California—who sent about ten boxes every month. He also used his connections in the 160th to bring in other goods; all sorts of foodstuffs and quality-of-life items like handy wipes and sunscreen. Other organizations sent various supplies as well, which we added to the collection.

The cigar stash and supplies soon outgrew the box and barracks. We had little room in our barracks at Jalalabad. So Baker and I put in a request for some lumber for "medical equipment storage." We were told it would be coming. This was about the time I took my leave. I told the guys to wait for me to help build it. But of course, by the time I got back, those bastards not only built it, but built a second-story porch above the Conex boxes with the leftover wood.

They sealed off the Conex entry, put in a door and shelves, and brought in an old air conditioner. It was the coolest room in Jbad—kept cool for the chocolate and the coffee. We called this place Walmart.

We made a humidor. We had a two-foot by four-foot plastic box, got beads that retain water, and popped those into the box with the cigars. Of course we stole sterile water from the medics' supply for the beads. It worked great.

We estimate that our task force gave out about thirteen thousand cigars during the time we were in Afghanistan. I have no idea how much food and other supplies we dispersed to soldiers in the field.

In our spare time, we packaged up cigars in bundles of twelve; rubber-banded them, added twenty-five to thirty matches and a cutter, and bagged them. We added little notes that said, "Thank you for your service" and tucked them into the aircraft for when we were out and about. We also carried small boxes that were packed with food items, wipes, and whatever.

Whenever we could, we'd fly over some of the more remote places like Restrepo and Keating. We'd kick out these prepackaged bundles at the top of the hill. It was a huge morale booster. When specialists came to Jalalabad, we gave them bags, took them to "Walmart," and told them to fill their bags. They loved it.

The Chinook guys took some of the bundles, picked up pizzas from Pizza Hut, then dropped off the goods to the guys in the foxholes. Others dropped bundles for us as well. We felt good to put it together, getting this stuff to the fighters in remote places.

Soon we began getting thank-you notes. Some took pictures and posted them on Facebook.

Donald was given an award for this work. He also was coined[35]. The greatest reward, however, was the satisfaction of knowing the guys in the field appreciated it.

We were in the middle of the killing season, watching our soldiers die and seeing the very worst that men do to other men. We were away from our spouses, our kids, and our comforts, and the Afghan differences of thinking sucked. Walmart was just one way to keep up morale.

There were other ways as well, some less than dignified.

CAC'd and Cocked

There were always practical jokes to be played—no one ever passed up an opportunity. To get on the computer, we had to put in a personal

---

35 He was given a Task Force coin by LTC Blackmon and SMG Thom.

access code. This is a military ID card, also called a computer access card (CAC). To access the computer, we put a CAC in and checked military e-mails, etc. If we had to get off in a hurry to go on a mission, or simply forgot to log off, oftentimes someone would sit down and write an apology letter to the Task Force for something "you" did wrong. So when we spent time at the computer, it was very important to log out when we were done, otherwise someone would inevitably get "CAC'd." Many guys authored anonymous letters in the name of whoever's card was left behind.

Most of the really funny ones were those expressing the urgent need to come out of the closet and profess one's undying love and devotion for a fellow (usually same sex) soldier. Typically it got pretty descriptive: "I can no longer restrain my primal urges when I see the sweat glistening from your tanned and well-muscled body. I feel as though we can slip the bonds which separate us and…" It got worse from there. DUSTOFF, Blue Max, and sometimes the entire task force got the e-mail. We of course howled with laughter at the said "CAC'EE" and their embarrassment.

I never got CAC'd, but I CAC'd others. I CAC'd Lovett and he blamed Smoot—perfect.

Getting CAC'd sounds a lot like getting "cocked." To a group of mostly men who carry guns, it's similar language. It's like saying, "What did I get for all my hard work? A stiff dick in the face!" Which most of us didn't prefer.

Smoot-isms

I love Smoot. He's a close friend. But he's also one of the most irreverent men I know. He and I went back and forth with our friendly "fireman versus cop" banter; it was endless. I made jokes about how firemen are girls who like to cook in their skimpy aprons. Smoot just called cops pussies. But then again, that's what he called the air force guys too. That's where we agreed!

Al had a lot of nicknames for people, but my personal favorite is when he called the insurgents "feral humans." The other that got us spewing milk through our noses was when someone did something stupid, he called him a "fuck-tard."

I'll never forget one night as we got to telling stories on the Porch over a few cigars. He told a story of a call he was on as a fireman. It was probably the fourth call he'd gotten to rescue cats in trees. This lady was hysterical, and he just couldn't take it anymore, so he said, "Lady, when's the last time you saw a cat skeleton in a tree?"

The Quote Book

Smoot wasn't the only funny one. Everybody said something at one time or another, and finally we realized we needed to write them down. Catch phrases, misspeaks and dumb-ass comments all made their way into the Quote Book. It was the kind of thing that helped us pass the time with laughter. And laughter was gold as our rotation wore on and we grew more tired.

Facilities

Every Thursday was Crab and Steak Day at the Dining Facility (DFAC). You'd think that we would be overjoyed with this, but alas, the steaks were always well-done—practically burned! But we ate them gladly, because the real fighting men were eating MREs out in the field.

We lived in what we called bee huts. There were eight guys per building. They were hot as hell in the summer and cold as an arctic wind in the winter. We spent time making them up to be better and nicer by putting in ceiling fans, an A/C unit, and better lighting. We also rebuilt the cubicle beds and areas.

The port-a-potties at the airfield were strapped down with cargo straps so they didn't blow over. We also had regular latrines and showers in trailers parked in strategic places. It was pure entertainment inside the port-a-potties: they were hot as hell, smelled of chemicals and poop, and the insides were covered in Chuck Norris jokes. We sat and read them until we were done. A few of my favorites:

Chuck Norris has a grizzly bear rug in his living room. The bear isn't dead, it's just afraid to move.
Ghosts sit around the fire and tell Chuck Norris stories.
Chuck Norris doesn't flush the toilet; he scares the shit out of it.
Chuck Norris once kicked a horse in the chin. Its descendants are now called giraffes.
Chuck Norris doesn't wear a watch; he decides what time it is.

I don't think there's one latrine or port-a-potty in the entire army that isn't covered in Chuck Norris jokes. He could make a million if he sold pre-joked, pre-signed port-a-potties!

The Porch, Push-ups, and Prayer

The Porch was our hangout. When we weren't working, we were sittin' with the guys, having a cigar. We invited the pilots over often. We debriefed calls, told stories, and talked about our kids. There was a lot of bonding that went on at the Jalalabad Porch.

Every other night, we joined together and did push-ups on the Porch.

Wednesday afternoons, about cigar time, there were several men who took part in a Bible study. Many of them were pilots. They brought their Bibles and met on the Upper Porch before dinner for about an hour. It was a great encouragement for those who had a faith in God.

I didn't take part in the Bible study, mainly because I see myself as an infidel. Nonetheless, just seeing them do this gave me comfort.

Sprucing Up the Yard

Penrod and I built a brick barbecue in our spare time that I don't think we ever fully finished. It was hard work in the insufferable Afghan heat, and we had less spare time toward the back end of our deployment. We were able to use it a few times before we left.

Erdmann had the idea to plant a garden. Many received seeds sent from the States, and we planted and watered them until things grew. As plants came up, LT Carmel Cammack (a Kiowa pilot) decided we needed a garden gnome to guard the crops. A friend of hers sent a cool gnome, and he relaxed in the middle of the garden with his legs crossed and arms behind his neck. It was quite a sight.

As the garden produced, we noticed that things began to disappear. Fruit and flowers and vegetables went missing, and then finally, the gnome. Oh, Carmel came unglued. She put up MISSING posters and demands for its return. But we never saw the little guy again.

Miss Kim

Elizabeth Kimbrough was the only woman in our group of Apache pilots, and she was beautiful. A reporter dubbed her Killer Kimbrough because she did her job well. Man, she hated that name. Here was this short and petite, beautiful, young American blue-eyed blonde who was also a tough Apache pilot. She flew about the country *offing* bad guys. We loved her!

From time to time, we had imbedded reporters, and they inevitably wanted to talk to Kimbrough. Some photojournalists from Japan followed her around like little puppies, taking her picture over and over again. We thought it was hysterical. She found it extremely annoying.

Kimbrough was a person who brought a smile to our faces. After some time of seeing American women only in the pictures in our hooches, it was nice to be reminded that beautiful women still lived, breathed, and existed in the world.

Johnny Be Good

Johnny Hanson was a rock star pilot. He was a quiet, unassuming guy, all the good stuff. We were thrilled to have him on our team. He came to Jbad for about a minute and a half before he got reassigned. We had a fun team, and he would've been a wonderful addition. We liked him a lot and were bummed to see him go.

Kavanagh took his picture and had it blown up and put on cardboard, and then we took pictures of it everywhere. Just to let him know that we were thinkin' about him. We walked Johnny around all over Fenty and took pictures.

I even took pictures of him in my bed, which I'm sure was horrifying to him, but made everyone laugh. From the waist up, I have no clothes on and I'm holding Johnny in my bed.

We got a picture of Kimbrough kissing him, and LTC Blackmon sitting by him. Johnny Be Good was everywhere.

Whorton's Classes

Even some of the technical training was a morale-builder. Nate Whorton put together an evacuation plan to load and offload patients when Medevac landed. He noticed when our helicopters came in and we had a hot offload (patients were dying so we didn't power down the aircraft), we didn't have an organized way to offload the personnel and get them to the field litter ambulance (FLA). Nate thought it wasn't right and was squawkin' about it. I told him to put it together. "Make it happen, Nate! I need you to train the class, because it has value. You have the experience and expertise, so do it."

He took it on. He put together a training class and ran several rotations of training. He trained everybody on how to wait for the landing, notify the FLA of incoming medevac, line up the litter teams, and put people in charge of specific litters. He had a procedure for when the medic disembarked; he would point to the soldier in charge of the litter. The litter soldier would acknowledge and move the litter bearers forward in a certain way. He taught them how to offload when they were ready to go, when they couldn't hear anything, and that we don't just walk away. He showed them how to do it and walked them through, step by step.

We rotated several units through—not just our people, but the Kiowa guys, the Black Hawk guys, the Apache guys, and others. If they happened to be walking by when a hot Medevac came in, they could take a position and know what to do. We were able to have safe, efficient offloads and get the wounded off immediately. Nate worked it. It was like clockwork.

It built morale because many soldiers were stuck on the FOB providing important support but not able to be directly involved in the fight. They got to see a piece of war, horrible as it was. It gave them purpose and a way to help and contribute to the men and women who were getting shot, killed, and blown up. It's hard to be a crew chief for an Apache unit and never go out. They were in the FOB every single day, and their pilot counterparts were flying out, tearing up the terrain, and all they were able to do is wrench. But at least when they could run over and offload injured personnel, they were seeing the war and doing their part.

This also improved patient care. Before this, there were patients who were occasionally dropped, jarred, extubated, or injured in the confusion and hurry. We found that smoothing it out gave us the speed we needed and kept the patients safer in the move. It was a huge morale-builder. I got Nate coined for that.

Giving Back

It's not easy to be a kid in Afghanistan. Our hearts went out to them. We kept toys in the helicopters—Beanie Babies sent from the States—for the pediatric patients. These kids liked the gifts we gave, and sometimes we got a smile in return. We always had to ask permission from the parent, though. The Russians used to leave little bombs in toys for the children; the older Afghans remembered this.

We also put together a school supply drive for the local kids. We brought in about $2,500 worth of pencils, paper, crayons, etc. There were two collapsible cardboard and plastic palettes that were stacked four feet high. One we gave to the Provincial Reconstruction Team (PRT) across the airfield to distribute. The other was taken to Bostic, where they gave it to a minister of a church there. It felt good to contribute something the kids could appreciate.

CHP Flag

We had a lot of laughs in the downtime, for sure, and took the time to lift the morale of others. But one of the most meaningful boosts for me personally was the California Highway Patrol flag the commissioners gave me before I left. They'd ordered me to take it with me and to personally bring it back when I returned.

During the killing season, the action heated up along with the weather. There were more battles, more IEDs, more patients, and it was intense. Our rescues grew more dangerous, and I had serious doubts about my return. I'd been lucky so far, but I felt my luck may run out at some point.

I sent an e-mail to Max and told him I didn't want this thing to get into the wrong hands. I didn't want some goddamned hadji using it as a hammock or as bandages. I wanted it to have some history, but I didn't want to lose it.

Max didn't reply. He forwarded my e-mail to Kevin Green. Green answered, "No, Emmett. You bring it back on your own. You'll be all right."

I wasn't being overly dramatic. Things were crazy. But Green gave me a sense of hope. It was a lesson learned. He gave me the beyond-right-now, beyond-this-hour, beyond-this-mission, beyond-this-deployment, and when-I-get-home attitude.

It was a gift that was given to me. I would soon pay it forward to some young men in the middle of an intense firefight in the Watapur Valley.

An Apache helicopter popping flares in the mountains of Afghanistan.

Courtesy of Sebastian Rich, Photojournalist

SELFISH PRAYER

"Courage is being scared to death, but saddling up anyway."
John Wayne

"The flight medic is the man. He is the one who knows what to do. And he does amazing things, heroic things."
Doc Kavanagh

Watapur Valley
17 Jul 2009

Slightly northeast of Asadabad in the Watapur Valley was a little FOB named Honaker Miracle. A group of sixteen soldiers (Chosin 93) set out on a dismounted patrol to do a recon of Pun Sar to locate enemy mortar and ambush positions. As they headed back, they were suddenly ambushed with small-arms fire and RPGs. There was a large group of Taliban fighters that had watched and waited for them to be virtually surrounded. It was later learned from intelligence they wanted to get close enough to capture a soldier alive.

The squadron settled into a perimeter and engaged, but the enemy seemed to be close. They waited for a lull in the fire and bounded to the south to achieve some distance. That's when one soldier was shot in the stomach, another took shrapnel to the hip, and a third broke his ankle dodging bullets. They called for Medevac and established a site.

It was eight o'clock in the morning, and I'd already treated several Medevac patients that rotation. We were returning to Jalalabad from Bostic and were to be relieved. The new crew was running slightly behind schedule, but we were planning to pass them in the air soon and wave. The pilots with me were Brandon Erdmann and Scott St. Aubin, and the crew chief was Tom Gifford. Together we made up DUSTOFF 24.

We were listening to the radio traffic and heard the Medevac request. We clearly heard gunfire in the background. Erdmann responded that we were in the area and would take the nine-line. Until we were given clearance, we circled near the mouth of the valley and listened to the huge battle going on below.

I had a gut feeling and it wasn't good. I'd been under fire before, but I'd never heard a level of intensity like that. We could tell it was bad. The enemy was closing in. And they were calling for a nine-line.

I asked Erdmann, "Hey, is this guy gonna die if we don't go?"

Erdmann got on the radio and asked the question.

With only a slight hesitation the radio operator answered, "He won't make it if you don't go now."

Oh God...

"Well, Emmett?" asked Erdmann. "This is probably a hoist mission. It's your call."

"Ask him if there's any place for us to land. Is there an HLZ?"

I was ashamed of myself. I'd spent nine months in this crazy war, and I'd done several rescues and been fired upon. But hearing the intensity of the explosions and fire, I just didn't want to go.

At that point, I offered up a selfish prayer.

When you're young, you pray for yourself. As you get older, you pray for your family. You pray for your friends. You pray for other people. You live your life, and try to do the right thing. You talk to God, explain yourself. But you don't pray and ask for selfish things when you're older.

I'd prayed silent prayers as I've worked—"God, guide my hands…make me do the right thing. Help me to remember the treatment. This is a good US soldier. Help me, guide me. He's a baby…"

But it had always been for them. This time it was for me. This time it was selfish.

Lord, help me to find an HLZ. I don't want to hoist through the fire, because I'm afraid!

I'm embarrassed to admit how much fear I felt. I knew these young men were there, had been there, and would be there for some time. Yet in that moment, I was completely depleted of self-esteem. I'd realized the level of my human frailty.

A voice came back on the radio and said, "No. It's gonna be a hoist. There's nowhere to land."

The crew knew what that meant. I would have to be hoisted down in the middle of this mess.

Erdmann asked again, "Well, Emmett, what do you think?"

I wanted to puke. "Let's do it."

The cavalry had come. Two aircraft had already sustained damage from enemy fire when Chief Warrant Officer Scott Stradley entered the Watapur Valley. His team faced heavy enemy fire as they located the enemy's position and engaged. They received small-arms fire from at least six fighting positions to the north, east, and west up the ridge from Chosin 93.

Stradley saw that the enemy was closing in on the squad and were advancing to about 400 meters from the wounded. Taking control of all air assets, he controlled a team of two Apaches and two A-10s, raining massive amounts of firepower on the enemy.

Chosin 93 continued down the draw, and the enemy was hot on their trail. Some of the hadjis maneuvered around the next draw to the east, others coming down from the high ground. They were relentless, firing continuously, moving in quickly.

I had a thousand thoughts racing through my head. I thought through the practical: crawl over, grab my bag. Grab the Sked, my rifle.

You will not survive this. Not through this intense fire.

I had to think about protocols—flesh wound, abdominal wound.

You're not who you think you are. You're not as tough, you're not as courageous, you're not as brave, you're not as squared away as you think.

You're not even on the wire yet, and you're about to crap your pants. These kids are half your age and are fighting for their lives...

Medications...

My family. This is the last they'll ever know of me. They'll know I died in Afghanistan. Maybe that I died in a draw near a little FOB called Honaker Miracle. My two oldest kids know me, but my youngest doesn't. Shit...

I had to get hooked up and make sure I had the tag line.

My thoughts went to my daughter. When she was about two or three, she was pre-diagnosed with a debilitating disease that usually meant she would die in her teens. I was absolutely devastated. I remembered sitting on the kitchen floor, holding her close and praying. *Please God, take me instead. I can't live through this pain. She hasn't lived her life yet...*

I made a bargain with God that day.

He didn't take my daughter. A few days later, there was a miraculous turn of events when the blood tests came back. They said, "We don't understand fully, but this isn't what we thought it was. It was something minor." Since then, I've lived my life with this pact in mind. I didn't expect to make it past my thirties or my forties, and certainly not into my fifties.

I made a bargain. Time to uphold my end of the deal.

Stradley continued to engage the hadjis as they moved south. The A-10s notified him that they were taking fire from the northwest. He broke out of the engagement, hearing multiple automatic weapons, including a DShK. At that point, a round grazed his copilot's chin bubble, and the window exploded.

"Medevac, hold your position; we've got intense fire."

Stradley pulled around and came back in, engaging multiple targets until he went Winchester.[37] He flew a couple of low passes to check the LZ and marked it with smoke for DUSTOFF. He then turned over Chosin 93 to others and headed for the FARP.

I hooked up to the hoist. I could hear the shots without the radio now. I could hear them above the high-pitched whining of the helicopter. We were close.

Remember Uncle Bill and that damn bear. He didn't back down. He put himself in between his family and the predator...

After determining that the shattered chin bubble wasn't a problem and rearming, Stradley gave the OK to bring Medevac in. He directed the A-10s and Overdrive to engage several threat locations and initiated fires to mark the targets for the other aircrafts. However, Overdrive was unable to see the fire. Stradley decided he'd bring them in himself. He took over the lead with Overdrive following, and they engaged several of the targets, providing suppressive fire for Medevac.

---

37 He ran out of ammunition.

Selfish Prayer

Explosions. Intense firefight. I recognized the sounds of M-4s and the Kiowas tearing up the ground. I heard AK-47s, and something else I wasn't familiar with—probably a DShK.

I was hooked up and hanging outside the aircraft in the rappel position, my gun at the ready. I disconnected my cord, thinking about my family. Gifford and I gave each other a look, and I yelled, "Tell my family I love them!"

He looked at me with a confused stare. "You love me?"

"No! No, you idiot, my family! Tell my family I love them!"

He yelled back, "I can't hear you!"

Well, all right then.

I had my rifle pointed toward the ground. I gave the thumbs-up sign and then waited. DUSTOFF came in aggressively, descending quickly. I felt bullets whizzing by.

The internal dialogue started again.

God, I don't want to be a part of the problem. I want to rescue. So, I'd really appreciate it if I weren't hit in the head. Because I don't know if I could shake off a head wound. Maybe the vest. It would hurt, maybe get some shrapnel, hopefully I could survive that. If I get hit in the limb, well, I could probably still work. I'd really prefer not to be hit in the testicles...

I looked to where the aircraft was headed.

If I get hit in the leg, I could limp around...but keep it low so that if it needs to amputated, I could get a prosthetic leg. I won't tell anyone in the highway patrol that I got shot. I'll just wear pants until my last day of work. Then I'll come to work with shorts on... I could still help these guys...please let me work...

I looked at how far we were to the ground...man, there was a lot of gunfire.

Emmett, you have no control. You've been on the edge for years, hedging your bets, weighing the percentages, making your decisions and going. For the first time in your life as a professional risk-taker, you have absolutely no control. You're in God's hands now. So let it go...

For the first time in my life, I let go. I leaned back. My arms were kind of out like a baby's, and I dropped.

A calmness—an encapsulating silence—enveloped me for a brief moment. I heard nothing. I felt a sense of relief. I still expected an agonizing piercing, to get hit, to die. I really thought that was going to be the end of me. It wasn't a generalized fear of death, or a premonition. It was simply that the circumstances were so aggressive—it would be like walking across a busy highway and expecting to be hit by a car. I was being hoisted from a helicopter in the midst of intense fire, and that's what should've happened. That's what made sense.

I saw faces.

I'm gonna make it. I'm gonna fucking make it! I'm thirty feet away, and I can make it. I can help these guys. I'm not gonna get clipped. I'm gonna get down behind this ravine, and I'm gonna make it.

Then the hoist stopped.

I was dangling twenty-five feet above the ground.

Seconds went by.

I looked up and didn't see Gifford. *What the fuck?*

Ten seconds.

Maybe Gifford got clipped. Maybe the pilots don't know. Is there a failure in the hoist?

I screamed into the radio, "Get me on the ground now! I'm like a fucking piñata down here!" That evidently went throughout the entire task force. Everybody heard it.

Then the cable lowered, and I suddenly hit the ground hard on my ass, feet, and back. The terrain was at a forty-five degree angle and rocky. It knocked the shit out of me, the pain briefly distracting me from the firefight.

Fucking terra firma.

I didn't know, but when I hit the ground, my radio cable was damaged. My communication was intermittent from then on.

I unhooked, gave them the signal, and they peeled off. I looked forward, and there were two soldiers higher than the rest. Everyone was looking at me despite the chaos around us.

"Yeah man, that was badass! That was cool!" one of them quipped.

I was still focused. But I imagine they saw a guy coming down the wire with bullets whizzing by him, impacts on the other side of the ravine, and they've gotta be wondering, W*hy is this guy not getting killed?*

I looked up, and all eyes were in. These guys were tucked into the boulders, pressing into the crevices. They were against the sides of the ravine. They were making themselves rocks and were pushing themselves in hard.

These guys were withdrawn emotionally; I could see it. There were continuous explosions, a lot of gun runs by the aircraft above, and shell casings tinkling a tune on the boulders just west of us. They were keeping themselves in a safe position from shrapnel, friendly fire, and certainly hadji fire. But they were withdrawn, and only couple were boisterous when I landed.

I had the impression they all thought they would die.

"Who's in bad shape?" I asked.

"He's over there on the ground."

The soldier was lying out in the open but still protected by the walls. I rushed over to him, and as I leaned over, a 58 flew right over the top of us and started blazing away. I jumped and bumped my patient.

"AHHHH!"

"Ah, dude, I'm so sorry."

My patient had just told me a couple things. He was responsive to pain, and also he had an airway, a heartbeat, and he was breathing.

Then an E-nothing put his hand on my shoulder and said, "Don't worry, Staff Sergeant, we jumped the first time they flew over too. You did pretty good for the first time."

Here was a kid my son's age comforting me. I'd been completely shattered emotionally just minutes before, yet I had to be the guy with all the answers to this mess. My perception was that I was the flight medic dropping in—I had to be the answer to the problem. I had to be the solution.

I'm certain their perception was the same. They were desperate for a solution. I was the guy who was there to get the wounded out, so they could move and fight. When I dropped in and took charge, they had no idea of my inner struggle. It was important to keep this outward persona up because of what I'd seen when I landed. We needed to get the hell out of there—alive.

I took a deep breath and shook off the pain. "If any of you are interested in law enforcement, I'm in the California Highway Patrol. I work at the CHP academy, and I'll give you a reference. If you come to California, everybody knows my name. It's Emmett. Everybody at the academy knows me."

They started to interact. As I worked on my patient, I gave them jobs. "I want you to look that way; I want you to look this way. Don't look in; look out. Protect me while I'm working on this guy."

I got them to stop thinking about right now. I wanted them to think about an hour from now, and then two hours, six hours, and the day after tomorrow. When they survived this deployment, they could come to California and start thinking about their futures. This was not their end.

A vibration went through them. The atmosphere changed. They got kind of frisky again, coming back to life.

My full attention turned to the big kid with a right-side abdomen wound, and he's pale. Very pale. I don't think he was even sweating anymore. He was in shock. He was alert but not oriented. His abdomen was distended—that told me there was internal bleeding. He had a rapid pulse and was very sick.

I knew immediately he needed a surgeon. Asadabad was only three minutes' flight time away. I could've played with this kid for twenty minutes, done all the right things, and killed him. Or I could tuck my ego away and say, "You don't need me, kid, you need a surgeon." That's what I chose.

One of the soldiers who helped me was a redheaded kid. Red and I got the patient on the Sked, bundled him up, put a tag line on, and called DUSTOFF to return.

"DUSTOFF 24, this is ground medic. We're gonna do a hoist on the Sked. I'll be ready in two mics."

"DUSTOFF 24. Roger that."

A couple of A-10s came in and dropped some five-hundred pound bombs. I leaned over and covered my patient. Shortly thereafter, DUSTOFF 24 swooped in and lowered the hook.

Red and I packaged the patient up. I pulled him out to an area not very far away, hooked up the tagline, broke cover, and went out. As DUSTOFF 24 came in over the top of us, we were taking fire again, so the Apaches and Scouts took turns swooping in to blow shit up around us to provide cover.

My guys on the ground were providing cover fire, but they were running low on ammo.

"Don't touch that hook—let it touch the ground. You're gonna get a shock if you grab it mid-air," I yelled to Red.

"OK."

But when it came in, he grabbed it anyway. He knew. He got a hell of a shock, but he grabbed that hook, really, for his wounded buddy. I hooked it in and gave Gifford the sign.

"Go as fast as you can, Gifford—I'll take the burn," I radioed.

This meant Gifford could hoist at four feet per second. If you've got gloves on, the rope goes through your hands, but it burns. I decided this guy deserved a second-degree burn. He'd given everything he had, and he was dying.

The tag line zipped through my hands. I tried to be quiet but as it burned through, I found myself yelling *"Fuuuuuuuuuck!!!"* I could hear myself above the battle noise. I took the burn.

Gifford pulled him in, unhooked, and dropped the tag line, all while taking fire. We ran back to the boulders as DUSTOFF 24 peeled off, and I brought my rifle up, firing several rounds toward where I thought the hadjis were coming in. There was a kid who was behind me, his head near the barrel, and he covered his ears—'cause I just let loose.

Stradley maneuvered to the north of the hovering Medevac, drawing the fire away from the rescue. The hadjis fired continually from a northeastern draw and a village from the east as well as a DShK from up the northeast ridge.

After DUSTOFF left, he cleared the airspace for a TOW missile to be fired out of COP Honaker Miracle. After the missile was fired, he went back in, engaging the enemy until he went Winchester.

Now for the other two.

They were stable. There was really nothing I needed to do for them—the medic on the ground did a great job. But I checked them, because their injuries could be distracting. Sometimes a fracture to the ankle can mask shrapnel taken somewhere else more dangerous. Because the pain is worse on the ankle, he may not feel it.

The hip wound was superficial—it didn't go into the pelvic cavity. He was sitting up and talking, but couldn't really move. I didn't think anything was broken.

The battle above ebbed and flowed. We didn't know when DUSTOFF 24 would be back. I got these guys ready. I put both on the jungle penetrator and hooked up all their gear, and we waited.

At some point, I distributed my ammunition. I thought I was getting out of there soon and they needed it more than I did.

DUSTOFF 24 came in and we got the patients hooked up on the line.

"Ground medic, get on the cable." *What?*

"Negative, DUSTOFF 24."

"Ground medic, we need you to get on the cable."

Now I had radioed in that there were two patients, but because my radio communication was intermittent, they didn't understand this piece of information. I knew the hoist wouldn't pull the three of us. But then I wondered if maybe they knew something I didn't; maybe the enemy was closing in. I found out later that even with the gunships blasting the shit out of everything, the enemy was still moving forward. It was a very committed assault.

I hooked in, and we started up. The hoist stalled again at about twenty feet up, for about five seconds.

OK, God, again?

There was too much weight. They lowered us down, I unhooked, and they quickly hoisted up the injured and into the aircraft.

DUSTOFF 24 held hover during the hoist. Scott St. Aubin observed the enemy within a hundred and fifty yards of the trapped platoon.

"Pale Element, this DUSTOFF 24. I have numerous enemy 150 yards 030 degrees from Chosin 93. Requesting gun-run."

A Kiowa 58 immediately and effectively strafed the area.

"I don't know who that was," St. Aubin radioed. "But you were right on target."

I felt a small sense of relief that we provided these guys with the ability to be mobile. When you have significantly injured people, your mobility is extremely limited in that type of terrain. We gave these guys the ability to fight their way out.

"We've got to move from this location. This is not a defensible position," I directed. "We need to move toward the trucks, and we need to move now. We need to get into patrol configuration and go. We can't defend ourselves here!"

The squad and I started to move, but Red and another young soldier stayed still. *Shit! What's going on? Did they get hit?* That's when I realized that they were severely dehydrated. One started dry-heaving right then.

They had become heat casualties. They were not able to hike out of there. No way. Medically, they were now very sick.

"We're out of water," Red said.

"What?!"

"And we're low on ammo." *Shit.*

There was just no way we were gonna make it on this terrain with these guys down. They could die. Should I take off their flak jackets, helmets? I had no water to cool them down. Could I start an IV? No, an IV in this area was a Band-Aid approach. It would get ripped out easily in this kinetic activity.

So I called DUSTOFF 24 through the radio operator, as I figured out by then my radio wasn't working.

"We need ammo and water out here! And a jungle penetrator! I've got two more heat casualty patients!"

Shit. I'm calling DUSTOFF 24 one more time into the fire.

Over at Honaker Miracle, everyone was listening. It was like a Super Bowl event. Some were watching on satellite imagery on the Predators from way above. There were also security cameras from Honaker Miracle that were trying to zoom in on parts of it.

When I asked for the supplies, DUSTOFF 24 responded. When they landed at Honaker Miracle, several soldiers raced to the aircraft and loaded up ammunition, water, rockets and grenades.

To this day, I imagine St. Aubin, still feeling the effects of his shrapnel wound, shouting, "No, no, no! NO FUCKING GRENADES! Spraktes doesn't get ANY grenades! Just put on water and loaded M-4 magazines!"

At the request of the crew, they took off the grenades and rockets, and DUSTOFF 24 peeled off one more time.

I placed my heat casualty patients on the JP, and as I was working, I saw this softball-size object fly right over the top of us, moving fast. I saw it with a naked eye, moving from south to north. In my ignorance, I thought, *"Holy crap! A 58 just fired a rocket in. They must be getting really close if they're firing danger-close."*

I heard another explosion just to the north of us. *Boom!*

Holy crap!

I learned later the hadjis had fired one of many RPGs at us. We had this whole group of Taliban fighters at 030 inhabiting the high ground to the north of us. On the high ground to the east and west were two DShKs, which were Soviet weapons, firing down on us. At our 180, we had at least one, probably several, who were firing RPGs. We were surrounded.

Stradley had to wait for a FARP pad to open up and eventually landed on pads one and two. He exited the aircraft, rotors still going, and did a damage assessment, finding nothing. He and his copilot were reentering the aircraft when he heard, "This is (AH-64). I've got a hydraulics failure and am approaching the FARP. Clear the pads of all personnel immediately. Leave all aircraft on the pads. I'm on approach for an emergency landing." His hydraulics were shot up from the fight.

Stradley had heard that tone before, and it wasn't good. He looked up and saw the AH-64 turn his final approach and realized he wasn't gonna make it.

"Clear the FARP of all personnel! Clear the FARP of all personnel! Now!" the pilot screamed over the radio.

Stradley yelled to the pad chief, "Disconnect me!" The pad chief disconnected him and sprinted.

Stradley peeled off to the west, making sure he didn't clip those who were running away and taking cover, barely making it over the Hesco basket perimeter wall. His armor doors were still open, and they didn't have time to buckle in.

The AH-64 dropped in fast and landed hard on the very spot Stradley's aircraft was resting just seconds before.

Stradley and his copilot transferred the controls back and forth so they could buckle up and close the doors. They then landed to continue refueling.

That was too close.

DUSTOFF 24 came in flying low and fast, under fire, and they kicked out the jungle penetrator, water, and ammo. The water bottles hit the ground and blew in every direction. Another kid and I broke cover and retrieved the drop, throwing bottles and ammo to everybody. They started pounding water. What a relief. Now they could fight back.

I grabbed the JP and ran to the heat casualties. I told them to take sips while I poured water over them, cooling them down.

It was a long wait before DUSTOFF was able to come back in again. I had these guys strapped into the JP, waiting a while before we were able to clip in.

I knew the 58s were tearing up the terrain. The A-10s were coming in, tearing up the terrain. The Apaches, Black Widows, and the Kiowas were tearing up the terrain. They were chewing it up, trying to beat back the enemy's advance. They were two hundred yards, one hundred yards, seventy yards. There were a lot of them, and they wanted to kill us. That was the bottom line.

I got these boys hooked up and everybody hydrated and supplied with ammunition. DUSTOFF 24 came in, I hooked them to the hoist, and they peeled off.

I radioed to DUSTOFF, "We now have eleven people; I'm number twelve. We're going to move in patrol formation."

I told the patrol, "We're gonna hustle down, and I'll take rear security. You guys just slowly work it. Take your time."

Then I hear DUSTOFF 24. "We're coming back to get you."

"Negative. I'm in good company down here. They're down five people, and it's too dangerous for you to come back," I argued.

We were already too lucky. I didn't want to risk DUSTOFF 24. I could walk out with these kids. I'd bonded with them. They were young—my son William's age. It was already a terrible situation. And selfishly, I didn't want to get hoisted back up through the fire again.

"No. Medevac's no good without a medic. We're coming back to get you."

OK. Obviously they knew something I didn't. I trusted them.

They came back again under unbelievably intense fire. I witnessed it. *Are you kidding me?*

I hooked up, and then I gave them the hand signal that I was ready to go, rifle at the ready. I looked down at the soldiers' faces.

I'm abandoning these boys. I'm leaving them behind, not seeing it through. I'm running away...

I looked down at them as I was hoisted up. I raised my rifle, pointed it toward the bad guys, and let out four- and six-round bursts as I went up. I ran dry before I made it to the wheel of the aircraft.

Gifford pulled me in. I rolled over on my back, exhausted, and safetied my weapon out of habit. I was lying on my back, looking up and thinking, *Thank God that's over.*

I turned my head and saw a couple pairs of legs.

What the hell?

Four patients were still on board. My heat casualty guys. My ankle and hip guys too. *What the fuck are they still doing on board?*

I was mad. What care had they been given? Why didn't they get off at Honaker Miracle and get treatment?

The dynamics of the battle had dictated DUSTOFF 24 be ready to go in. It was just one of those things. They didn't have time.

I ripped off the jacket of one of the heat casualties and checked the ankle and hip dudes. They were stable. I checked their wrists for temperature and pulse.

"Are you all right?" I asked each one.

"Yeah, I'm all right."

"Are you sure?"

I moved on to Red. He was ready to puke. I cut away his clothes, dumping water on him and making him drink. I was gonna start an IV, but we were only two minutes away from Asadabad.

The moment we landed, it was a beehive of activity. A variety of vehicles and people were there. The FLA, little pickup trucks, SFPAs, and SF Dogs, swoopy secret guys with beards, and regular nurses. They all ran up, grabbed these guys, and threw them into trucks.

I hopped in a truck because I needed to give patient care turnover. I didn't have time to reset. I had the crew chief there to start cleaning up blood and getting ammo off the deck. He'd start to reset the aircraft with the pilots and take note of what was used.

At the FST, different people descended on different soldiers. Orchestrated chaos. I went down the list, giving my reports. They had it under control.

I stepped back.

"Where's my guy?" I asked.

"He's still in the OR."

I walked over and looked in, and he was still opened up on the table.

I didn't realize until later that we were the nucleus of this battle. We were the center. Everything that occurred, all the side stories, was a part of this protective layer for these guys on the ground. And I was with them.

People were looking at me. I was covered in sweat and blood and dirt—just a fucking mess. I was dehydrated. And they looked at me like, "Holy shit, dude. We can't believe what you just did. That was insane. That was awesome!"

Sigh.

"Are you all right?"

A little thirsty.

Shortly after that, a couple of SF guys with beards grabbed me and muttered, "We need to talk."

They took me to a private compound I didn't know existed, sat me on the couch, gave me Gatorade, and asked, "What do you know?"

"I don't know anything. What do you want me to know?"

"How many were out there?" he drilled.

"I don't know. A lot, I think, but I don't know. My eyes were in. I was the medic. I was treating patients. Yes, I was shooting out, but I can't tell you how many bad guys are out there. I don't know."

They looked at me in disbelief. "We can't believe DUSTOFF 24 went in six times."

We were just Medevac, ya know? No one expected this. They were stunned.

We're just the fat neighbor who ran into the burning house and saved five kids...

Their perception of us had just changed. There was a quiet understanding of what had just happened. I didn't fully grasp it at the time. I honest to God did not appreciate the gravity of the situation. I say that I did, but I didn't have a global perspective, a bird's eye view looking down.

As I progressed through the day, I realized some things. I knew we were all in a really hairy situation. I knew that it could've gone bad at any time. I knew what I risked as a person, and what my crew risked. But I didn't know what others knew until later.

I returned to the FST absolutely exhausted. The doctor found me and told me they wanted to move my guy. They'd done the laparotomy, opened him up. He was still open, sedated, on pain management, paralytics, blood products, drips, and fully catheterized and on a vent.

He was the nightmare patient that needed a critical-care transport paramedic for pickup. He could go bad quickly, and they wanted me to take him.

I went from being a healer/killer—a soldier on the ground, under fire and shooting back—to thinking I'm done. Suddenly I was tasked with a critical-care transport and needed to start thinking clearly again.

I never said no. In my mind I said, *Oh man, I don't want to do this. I'm exhausted.*

How many operations can a surgeon do before he has to step away? There's a point of exhaustion where you must stop; otherwise you become a problem. I did not want to be the problem. For the second time that day.

But when the doc asked me personally to do it, I said, "Oh yeah, Doc, I caught him, I'll clean him. I'm more than happy. Let me know when you're ready for transport, and we'll do our normal thing." Which meant he'll give me all the information, I'll write it down, and I'll be ready to load this kid up, balance him out, and manage his care.

There was a slight wait. I was in no rush. Neither were they. I radioed the medevac guys and said we were taking this patient back to Jalalabad.

"OK, we'll shut down, take off our stuff, and reset the aircraft."

I took off my gear and tried to dry out a bit while I waited.

The trip back wasn't remarkable. I was able to maintain his stability. I made some slight adjustments and maintained his medications and vent settings, even though we had to go to altitude at some point and come back down to follow the river.

We returned and landed. I did the patient care transfer with the next medic, who was familiar with the incident.

I wasn't really numb, but I had to tell myself to clean up my aircraft, reset my gear and the helicopter. I had to make sure I had enough information for my reports. I had to take a shower, eat, and then sit and write reports. And that's what I did.

Captain McCarthy had seen what DUSTOFF had done. He approached me later and said, "I'll never forget what you did. I'll never forget seeing you go down on that wire through that mess. As long as I live, I'll never forget it." I didn't know what to say.

In other soldiers' eyes, Medevac doesn't do this. Medevac doesn't really risk everything to rescue. That day, we were one of them. In their eyes, we don't put ourselves in between them and the bad guys. They didn't realize we were willing to put it all on the line. But we were, and we did. We had many times before, but that was the first time everyone had actually seen us in action.

Those eleven soldiers fought their way out. Air assaults kept beating the enemy back, slowing their advance.

Up to that time, this battle was the largest air-ground event for our Task Force. It stayed that way until just before we left.

My guy with the gunshot wound had many surgeries, but he made it. He went home to recover. Red and the other three were just fine, too. All sixteen men of that patrol survived.

When SF guys went in that night to clean things up, they didn't find anyone alive. They did find eleven bodies and a lot of blood trails. Hadjis take their bodies. They probably carried as many as they could and either couldn't find those left behind or couldn't carry them. I found out later some of our aircraft were so damaged by enemy fire that they had a few emergency landings. None crashed, thankfully.

The Black Hawk captain, CPT McCarthy, and his crew were in engaged against the DShKs and put themselves in between heavy fire and the soldiers who were being loaded and unloaded onto the aircraft. An act of heroism.

I'm the first California National Guardsman to receive a Silver Star (for this rescue). I'm the first California Highway Patrolman to receive a Silver Star. People tend to take notice of this but really, there were many who went through a greater hell in comparison. It just so happened that lot of people witnessed this particular incident.

CW4 Brandon Erdmann, CW2 Scott St. Aubin, and SSG Tom Gifford were all awarded the Distinguished Flying Cross with V. Many others were given awards that day, including members of Chosin 93. CW2 Scott Stradley was awarded an Air Medal with V for his actions.

ROUTINE CAREER CALL

"Defeat is not the worst of failures. Not to have tried is the true failure."
George E. Woodberry

"We all had tough calls, and we all came out scarred by some of them, but at least we know that those who could've been saved were because we had brought the right capabilities."
SGT Michael Ferguson

Uzbin Valley, Kabul Province
July 2009

With the killing season in full force, our rescues became almost routine. Call after call, it was the same horrifying things. Burns, gunshot wounds, IED strikes. Shit we didn't see in America as civilians, we saw every day in Afghanistan. There were career calls every single day.

The call that weighed heaviest on Mike Ferguson was a soldier with Special Operations. Ferguson had been flying with a SpecOps soldier from the same unit who had been tagging along with them for the last couple of months. He had left just weeks before this call transpired. They received a call in the Uzbin Valley, which is midway between Bagram and Jalalabad. Troops had been pushing up into that area to make contact with the locals to make sure the elections weren't spoiled by the Taliban.

The Medevac crew included MAJ Laura Kaster, CW3 Bobby Brockly, SGT Bill Dahl, CW2 Mike Maxwell, Norsoft medic Oyvind Alusakr, and Ferguson. They had just finished an NVG[39] transfer flight and dropped a patient off at the hospital as dawn broke over Bagram AFB. They were due to end their shift in thirty minutes.

"Nine-line…Nine-line…Nine-line!" the call came over the radio. "You have one urgent-surgical route of flight BAF – POI – BAF."

Because the new team had not yet done run-ups, the task fell to Ferguson's crew.

They were given launch approval to fly to the vicinity of a nearby COP and meet up with an Attack Weapons Team (AH-64 Apache helicopters). This was one of the first times they were allowed to fly to a TIC[40] and loiter in the vicinity. The policy used to be that calls came in, and the commanders wouldn't let them go. Sometimes they deemed it too dangerous and required a V-feed from a UAV[41] in the area to see what was going on first. It took most of its deployment for Charlie Company to convince headquarters at Bagram they should be allowed to head to the fight and "loiter" a little ways away until it was clear.

Prior to this, the Bagram medics sat on the tarmac many times, waiting to get launch approval, only to be denied or have ground forces find another way to evacuate their wounded. Several months earlier, Mike and his crew had waited with the aircraft at idle for so long that the Apache crew landed, put the wounded soldier in the copilot's seat, and flew him to the Medevac bird. Mike and a medic from the Battalion Aid Station pulled him out of the cockpit and began CPR.

---

39 Night Vision Goggles
40 Troops in contact
41 Video feed from an unmanned aerial vehicle

This particular day they flew to COP Castle, circling and waiting for clearance to go into the LZ. Troops were still in contact as they flew. The Apaches spooled up and headed in, performing gun runs.

The medevac pilots asked if the LZ was clear. In the radio chatter, they heard the ground medics had lost a pulse on the patient. Bobby immediately turned down the valley and headed up toward the LZ, trying to get as close as possible to the wounded soldier's position. The pilot tried to learn if it was clear to enter and asked multiple times for an LZ status. He headed towards a firefight in his unarmed aircraft with no idea if it was safe or whether they would meet a wall of lead or more. They finally got a response from the ground:

"We haven't taken any rounds in the last few minutes. You are clear to land."

Mike locked and loaded his M4 and looked over at Doc Kaster. "The shooting just stopped, and we are on our way in," he told her. "Stay in the aircraft." Docs flew with Medevac on critical-care missions to be an extra set of hands and get a feel for what the mission entailed, but at Bagram they normally didn't go on POI calls. Mike witnessed an "Oh, shit!" look register on her face, and then she resumed scanning to find the landing site.

The ground guys popped smoke, and the helicopter did a couple circles around the area to find it. Smoke was surprisingly difficult to find from the air, especially if it was green in color, and they popped it in the one green spot in the valley.

"I've got it. Green smoke out your left door now," Mike called on the ICS. The pilots vectored in to land.

The Afghans farm on terraced fields because the terrain is so steep. There was barely enough room to land a Black Hawk helicopter on one. They came in, a tree on the left—just outside the rotor disk. A little closer, and they would've hit it with the rotor blades. "How are we looking on the right?" Bobby asked as he descended into the LZ. Bill, who sat in the right rear of the aircraft, told him to "come left a little, or your tail is going to drop off the edge." They descended onto a small terraced field of crops about a knee high, the only place in the immediate vicinity to land.

Bill opened the cabin door, and Mike disconnected. He popped out of the aircraft, aid bag over his shoulder and rifle in hand. There was a low stone wall that ran just in front of the helicopter, about ten yards away. The patient was on a litter lying on top of the wall while the ground medics tended to him. Mike ran to them and saw he was intubated and they were using a BVM. He was white as a ghost—definitely a bad situation.

From his civilian experience, Mike knew that a traumatic arrest had statistically no chance for survival. But this was a US soldier. He was going to do whatever he could to save him. He saw only a fellow soldier who needed help and the helicopter that would get his patient out of there. Everything else was a blur. He grabbed a handle on the litter with other soldiers, and they ran back toward the aircraft.

It wasn't until they were loading that Mike realized there was actually a shit-ton of gunfire going off. While he had been securing the patient and moving to the aircraft, American and ANA forces had set up security around the helicopter. They were now shooting up into the mountains in three different directions to suppress incoming fire from the Taliban.

The HH-60 helicopter they used in Bagram was harder to load, so they had to get the patient in, slide the corner, and then push him in the rest of the way. It didn't take long, but Major Kaster and Oyvind had to direct the ground crews on how to do it. Oyvind had taken up a prone position on the ground facing the tail to provide suppressive fire. Ferguson jumped into the aircraft and realized he was a man short. He shouted to one of the soldiers and pointed, "Hey! I need that guy right there! He's with us!" They tapped Oyvind on the shoulder, and he jumped in. As they shut the door, they heard a bullet hit the aircraft.

Tink!

Oyvind and Mike looked at each other for a second, each with their own "Oh, shit!" expression, and the aircraft pulled pitch faster than Mike had ever experienced before. The aircraft tore out of the valley en route to Heathe Craig in Bagram.

Ferguson knew things weren't good. He checked for a pulse. Nothing. They started CPR, and Mike bagged a couple times to breathe for the patient, but the bag didn't seem right. The monitor had taken a shit and wasn't giving a reliable reading. Mike didn't know what kind of heart rhythm he was in, if any. He pulled the endotracheal tube, because it wasn't good either. It moved around too easily, most likely coming dislodged at some point in the rapid transfer into the aircraft.

As Mike pulled the tube, Oyvind bagged him. That seemed to be going well, so Mike crawled over the top of the doc doing CPR and dropped an EZ/IO. It didn't seem to be flowing well. In his excitement and shortness of breath from getting shot at, Mike figured he had screwed it up and started a second one. This IO seemed to work a little better. He crawled back over the doc and checked the monitor—still no recognizable reading, just random artifact and changing leads. Repositioning the electrodes didn't seem to help either. The only thing they could really do was continue CPR. Mike decided to re-intubate the patient.

As soon as Ferguson intubated him, blood began pouring out of the side of the occlusive dressing covering the bullet hole in the patient's chest.

Cognitively, Mike knew his patient had bled out into his chest cavity long before he got there. He wasn't going to survive, but it was impossible to let go when treating a brother. Ferguson fought for any opportunity, no matter how small.

Mike placed him on a ventilator as they taxied into the hospital drop-off. The crew hot off-loaded, placing the patient on a wheeled cart while the rotor blades were still turning. They quickly rolled him into the FST. Mike gave his report, and the doctor decided to crack the chest right there to see if there was any hope of stopping the bleeding, thus keeping him alive. Once they opened the patient up, he dropped about two liters of blood onto the floor and everything else in its path.

There was no hope.

Mike looked around, really seeing the scene for the first time now that his role in it was done. Bagram did not normally get many point-of-injury calls. They usually saw badly injured patients, but they were alive, coming from another forward surgical team on critical-care transports.

When the doctor declared him dead, there wasn't a dry eye in the room. Ferguson felt his own tears start to well up, so he picked up his blood-soaked ventilator and made a hasty exit.

Thankfully it was end of his shift, and others helped to prep the bird for the oncoming crew. He dropped off his equipment and made a beeline for his room. He closed and locked the thin plywood door, kicked over his chair, threw his belongings against the wall, and then sat down on the floor and succumbed to feelings of grief, frustration, and failure.

The entire Medevac crew earned combat awards on that incident. Sworn statements from the Special Forces team said the aircraft received sustained machine-gun fire from the time they entered the valley until they left. Medevac had no idea at the time; they only knew that a wounded soldier lie bleeding in the field, and it was their job to retrieve him.

As a civilian firefighter/paramedic in a busy city, Ferguson was used to seeing death. In Afghanistan, he was involved in what he describes as "career calls"[42], but they happened every day. Mike's Platoon Sergeant Kelly said it best: "You're out and about, and guys say, 'Hey, you're DUSTOFF; were you there when (insert incident here) happened?' We say 'Yeah—I was there at the time, so I might've been.' Then they say, 'Oh, you would've remembered it, because that was the worst day ever.' Then you politely respond, 'Every time I fly over the wire, it's somebody's worst day ever.'"

---

42 Incidents seen only once in a civilian career, or an infamous incident such as the North Hollywood shootout or the events in Somalia that inspired the book *Black Hawk Down*.

Service members bringing out an American hero.
Courtesy of SSG Angela Brennan, Medevac CE

RIDING THE HERO

"Just as the body goes into shock after a physical trauma, so does the human psyche go into shock after the impact of a major loss."
Anne Grant

"There is many a boy here today who looks on war as all glory, but, boys, it is all hell."
William T. Sherman, General, US Army, 8/12/1880

Wardak Province
21 Aug 2009

The convoy had in their possession boxes of ballots that were proof that—no matter what the Taliban and al-Qaeda threw their way—the people would have their say. It was the second election for the president of Afghanistan and many provincial offices. Men and women alike dipped their index fingers into purple ink and cast their votes for whomever they chose. The United States of America had brought democracy to Afghanistan.

But that day wasn't without its sacrifices. Security was heavy, but many polling stations remained closed for fear of retaliation. Already insurgent attacks were on the rise in recent days leading up to the election.

This particular convoy, with its precious cargo, was settling down from an earlier gunfight. They'd won, but it seemed the bad guys were relentless.

The road was windy—a single lane on very steep mountain. There was a sheer drop-off on one side, so the vehicles had to hug the mountain. Because it was single file, the convoy stretched out for two clicks—almost a mile.

Boom!

Nine-line! Nine-line! Nine-line!

Smoot was second-up, Whorton and Dragony were first-up.

In the chaos, the commander of the convoy lost track of where people were. He didn't know where anyone was, including the wounded or killed.

DUSTOFF landed and its two medics jumped out and jogged the entire stretch of the convoy, looking for patients.

Smoot was flying in circles, watching them as they jogged from vehicle to vehicle. They found three wounded soldiers midway. At the end of the convoy, they found a hero, another casualty, and a medic who was physically and emotionally spent. Dragony and Whorton returned and took charge of the three patients in the middle. Smoot was to tend to the three at the end of the convoy.

Kiowa 58s were flying nearby, watching for ambushes. There were gunners in the Humvee turrets, not really paying attention to much of what was happening.

A small charge had been planted in the road and completely destroyed the MWRP. It penetrated the hull of the vehicle and killed a young soldier instantly.

Smoot hoisted in; there didn't seem to be anyone shooting right then, which was a good thing. Checking the hero to make sure he was gone, he called for the Sked. It was hoisted down. In the meantime, Smoot found some gloves in the wreckage, so he wouldn't burn his hands again on the tag line. He packaged him up, and the crew chief raised the line.

Next, he sent up the injured soldier.

Smoot's attention turned to the eighteen-year-old medic who stood nearby. One look at his face said it all. He had just seen too much. He was absolutely spent and therefore was combat-ineffective.

"Send me down the JP again," he decided. He pops the medic on, clipped in, and DUSTOFF hoisted them both up.

On the deck, Doc worked with the patient.

Smoot was exhausted from the physical exertion he had put out for the three now in his care. But with the three soldiers, the crew chief, and Doc, there was no room left for him to work.

His eyes went to the hero. *Shit!*

He sighed and reluctantly maneuvered over others to where Doc was working. Squeezing in a boot on either side, he sat on the hero, the body giving under his weight. Smoot shuddered. *This isn't how it should fucking be. This guy just gave his life for our country, and I'm sitting on him like a piece of fucking furniture. Fuck those fucking fucks!*

Duty called. He joined in the care of the patient who still had a heartbeat. He got a line in, and he and Doc got him stabilized, despite the fact Smoot was inwardly horrified.

It was a fifteen-minute flight to Asadabad. They flew through the Konar Valley, and it was a beautiful morning.

The medic watched them work with a faraway look in his eye. His face was covered in dirt, sweat, and a look of despondency. Smoot recognized it, had felt it before. He had to get this kid some help. Now.

Once they landed, the patient was rushed into the FST. The hero remained with the crew chief and pilots while Smoot took the medic and found someone to talk with him.

A short time later, they were in the air with the hero to transport him to Jalalabad, where the mortuary services were. They were all somber. This was the part we hated.

While Smoot sat in the back, he heard the pilots talking over the radio.

"I hope they saved us some breakfast. I'm hungry," one pilot said to the other.

Smoot's anger burned. "This kid back here will never have breakfast again, asshole! How can you talk about food right now?"

No answer.

They just flew him in and landed like they'd done too many times before.

All those in the area were to present arms as they moved the hero out, but Smoot couldn't do it. He climbed out of the aircraft and just walked away.

Nobody stopped him.

SGT Ben Higgins tends to a patient in an FLA.

Courtesy of Max Becherer, Photojournalist

SAUVETAGE (FRENCH RESCUE)

"When we do the best that we can, we never know what miracle is wrought in our life, or in the lives of others."
Helen Keller

"Man's greatest obligation is action, regardless of how he feels."
Ayn Rand in Atlas Shrugged

Kapisa Province
4 Sept 2009

Ben Higgins was sleeping in his hooch. As the summer wore on, the tempo had been high. There were lots of calls; so when we were allowed sleep, we took advantage. A knock sounded.

"You're second-up, Higgins! Urgent nine-line request. Forty-six is already on its way. Mass casualties."

Ben wiped his eyes and tried to focus. He quickly changed and made note of what he needed.

Flight suit. Vest. Weapon. Sidearm. Medical bag. Aid bag.

He ran his fingers through his hair, smoothing anything at attention.

Go-to-hell bag. Helmet. IVs. Harness...oh, and my drug box.

It was shortly after 0700. The sun was just coming up over the mountains.

Normally, there was time to set up the helicopter and load personal equipment. Not this time...the other crew members had already began startup. At least the medical gear was onboard. It was time to move as fast as possible. Fortunately, this process was well practiced through much repetition, and Ben was mission-ready in a couple of minutes. Unfortunately, the rapid preparation and departure does not allow time to consider all the details normally addressed before assuming duty. There was that nagging and unsettling feeling...*what did I forget?*

It was a five-minute flight just outside of Bagram, barely time to get his bearings. He had no time to set up, no time to think.

The 58s escorted them in. The radio was squawking; everyone was talking. The whine of the helicopter was a steady nuisance—it was difficult to hear. Information overload. But experience had taught Ben to pick out what he needed to know, process it into what he needed to do, and manage it into action.

They passed DUSTOFF 46 coming from the point of injury as they made their way to the location. The pilots from the two aircrafts were conversing about the landing site location and direction, and the hazards. As they came in on the LZ, Ben still couldn't see exactly what was going on. He suspected it was an IED based on things he'd seen before.

The billowing black smoke rose high into the air, making it easy to find the landing site. Soon he saw the rolling orange flames coming from a troop carrier that was hit by an IED. Although he saw it, he couldn't fixate on it; it was only an indicator as to where they were going to land. It also gave an idea of the mechanism of the injuries they were about to encounter. Ben noticed the OH-58 Scout helicopters in the air covering the area with the .50 caliber machine gun and rockets. They flew low, looking for enemy, making it safe enough for DUSTOFF to land.

Ben estimated the LZ was seventy meters from the kill zone. As they flew closer to the LZ, he noticed they were close to a huge cliff face, and a river ran nearby. The terrain was lush and green with tall rows of corn. Many decent landing zones were in the fields next to the river. That is where the good soil is.

Flames increased, and small explosions were seen from small-arms ammunition burning in the carrier.

They landed by the river. It didn't seem like there was any shooting, at least that he could hear. Ben exited the aircraft from the right side, taking his aid bag, two litters, and weapons—his totaling about ninety pounds (more than half his own weight). He climbed a ten-foot cliff face to access the roadway about seventy meters from the carrier on his right.

The crew chief provided security for the helicopter, as it was all by itself for a time. He couldn't see much from his location below the roadway level. It was not an ideal situation, with the medic out of direct visual contact, but Ben used his radio to keep the rest of the crew informed.

The patients had been removed from the kill zone and placed in rows on the ground to his left under some large trees. Already out of breath, Ben ran the thirty meters to that location and found a French soldier, who offered a quick report and triage information in broken English. In an urgent situation, such as this, it is best to gather the most pertinent information, identify and transfer as many patients as can be managed safely, and then depart as quickly as possible. Thanking the French soldier—still not sure who or what his role was—Ben performed a quick assessment.

They were all burn patients, and they were only a few minutes' flight time from the most definitive care available in country. The point of injury was not the time or place to initiate treatment. All of the patients were stable enough for the transfer to the helicopter, where an additional assessment would be performed. The intent is always to depart as soon as possible, because a helicopter on the ground becomes a bullet magnet…red cross or not.

The area was secure with additional French soldiers who lifted three patients onto litters and moved them back to the helicopter. There was always a concern for safety around the aircraft, but particularly during dynamic situations such as this one. The French soldiers, adrenaline flowing, were not as familiar with the loading methods onto HH-60 helicopters or other safety considerations. This can make a dangerous situation worse. The three casualties were loaded onto the deck, because there wasn't time to secure them. It was more important to leave the landing zone. The doors closed, and the crew chief reported ready for lift-off: "Clear left up." They were in the air in thirty seconds.

With the greater life threats outside of the helicopter, Ben kept his focus out of the window, searching for dangers. As the helicopter ascended and increased speed, those threats decreased, and Ben refocused on the patients. While he secured patients and prepared to administer Fentanyl for pain control, the pilot reported a short estimated time of arrival at five minutes.

Burns are tough to manage. The immediate threat to life is from smoke and hot gas inhalation. This can cause the airway to close quickly with tissue swelling and displacement of the oxygen-carrying capacity of the hemoglobin with carbon monoxide. These patients were at risk for both. They needed intubation, but there was not time during the short flight. An RSI for intubation attempt under those conditions would not be in the patients' benefit. This procedure requires the use of short- and long-lasting paralytic medications as well as a hypnotic/sedative and pain medication. It is one of the most risky of procedures, even under controlled conditions. For this short transport, it was better to support with oxygen therapy and Fentanyl for pain control while monitoring their airways. Ben knew the risk was compounded if he allowed his attention to focus on one procedure, leaving the remaining patients without monitoring. He waited.

Victims of IED blasts are also at risk for internal injuries, bone fractures, and traumatic brain injury. This requires an accurate assessment of the patient. Ben began assessments but was unable to complete them because of the short flight time.

They flew the five minutes back to Bagram and performed a "hot" offload. Ben wasn't used to the short flight—he liked the long flights, where he could actually do something significant for his patients.

Once they landed, he transferred the three patients to the ER and gave his patient-care reports amid a mass of noise and confusion from elevated activity, limited space, and language barriers. There were ultimately nine patients transported from this incident, stretching the limits of the staff's capabilities.

It was later learned the truck indeed hit an IED. The soldiers were on a reconnaissance patrol to secure a route between Bagram and Nirjrab. There were a total of eleven French soldiers who were injured. One died instantly. Another died in Germany of his wounds. The rest survived.

The rescue was twenty-five minutes from beginning to end for Ben. He was awarded "Rescue of the Year" by the Dustoff Association and the Sikorsky Award.

Kiowa 58 (Scout) in action. Armed with a folding fin aerial 2.75 inch rocket pod and a .50 caliber machine gun.

Courtesy of Carmel Cammack

BENSON AND STEAD

"We few, we happy few, we band of brothers. For he today that sheds his blood with me shall be my brother."
William Shakespeare

"Medevac went places they probably shouldn't have to get to wounded soldiers and to get those soldiers to the proper medical care they needed. They are very talented soldiers."
CW4 Pat Benson

Shuriak Valley
8 Sept 2009

It's different when you pick up someone you know.

Donald Baker and Pat Benson had a lot in common. They had a lot of the same background. They both were sheet metal structural paint guys. They both were from the 160th. Benson got to be a warrant officer, and Brian tried but was disqualified by a hole in his eye. They both loved cigars.

In fact, Benson was a cigar connoisseur. A trait Donald loved.

Benson was a Chief Warrant Officer and flew 58s. When he wasn't flying, he was on our porch, smokin' and jokin'. We talked about helicopters, the task force, our kids. He was just the salt of the earth.

On September 8, a team of two Kiowa 58s were sent out on a mission to provide security for an infantry mission. Benson was the flight lead. Then they were called to go to a more active area to help out some troops engaged in a firefight. He was called to provide an air assault on the enemy, who were positioned on a mountain in the Shuriak Valley. After that settled down, Benson and copilot Adam Stead left the scene to refuel and let others have a turn.

After refueling, they were re-tasked to do Medevac security in the same area—there were two hurt American soldiers that needed to be hoisted out. The radio traffic advised them there were enemy in the area.

Nate hoisted in to tend to the casualties. Nearby, there were bad guys with AK-47s running around shooting at the air ambulance. About that time, DUSTOFF took a round to the nose.

In response, Benson and Stead put their armored 58 in between the bad guys and DUSTOFF and shot back. Medevac picked up one soldier, re-positioned, and then picked up the second. Just as Whorton was hoisting up, Benson heard a loud noise and a concussion. The Kiowa took rounds up through the center console of the aircraft.

The radio went crazy.

Benson looked to his right—Stead was slumped over, unconscious, with a bullet in the back of his head. Blood covered the cockpit. He looked down and saw a hole in the belly of the aircraft at his feet. He was also bleeding profusely from his own leg.

Benson's aircraft started to pitch up and turn right. He grabbed the controls and recovered. Bleeding out the leg, Benson was able to keep it together to descend out of the valley and land the aircraft at Michigan, several minutes away.

Kiowas are hard to fly. A Kiowa flies like a helicopter, whereas a Black Hawk flies like a Corvette drives, doing a lot of things for you. The way the Black Hawk is engineered, some people can't believe that it can do what it actually does. A Black Hawk is easy to fly. The 58, not so much. You have to think. You have to put foot inputs in it anytime you do something with the controls. So for Benson to fly that thing with an unconscious copilot and a bullet in his leg, and then land, was a tremendous feat. He could've easily rolled it over on the FOB. But Benson kept his cool and did everything he was supposed to.

Baker and I were second-up that day; otherwise we would've gotten the call. Instead, Whorton and Gorham took their patients to Michigan, leaving them in the aircraft at Schofield. They ran into the FST and helped triage Benson and Stead, and then carried them out to the helicopter and threw them in with the other patients. They then flew all the casualties to Asadabad.

The medical team got them stabilized, and then we picked them up out of Asadabad. When we got the call, Baker went into the Walmart shed and picked out a cigar that he knew Benson liked. A Pampalona... one of the good ones.

Once we arrived, we loaded up Stead into the helicopter. I then went back into the FST, got the turnover report, and grabbed Benson. As I leaned over to pull Benson's litter in, he reached up and planted a kiss on my cheek. *What the…?*

We both laughed. It was a recognition moment. He knew it was me. Baker secured the headset on him, stuck a cigar in his mouth, and talked with him a bit. It was good to be alive. His leg was screwed up, but he was OK.

When we tried to close the door of the aircraft, it wouldn't shut. The type of stretcher they used to carry Benson did not retract the handle, and it wouldn't fit.

"We gotta get these guys outta here," asserted Baker. He tried to use a little handsaw on his Gerber to saw off the ends so they could close the door. It wasn't working. I handed him my Medevac Gurkha, and he went to town. We didn't care—it was Benson.

To Benson's left, I worked on Stead. He wasn't doing well. He was sedated, paralyzed, and on the vent. He had drips, a catheter on board, and IVs. I balanced him out and kept him stable for the twenty-five minute flight to Jalalabad for the tail to tail to Bagram.

About halfway through the flight, I reached over to Benson with my syringe. He'd been given morphine, but it was time to give him some Fentanyl.

"Don't knock me out, Emmett! I don't want to go to sleep! I want to talk to Stead!" Benson barked.

Baker responded. "It's happy juice, Pat. Relax, man!"

When we got to Jbad, the entire FOB was there to unload them. Two of our guys had been shot. Everyone wanted to be there.

Benson and Stead were flown to Bagram. Within hours, Benson was flown to Landstuhl, Germany. He arrived at Andrews AFB on September 11, 2009. He's made a full recovery, and later was awarded the Distinguished Flying Cross for his actions that day.

There was one more souvenir Benson got to take home with him: Baker gave him the handle that he'd taken off his stretcher with my bone saw.

Adam Stead was in a coma for a couple of months but eventually recovered. He is visually impaired now and takes part in Wounded Warriors events.

CPT Will Swenson and SGT Marc Dragony helping SFC Kenneth Westbrook to the Medevac helicopter during the Ganjgal battle. SGT Kevin Duerst provides cover with his M-4.

Courtesy of CW2 Jason Penrod's Helmet Cam

Affectionate goodbye for a comrade during their last moment together at the battle of Ganjgal. SFC Westbrook was Medevac'd with gunshot wounds suffered on the battlefield, but later died in the United States due to a contaminated blood transfusion received while in theater. SFC Westbrook was posthumously awarded the Silver Star for his actions that day. CPT Swenson was nominated for the Medal of Honor.

Courtesy of SGT Kevin Duerst's Helmet Cam

AMBUSH AT GANJGAL

"The best thing you can do is the right thing. The next best thing you can do is something. The worst thing you can do is nothing."
Theodore Roosevelt

"Highlander 5 gave the clearest sense of urgency, had coordinated the first rescue and in the absence of air support, risked his life to rescue the ANA soldiers those marines had died defending. Fox 31 and Fox 33 were on the radio but very emotional, though who could blame them? Their fellow marines were being cut down and begging for help. As cold as this may sound, I had no choice but to ignore 31 and 33 in order to focus on the one player on the ground who seemed to have a grasp on this insane situation, Highlander 5."
CW2 Jason Penrod

Kunar Province
8 Sept 2009

It had been a long and arduous summer. We had just one month left in theater. We were worn out, yet the fighting continued. It seemed the Taliban wanted to spill as much blood as they could before the cold weather returned. On September 8, it seemed the entire country was battling.

Barge Matal was still raging. We'd been there dozens of times, even after the election. The violence continued about seventy-five days straight, and we'd lost many soldiers there. But President Karzai had asked if we could take back Barge Matal to allow the election to take place, and our commanders obliged. This meant that COP Keating would have to stay put for the time being. To get supplies to Barge Matal, we had to have COP Keating in place. The Apaches were up there often—they were the only gunships that could fly in that altitude. The Chinooks were going back and forth up there as well, taking in supplies.

There was also a full air assault going on in the Shuriak Valley. Many of Task Force PaleHorse assets were engaged there. We suffered casualties in that battle, two of them our own PaleHorse element.

Then there was Ganjgal, a small village located east across the valley from Asadabad. The ground was scarred with long-abandoned agricultural terraces separated by a dry wash. The elders of the village had invited ANA representatives and American advisors to participate in what was called a key leader engagement. There were marines, ANA soldiers, and a couple army soldiers who met with the local village elders. But as the meeting started, insurgents imbedded within the village opened fire and cut them to pieces. It was an ambush! Our men scattered for cover, and a several-hour battle began.

DUSTOFF 25 had already launched from Asadabad. The team on board was CW2 Jason Penrod, LT Marco Azevedo, CPT Doc Kavanagh, SGT Marc Dragony, and SGT Kevin Duerst. They were on standby for another operation in the Shuriak Valley but then were redirected to Ganjgal when it went bad. By the time DUSTOFF arrived, there were two Kiowa 58s already on station.

After getting an update from the lead 58 pilot, the DUSTOFF crew realized the marines and ANA were caught in the open. Listening to radio traffic, Penrod heard Highlander 5[44] demanding the 58s shoot at the village so they could escape the kill zone. The pilot refused and

---
44 Army Captain William Swenson

asked where the fire was heaviest. He seemed unimpressed with the critical nature of the situation, almost like he was engaged in a different fight.

Highlander 5 screamed back over the radio, "From the village! Shoot the village!" Again, the lead pilot refused, because of the rules of engagement—gunships were not allowed to shoot into the village.

While circling above the fight to the west, DUSTOFF 25 saw how dire the situation was. The enemy had gone to great lengths to set up the ultimate ambush. Our marines and ANA were out in the open without any cover. The insurgents held all the high ground south, north, and east. The only way out was the open dry wash, though it afforded no protection.

While Penrod attempted to locate the casualties through the 58 pilot, it became clear to him that the entire area was blanketed with small-arms, machine-gun and RPG fire. An occasional smoke trail disappeared into the rising dust from machine-gun rounds impacting the ground. Watching from afar and listening to these guys die was not where Penrod and the crew wanted to be.

As Penrod listened to the radio traffic on the ground, he was able to identify one key player in the rescue team. It was Army Captain William Swenson. He and Penrod connected via radio. Swenson explained he had a soldier shot in the neck who was bleeding to death, and his position was on the southwestern edge of where the rounds were impacting the terraces.

Flying over, Penrod determined the terraces might be tall enough to hide the body of the helicopter. After a brief conversation, the crew decided to go in. Penrod's plan was to nose the aircraft over, increase their airspeed, and fly up the wash twenty to thirty feet off the ground. He did just that.

As they arrived at Swenson's location, it was impossible to find him as they were blending in behind the terrace walls, taking cover. About that time, the insurgents began to direct their attention toward DUSTOFF, so it was time to get the aircraft out of the kill zone. As they flew back down the wash, Penrod asked Swenson if he had a panel marker. He did. Penrod instructed him to pull it out, lie on his back and point it toward the helicopter as they made another attempt.

Penrod turned the aircraft back up the wash and accelerated. Their previous pass was low enough that it kicked up the fine dust in the wash. Afghan dust is like talcum powder, and it made a less-than-adequate smoke screen. "What the hell," Penrod thought. "We'll take what we can get at this point."

As DUSTOFF approached the LZ, Penrod and Duerst could see Swenson lying on the ground with the panel. Penrod rolled the aircraft in and made a quick approach to the terrace, tucking the aircraft up against the wall. It was just tall enough.

This was when Penrod and Swenson had their first face-to-face meeting. He was dressed in nothing more than his uniform; he wasn't wearing his helmet, or visible body armor[46]. After giving a short report to the medics, he hesitated at the door and peeked around the front of the aircraft back toward where the rounds were coming from.

With a quick nod to each other, Acevedo and Penrod came to a painful realization.

Swenson was using the aircraft for cover.

Marco shouted, "What the fuck?!"

---

46 Although not visible to Penrod at the time, Swenson wore a plate carrier for body armor.

Penrod responded. "Think small, brother."

Duerst exited the helicopter, M-4 in hand to provide cover. Swenson jogged back to the group, who had just lifted a wounded soldier onto the terrace. Dragony joined them, and both helped the soldier to his feet. They each took a side, and all three limped to the helicopter where they set him in the aircraft.

As the soldier, SFC Kenneth Westbrook, sat for a moment, he and Swenson exchanged a few words. It was a poignant moment—these two were friends. Swenson leaned in and kissed Westbrook on the temple, patted his head, and then jumped back down off the terrace, not looking back.

Duerst reentered, and Dragony slammed the door. Time to leave.

"Let's get the hell outta here!" yelled Dragony and Duerst. Penrod lifted the aircraft from the terrace, accelerating simultaneously. They later described the view outside as though they were taking off from a Super Bowl stadium. Muzzle flashes looked like hundreds of cameras going off. Dragony emptied two magazines out the side with his M-4.

While Marc returned fire, Duerst stuck his fingers into Westbrook's neck to stop the bleeding, and Doc assessed the patient. He was dressed like a Special Forces operator and unshaven. He had a gunshot wound that tracked from his neck down into his chest, just beneath the clavicle, where two large blood vessels were located. He was struggling to breathe; his blood pressure was low, and his heart rate was elevated. Doc decompressed his chest just as they touched ground at Asadabad.

When they arrived at Abad, the FLA wasn't there. After several radio calls, Duerst went on the hunt for some help. He jogged toward the FST, spotting a Gator—a small Polaris-type vehicle. He quickly checked in with the soldier assigned to the flight line, who grabbed the keys.

They both jumped in the Gator, jetting it to the helicopter. Doc and Dragony loaded the patient into the back of the Gator, and the flight-line soldier rushed them all to the trauma bay. When they arrived, it became obvious why they weren't met at the pad. The FST was completely overwhelmed with patients.

After their turnover report, Doc and Dragony jogged back and boarded. While they were gone, 58s had met and flown to Abad after going Winchester, rearmed, and then all aircrafts returned to the fight.

Things had gotten much worse. The marines and their ANA counterparts were dying. The crew listened to two marines die on the radio begging for help.

Penrod couldn't stand it. The 58s were of little help, and DUSTOFF couldn't get to them. It was time to stop screwing around and get the Apaches on station.

He had Duerst send a message to the TOC and told them to launch Blue Max. In response, the TOC asked the 58s if they needed Apaches. They replied emphatically they did not. Frustrated, Penrod had Duerst resend the message. PaleHorse TOC inquired a second time. The lead 58 pilot became irritated and wanted to know who was asking, assuming it was the ground guys. They told him it was Penrod. He quickly directed his frustration at Penrod. "I don't need Apaches! This is MY fight!"

Time to pull rank.

"I'm the air mission commander (AMC), and I want the Apaches here. You're ineffective, and these guys are dying!"

Then Penrod had Duerst send a third message to the TOC and made it more explicit. "I'm the AMC. I want Apaches here right fucking now!"

A second 58 team was on its way to the Shuriak Valley and were directed by TOC to learn what was going on. They asked the lead 58 pilot on station via radio if he needed help. He quickly got his answer. "I don't need your help! Stay outta my fight!"

Surprised by the angry response, the second 58 pilot replied, "Whoa! Hey, man, I was just told to ask."

That was the end of the conversation, and the second 58 team kept to its previous course.

PaleHorse TOC again inquired with the lead 58 if he was sure Apaches were not needed. He again angrily replied he didn't need them. TOC responded that DUSTOFF was adamant about Apaches responding. There was no answer from the 58.

PaleHorse TOC came back on and asked Penrod why he wanted Apaches. Penrod replied, "These marines are dying out here and the 58s aren't effective. These guys are in an ambush and taking fire from every direction but the west. I want Apaches and I want 'em now!"

The PaleHorse TOC conversation took place over SatCom, which means everyone on the aviation frequency in country heard it. One of those sets of ears was in Thunder TOC, our parent command Combat Aviation Brigade (CAB) headquarters in Bagram. During the pause generated by Penrod's emphatic request, the radio operator in Thunder TOC interjected, "PaleHorse TOC, Thunder TOC."

The reply by the PaleHorse TOC radio operator was to standby. This wasn't well received and quickly drew the ire of Colonel Lewis, the CAB commander, "PaleHorse TOC, Thunder Six." This was Colonel Lewis's call sign as Task Force Thunder commander.

The Apaches were now on their way.

After getting the Apache issue resolved, the crew's attention was brought back to the fight. In the meantime, Swenson had decided to take matters into his own hands. He drove a small pickup truck into the kill zone and attempted to rescue the marines and ANA who were trapped and wounded. At that point it was unclear just how many he'd rescued, but it was blatantly obvious that he'd gotten himself into real trouble. The pickup was so badly damaged from small-arms fire, it was no longer moveable. He was trapped in the kill zone with the wounded he'd rescued.

Swenson's calls for help were more than Penrod and Acevedo could stand. They decided to attempt another run up the wide-open valley to rescue the wounded, even though they were further up and well within the reach of the highly effective small-arms and RPG fire.

In what was to be DUSTOFF's final turn before the dive, Kavanagh saw two aircraft flying down the Konar Valley and thought they appeared to be Apaches. Penrod knew it couldn't be those coming from Jbad, but it wasn't uncommon to have other Apaches from Bagram in the area.

"What the hell," Penrod decided. "Let's try and reach 'em."

Marco called over the Apache radio frequency, but there was no response. The common air-to-ground frequency was no better. As a last resort, Penrod gave a call over the air to air frequency, and they quickly got a response from Pedro, the US Air Force Pavehawks. These guys weren't Apaches, but they had fifty-caliber machine guns and miniguns. Penrod was ready for some well-directed crew-served weapons, given the fact that our 58 support was inadequate. He gave them a brief synopsis of the situation, and they decided to drop their patients at Abad and come help.

Given how grave Swenson's position was, the DUSTOFF crew decided it was too long to wait for the Pavehawks to get on station. Talking directly to Swenson, they were able to determine he was quite a bit further up the wash and very exposed. Penrod made the same dive as he had earlier, a fast and low flight up the wash toward the rising dust of where they believed his truck had made its last stand. There he was, tucked into a smaller tributary wash, with several bodies in the back, along with two ANP pickups that had made it to his location. A hard right, a decelerating turn, and they were on the ground, just feet from the vehicles.

The ground guys and the DUSTOFF crew wasted no time in loading as many patients as possible—five patients, all ANA, no marines. It was time to leave, but the Pavehawks were still not on station. They couldn't go back to Abad with these patients; the FST was already overloaded. They had to go to Jbad. As Penrod accelerated down the wash, Pedro checked in. As they tried to reach DUSTOFF, the 58 pilot interjected, "No need. They're all dead."

Penrod was done with this guy. He broke onto the radio and told Pedro to disregard the 58 pilot and listen only to DUSTOFF 25. He explained where the vehicles and patients could be found and that several remained. The Pedro pilot was unclear of where they were, so Penrod made the decision to delay their return to Jbad and link up with him to take another run into the fire. With the Pavehawk in tow, they made another low and fast run up the valley. As they neared the vehicles, Penrod explained to the Pedro pilot he would break hard right over the location, as they were in a hurry to get the patients to the FST. Pedro landed and quickly stated they couldn't find any patients. The 58 pilot came on the radio and scolded, "See, they're all dead." The Pedro pilot summarily dismissed the 58 pilot and stated, "DUSTOFF 25, we've got 'em. A lot of patients here."

DUSTOFF stayed as long as they could and then quickly departed toward Jbad. About halfway there, they saw the Apaches headed up toward Ganjgal. But it was too late.

The Aftermath

No marines were rescued from the ambush in Ganjgal. We later learned they stayed behind in the wash returning fire to ensure the others could escape. Their radio calls for fire support and rescue were the last words anyone would hear from them. Those pleas for help have kept Jason Penrod awake many nights wondering if they should've done more. Should he have gone in after them while they were still alive?

Jason has heard all the justifications as to why they shouldn't have—the state of Swenson's pickup as the strongest argument against such an attempt. They probably would've become, as LTC Jimmy Blackmon says, "the main effort." This was something he never wanted to be.

Jason Penrod has contemplated all of the rationalization and the risks that justify not even doing what they did. But this does little to drown out the voices of those marines. They continued to resonate long after the battle was over. The fallout of the ambush at Ganjgal was huge. There have been several different accounts of what happened that day, and several explanations. When the dust settled, three marines and one navy corpsman lost their lives in Ganjgal, as well as nine ANA soldiers.

The gunshot victim picked up by DUSTOFF, SFC Kenneth Westbrook, was rushed into surgery at the FOB. The surgeons repaired the vascular injury at the FST and placed a chest tube. He made it back to the United States but tragically suffered a fatal reaction to a blood transfusion believed given in Asadabad. He was the fifth American to die in the Ganjgal ambush.

Marc Dragony was absolutely livid about what happened in Ganjgal. We had bonded with the 58 guys and were indoctrinated into the Cavalry culture, even calling each other family. But after the 58 pilot declared the battle "his fight" and refused any additional air support, Dragony took off his Stetson and abandoned it in Jalalabad. He had lost all respect and didn't want to be associated with them. Years later, Dragony regretted leaving the Stetson and painting such a broad picture of the Cav. He is, however, still angry about the actions of that day.

Marc had suffered. He recounted to me how he was in Diego Garcia on his way back to the States from the war. He was in that beautiful paradise when he learned that SFC Westbrook had died from that damn transfusion. He struggles with this. To this day, Marc wears a bracelet with Westbrook's name engraved on it.

Marine Dakota Meyer, who was also engaged in the fight this day, was awarded the Medal of Honor for his actions. Other members of ETT 2-8 were awarded Bronze Star with V medals. Two other marines, SSG Juan Rodriguez-Chavez and CPT Ademola Fabayo, were awarded the Navy Cross.

After years of indifference, Westbrook was posthumously awarded a Silver Star on April 19, 2013. Army Captain William Swenson was nominated for the Medal of Honor, but after his public criticism of the US Army, his paperwork was claimed to be lost.

Northern California
Spring 2013

When I interviewed the men who were on this call, it became apparent to me that Ganjgal has lived on in the nightmares of all of them.

In their eyes, it wasn't only controversial; cries for help were not responded to, and people died. For Medevac, this was devastating.

As the story unfolded, I decided that I would try to help my friends heal by creating a critical incident debrief[48] (three and a half years later). I invited all of those who were on the helicopter with Westbrook, and his close friend and Afghanistan comrade, CPT Will Swenson. Though Marco was deployed in Kosovo and Doc couldn't get away from his residency, Dragony, Duerst and Penrod were able to come. It was time to get some closure.

I set up a tour at the CHP academy with Chief Newman and Victoria to break the ice. We then headed for my home for barbecued ribs and drinks.

We talked about what occurred that day. Captain Swenson joined in, giving clarity but more importantly, his thanks. He thanked the guys for coming when others did not. This meant a lot to them.

Penrod and Duerst didn't know exactly who Swenson was. They did not recognize him as the one they talked with on the radio or the one who placed Westbrook on the aircraft. There were assumptions made, and not everything made sense.

Immediately after landing in Jbad, Penrod wrote his sworn statement. He primarily wanted to capture the epic failure of what occurred that day but also to ensure that Highlander 5 received our nation's highest award, the Medal of Honor. As the pilot who had a front row, overhead seat to this tragedy and the resulting act of heroism, it was beyond any reasonable doubt that Highlander 5 embodied the values of such an award. However, Penrod later learned his sworn statements were never included.

---

48 A law enforcement term for a group discussion after a traumatic event

Penrod and Swenson had a frank discussion about Ganjgal. Jason needed some critical items verified. One of the most significant was if the marines and corpsman who stayed behind had in fact covered the ANA's attempted escape from the ambush, giving their lives in doing so. Swenson verified this and reiterated that because they had remained so close to the enemy, there was no way for Medevac to reach them without becoming casualties in the process. For Penrod, Dragony and Duerst, knowing there was nothing they could've done does ease some of the long-term burden, but it certainly doesn't silence the pleas for help in their minds.

There was one more detail. As Penrod and Swenson sat face to face, the fog of war began to clear. Until this moment the entire Medevac crew believed that Highlander 5 had already received the Medal of Honor, even though in all of the reports they read, the placement and types of vehicles and locations didn't jibe with their recollections.

Penrod remembered Highlander 5 at the first Medevac site in Ganjgal with the panel marker, a radio on his back with a long whip antenna, dark Oakley sunglasses, longer dark hair, and his face clean-shaven. At the time, Penrod wasn't sure who the man was, but assumed his identity. Three years later, he became unsure. He looked across the table at the long-haired, bearded man before him and demanded, "If it wasn't that dude, then who the fuck was Highlander 5?!"

Swenson stared back with a shocked look and replied, "I'm Highlander 5."

CW2 Jason Penrod (left), Nevada National Guard, and CW2 Scott St. Aubin, California National Guard, take a rare moment to smoke a cigar and decompress on the upper deck at FOB Fenty, Jalalabad, Afghanistan. Medevac helicopter waits on the airfield below.

Courtesy of CW2 Cole Gould

Barge Matal, September 12, 2009 – daytime mission under fire. Lithuanian soldier in front is limping in a dead run toward the Medevac helicopter with a gunshot wound to the leg. Afghan soldiers follow behind with another gunshot victim on a litter.

Courtesy of CW2 Jason Penrod's Helmet Cam

LANDINGS, LASERS, AND A RONALD REAGAN MOMENT

"The credit belongs to the man who is actually in the arena, whose face is marred by dust and sweat and blood, who strives valiantly, who errs and comes up short again and again, because there is no effort without error or shortcoming, but who knows the great enthusiasms, the great devotions, who spends himself for a worthy cause; who, at the best, knows, in the end, the triumph of high achievement, and who, at the worst, if he fails, at least he fails while daring greatly, so that his place shall never be with those cold and timid souls who knew neither victory nor defeat."
Theodore Roosevelt

"The darkness did not mean the enemy had withdrawn, quite the contrary. Every time the crew came into a hover, the enemy fire increased including small arms, RPGS and B-10 rockets. The Medevac crew didn't hesitate in holding position while hoisting the medic down to join the ground force even as we conducted rocket and cannon attacks directly over the top of their aircraft to suppress ground fire. I knew...I had witnessed incredible heroism."
CW5 William Ham

Community Center below Bari Alai
Barge Matal
12 Sept 2009

We were forward deployed to Bostic, on standby for Barge Matal. We received a nine-line call for a soldier who had his arm blown off by an

RPG. When you get a call about an RPG injury and there's a severed hand or arm, it's just like any police call—the information you receive isn't always correct. There was a report that shots were fired, but by the time we arrived, that was no longer the case. There were reports that the enemy was in the area, but there were no longer firefights.

As we waited for clearance to go, I asked the surgeon if we recovered the arm, could he reattach it? He said, "No way. If his arm was blown off, there's no possible way."

I didn't question him. But my mind went back to my days when I was a paramedic intern at UC Davis Medical Center in Sacramento. I was working in Area One, where all of the shit came in. There was a douche bag who was high on meth and attempted suicide by stepping in front of a moving vehicle. It absolutely shredded his legs—bone, flesh, hamburger. And yet, they took him up to surgery and were able to replace the bones with metal rods, saving his legs. I'd also seen some of the heroic things these surgeons did here in Afghanistan in the middle of nowhere. But again, I didn't question his decision.

We took off after clearance, landed, and I hit the ground running. As I went forward, I saw two soldiers standing in front of the community center. They were facing each other, and I was at their 090. I jogged right up and asked them the location of the patient. The one soldier turned to face me, and I saw that he was missing his arm from mid-bicep down. It was wrapped with an Israeli bandage and evidently not bleeding.

Oh shit. This is the patient.

The first thing I thought was: where were the other injuries? If he had his arm blown off by an RPG, experience has shown me that it is a pretty distracting injury. Surely he had shrapnel in other places.

The helicopter was close by, and I couldn't hear a word they said. But I realized there wasn't any paperwork. The patient was a big guy, and he walked with me to the aircraft and got in.

Now, I know what I'm supposed to do. I'm supposed to strip him, flip him, make sure there are no other injuries, and then start oxygen, pain meds, etc. I set him in the chair and started cutting off his clothes. He stopped me for a second, reached into his pocket with his left hand, and pulled out a picture of a woman—probably his wife. He looked at it for a moment and then put it into his coat. Then he let me strip him down. I checked him over, and he looked pretty good. Everything seemed normal, except that his arm was missing.

It was a very short flight—maybe two and half minutes. I asked him if I could put him on the litter and he said, "No. I'm gonna walk."

I'm not supposed to allow that. We take control of the patient, and that means carrying them out. But I understand a man who wants to walk out on his own two feet. It reminded me of President Ronald Reagan walking into the emergency room after he was shot. It was an attitude of "You're not gonna put me down."

I allowed him to walk into the FST.

I'll never forget this soldier. He was an inspiration to me. He had a defiance toward the enemy—"I'm not gonna lie down. I'm gonna walk out on my own two feet." A man's man.

About that time we received a call for two gunshot wounds to the chest in Barge Matal. As we were waiting on Apache support, the FST surgeon came out and said the arm was a clean sever. Did they still have the arm?

Didn't I just initiate this discussion?

We contacted the ground element, and they said they did have the arm. However, the fighting in the area had kicked up again.

Well, OK then. If we could save his arm, it was worth it.

Penrod flew us back down to where the 58s were still providing cover for this patrol so that we could try to retrieve the arm. The patrol had moved from the earlier LZ, so we couldn't do a hoist because of the terrain. And we couldn't justify our safety of an entire crew for just an arm.

We saw a rock peninsula by the river near some giant trees. We radioed in, and asked if the patrol could walk out there, stand on the edge of the rocks, hold the arm in the air, and not move. Our plan was to fly over and grab it from them. They agreed.

We flew in close, and the crew chief hung out as I provided gun coverage. He grabbed the bag and tossed it to me. It was an MRE bag. I opened it up, and it was only half of a hand.

"Goddamn it!"

Penrod bristled—that's not something you want to hear in the middle of a maneuver like that with bullets flying nearby. "What?"

"It's only half a hand in an MRE bag. Only a bit of it is left," I answered.

Disappointed, we pulled in the crew chief and returned to Bostic. As we refueled, the Apaches arrived.

Now on to our original mission, Barge Matal.

On takeoff, one of the two Apaches had a mechanical malfunction and was unable to fly.

Penrod wanted to continue the mission anyway. He contacted CW5 Bill Ham in the second Apache, and together they determined to go. The patients were still in danger, so we decided to go and see what we could do.

In the meantime, on the ground in Barge Matal, the men were in bad shape. There were four Chechen snipers who were relentless. They were good shooters, able to penetrate between the body armor plates. Those who were trying to get the wounded to the LZ were taking unbelievably effective, repetitive sniper fire. We learned later our men took over 150 rounds.

There was a rocky pass that we'd fly over rather than go through the valley because they had shot at us before with everything they had, including muskets. As we were crossing this pass, we could tell Bill was attempting to test-fire his gun because it'd come out from its stowed position, move over, and then stow back up again. Penrod was watching it, and nothing happened when he tried to shoot. Again, it came back out, nothing happened, and then it retracted, about three to four times.

Bill came up on the radio. "Bad news. My gun's broke and I can't fix it in flight. It's 'hard broke.' But I have good news; I still have eighteen rockets, two hellfires and a rocket pod. What do you want to do?"

Penrod answered, "Damn! Let's just fly out there and see what's happening. If these guys aren't alive when we get there, we'll just have to call it."

We flew up to the area, and Bill was talking with the soldiers on the ground. We heard rounds cracking over the radio as they were getting shot at. Bill tried to get situational awareness as to where the bad guys were so he could shoot his rockets.

And then near the edge of the LZ, a Lithuanian soldier carrying a patient took a round through the thigh.

The LZ was a little bigger than a football field; a battle zone where we were initially planning to land. Unfortunately the bad guys knew we were there now, and we learned from intercepted hadji radio traffic that when the air ambulance landed, they planned to burn us with RPGs. Not a real confidence-builder. We decided not to land at this LZ; there was no possible way.

On the north end of the LZ, right where the valley narrowed, it was like flying down a hallway. There were peaks that went up to the 16,000-foot level. The valley narrowed and cut where the river went through. Right by this cut was a cliff, and a tiny grassy field by a mud hut that was protected by some trees. On the other side was the river. It was about the size of a tennis court. That became our new LZ.

Penrod radioed the men. "Is it possible you guys could move to that mud hut?"

They were still getting shot at where they were, so they answered, "We would love to..."

"When you get there, let us know. We're gonna do this," Penrod directed.

As they moved, Bill and Penrod planned it out. "Hey, Bill, forty-five seconds before landing, we'll give you the signal. Start shooting your rockets."

"Perfect."

One thing about my buddy, Penrod—he is amazing on the sticks. He can wiggle the sticks like you wouldn't believe. I trust him like no other.

I feel comfortable in almost any situation he flies us into. But that day, he tested me.

We set up our approach, slow. We didn't want to lose power and crash to the ground. The hard thing was how to get from up high out of the fray, to low enough so the bad guys couldn't shoot us without plowin' into the ground. Then doing it fast enough so they didn't pick us off. It was like a duck sucking into a pond where hunters were waiting to blow it out of the sky.

Penrod started about fifteen hundred to two thousand feet above the valley floor. Then he slowed back and nosed it over, picking up a little speed along the way; nothing excessive. Soon we were right down on the river in between the trees. The thought was it would give us ample opportunity to get out of there if we started to get shot at, or we could turn around, come back, and land. That's what we did.

The Apache pilots called this maneuver "return to target." We nicknamed it "return to patient." That day was my initiation. When Penrod explained it to me, I questioned him. "Now, what are we doin'?" It was a good thing I trusted him.

Penrod pushed it over and we came down, passing right over the LZ. Then we turned around, slowin' the aircraft back in, right over the top. We were really low. My pucker factor was really high.

At this point, Bill was on his attack run, shootin' his rockets. Penrod came in around and sideways, and found the locals had strung tow missile lager power lines down through the edge of the postage stamp LZ he'd had picked out. This was an attempt to prevent any aircraft from landing.

I was scared shitless. "We're gonna down this thing! STOP! No further back!"

But that fucker set it down with the tail sticking out over the water. He was on that LZ like a dog on a dead rabbit.

I pulled the harness out of my ass and prepared to jump out, but at that point the ground guys erupted out of the mud hut, threw the patients on board, and then disappeared. I didn't have to move.

As we were starting to pick up and fly away, Bill came back on the radio. "Hey, how much longer you gonna be?"

"We're comin' out right now," Penrod responded.

"Well, that's good, 'cause I'm out of rockets! Several of them wouldn't fire!"

We were on the ground for fifteen seconds, if that.

I focused on what I do best with the patients, and Penrod took off and got us the hell outta there.

That night, we went into the same location to pick up more wounded. We took fire on that one. That was when Duerst took out his laser and pointed at where the bad guys were on the mountain.

I was working on a patient, and the crew chief called out, "We're taking fire! We're taking fire!" Duerst leaned out and shot out bursts with his M-4. I said, "Hey! I wanna shoot too!" But that wasn't my job. So I leaned forward and covered the patient, who was ANA, with my body. Man, he smelled bad.

Penrod said, "Point at 'em with your laser and I'll tell the Apaches to fire on 'em." Duerst took out his laser and lined it up with where the shots came from. The pilots could see the whole line of the laser under night goggles. Penrod told the Apaches, "Go get 'em!"

The Apaches swooped in, and blew that area to bits. The next day our guys found three dead bodies.

We used the laser several times over the course of the elections—worked like a charm.

That little instinctive move of covering the ANA patient with my body did more than just shield him from harm. Evidently, before that, the ANA soldiers felt we valued our American soldiers more than them, and trust was breaking down. They didn't feel we were trying our best to help their wounded in comparison to our own. But because the patient was coherent and witnessed my action, things seemed to settle down after that. Penrod swears that the word got out that we did care—which was much closer to the truth.

PART THREE
Abandonment and Retribution

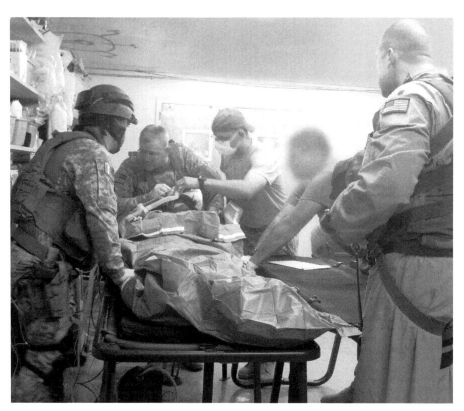

SSG Rob Walters preps critical-care patient for Medevac. Walters and other Army Medevac personnel often oriented Air Force PJs and other special forces medics to the Medevac mission.

Courtesy of SSG Angela Brennan, Medevac CEa

LET THE TERRORIST FLY!

"There will be times you must treat men and women who, moments before, were trying to kill you... You must somehow give the same dispassionate care to these as you would your own soldiers that you've lived with, ate with, slept with and generally suffered with. The life of a Medic...is not an easy one, indeed it is one of the most taxing, emotionally speaking, of any job in the military. Only commanders have more responsibility, but their burden is lightened by the distance they keep from their troops."
Michael Bailey, *The Madness of the Combat Medic*

"I did feel the military brotherhood connection to all of my patients, but I had to put that aside to provide the most objective assessment and care I could deliver. I think the best way to accomplish this is to perform well under stress and then lose my mind later on after the call."
SSG Rob Walters

Jalalabad to Bagram
Late September 2009

We were soon to be relieved by 3rd ID in Jalalabad, and it wasn't promising. One soldier had been a paramedic but let his certification lapse because the army wouldn't pay for continuation training. We had an experienced medic, but he wasn't grasping the concepts we were trying to teach him. We had a young kid who was a go-getter; a combat vet who wanted to learn and listened to everything we said. Then we had a knucklehead who knew everything and did everything, but had never been actually deployed before. The situation was frustrating, and Smoot was simmering just below the surface.

This was the part he hated. Turning over the mission to those who didn't have the education or experience needed brought up the guilt he'd had to stuff away time and time again. We put the new guys through some augmentative training, but some of these kids were just not interested in what we had to say. They had no idea what they were getting into, yet some seemed arrogant. In Bagram, Ferguson saw some texting in the back of the classroom during training, and some didn't show up at all. We knew they were not even close to being ready for what they were about to face.

During the RIP, Smoot flew with the right-seat rides. One morning, he got a nine-line request for a patient who needed to go to Bagram. He'd been trying to teach the relief how to do the basics for several days.

"Just record a time," Smoot guided. "When this time expires, you push the next drugs to keep the patient sedated and paralyzed. If you do that, you spare him the torture of coming out of sedation and thrashing around, losing the tube and dying. Write down the times, and give the medications at those times. Push the next drug to keep the guy paralyzed; manage his pain. If you do the monkey work, you'll be good."

Then Smoot learned that the nine-line patient was a Taliban insurgent who had emplaced an IED on a road frequented by coalition forces and it blew up in his face by accident. An American convoy found the insurgent barely alive on the road. They initiated care and evacuated the patient to an FST that was close. Al's aircraft was dispatched to transfer the patient from that FST to Jbad in preparation for a tail to tail back to Bagram.

Smoot had been to many IED calls. He'd seen what they've done to our soldiers. In fact, those who'd died by IED visited him in his nightmares. After the trauma of the past year, Smoot could give a flying fuck whether this insurgent lived or died.

Smoot went to the FST and asserted, "His face has been blown off, you're not gonna get any intel. There's nothing useful to get out of him. He has no face. He can't talk. Give him to the Hadji hospital and just let it go. Why put my guys at risk on this mission? Why put the Bagram guys at risk to save this piece of shit that's not gonna be worth anything to us?"

He was putting an IED in place, thought Smoot. *Throw him out of the fucking helicopter.*

Others were not so moved. Smoot and one of the new flight medics would have to do the transfer.

It was the American thing to do. It was the right thing to do. Smoot knew this cognitively, but his emotions wouldn't align. Smoot was done with terrorists and he'd had it with arrogant active-duty medics who didn't listen. But he would do his job whether he liked it or not. He allowed the EMT-Basic medic who "knew everything" to work on the patient.

Here you go, Mr. Know-it-all! He's all yours! Treat him!

The hadji was paralyzed and intubated. Smoot watched, but didn't say a damn word.

If he fucks this up, maybe he'll learn before he treats someone that deserves to live. Then I'll fix it before the bastard croaks.

The medic didn't have a notebook to write down the information or medication times from the FST. It was the end of the RIP, yet he *still* hadn't come prepared.

Smoot was furious. He'd rather get up to level flight over the Konar Valley, open the door, and throw this hadji murderer out.

He came from Pakistan, decided he was gonna blow up some Americans. Here, let's see if you can fly...

On the way back to Jalalabad, Smoot let the newbie see if he could keep up. They landed at Jbad, and Walters, a compassionate patient care advocate, was there to pick him up.

"Looks like you kept him alive," Smoot sneered.

Rob hopped into the helicopter and began his assessment of the patient.

Smoot knew Rob would work on this patient like any other. It didn't sit well. "Rob! This guy was setting an IED! He was gonna blow up somebody! Why fix it? Why not let your relief do it? Let him screw it up and learn a lesson or two..."

Rob noticed Smoot was frustrated. Al had given a terse report while they set up the patient for transfer. When Rob put the patient on the ventilator, he noticed the patient's peak inspiratory pressures were over double what they should be. This meant air was not moving into his lungs correctly.

In a patient with a known head injury (such as this patient), proper ventilatory management is crucial to care, especially when taking a patient up in altitude. So when the patient was transferred over to Rob and his relief's care, Rob noted a much higher than normal chest pressure.

With his active-duty medic in tow, Rob notified the FST staff that were assisting with the patient movement to his aircraft of his findings. He consulted with the FST surgeon and Doc Kavanagh, deciding to shoot a chest x-ray to see what was going on. This caused a small delay but identified a pneumothorax which required the placement of a chest tube prior to flight. They also initiated hypertonic saline because his brain was swelling and continued paralysis, sedation, and pain management in preparation for the flight.

Rob and Al's new medics were completely beyond their level of training. Neither understood the chest pressure findings or concepts. This was not a surprise, given the limited medical training they were given prior to deployment, but nonetheless extremely frustrating.

Rob cared for the insurgent during the flight back to Bagram. He and his relief followed the patient into the hospital and into the CT scanner so they could see what his true injuries were. The patient had an internal decapitation where multiple major structures inside his head and neck were destroyed in the blast. The damage was catastrophic. There was nothing they could do.

Rob was aware that the patient was an enemy who would've killed him in an instant and had likely killed and caused injury to many US troops. But he was able to compartmentalize this information and shelve it until a later time when it was more appropriate to deal with. During the flight, Rob simply had a patient to care for who needed his help to survive.

Smoot, on the other hand, had snapped. He knew the relief wasn't ready. Everything they'd worked for for years was coming to a close, and he would have to release his control to those who didn't have adequate education, experience, or support, to handle it. It was the same problem, different people, his entire career. Twenty years of fighting for more training for Medevac. Twenty years of watching patients die needlessly. Twenty years of those who seemed indifferent. After twenty years, what had changed? It was too much.

Later, when Smoot's emotions subsided, he had regrets on how he handled the call internally. He knew he'd taken it too far and let his emotions get the best of him. For the sake of his own emotional health, he was taken out of the rotation.

Unfortunately, this wouldn't be the last insult.

A devastated COP Keating the day after the insurgent assault. Eight US soldiers killed in the attack. These switchbacks are described by CW2 Bardwell and CW3 Lewallen.
Courtesy of CW2 Elizabeth Kimbrough

KEATING

"There are wounds that never show on the body that are deeper and more hurtful than anything that bleeds."
Laurell K. Hamilton, *Mistral's Kiss*

"When we were pushing off, that's when we discovered we'd taken one round to the tail rotor blade and another through the hydraulic line that goes to the tail rotor. It was the utility line, not the primary so it wasn't that big of a deal, other than the pylons wouldn't move, the gun wouldn't shoot, and the aircraft was really ineffective at that point."
CW2 Chad Bardwell

Nuristan Province
3 Oct 2009

COP Keating sat on the valley floor in the Kamdesh, completely surrounded by towering mountains and rocky terrain. It was a contested area, and extremely remote.

Keating was a Shangri-la—paradise on earth. It was beautiful up there. It had a gorgeous, raging river and a high peak wall. Because it was at such a high altitude, we had to fly around a mountain and then descend down into this beautiful area with a gorgeous waterfall. OP Fritsche was up there as well, a little higher than Keating.

On October 3, at 0600, three hundred Taliban attacked COP Keating and OP Fritsche simultaneously. They surrounded Keating and fired from all sides with machine-gun fire, small-arms fire, mortars, and RPGs. They disabled our mortar pit, which inhibited our ability to fight back, and because Fritsche was also under assault, they were unable to assist. Our troops fought back, but there was a breach where the Afghan security guards and Latvian army were located. Keating was overrun in under an hour, and they had our soldiers pinned down in a couple of buildings with several casualties. The Taliban set fire to several buildings.

CW4 Ross Lewallen and CW2 Chad Bardwell, Apache pilots, were heading into the chow hall for breakfast. Bardwell had been holed up with mononucleosis for over a month but was feeling better. It was good to be able to fly again.

They'd just sat down when they got a call. It seemed at first like nothing out of the ordinary—Keating was getting attacked with small arms, so they had to launch up there. This wasn't really anything new; Keating was always taking fire. Nonetheless, they dropped everything, ran out to the helicopters, and joined CW3 Randy Huff and CW2 Chris Wright on the pad. Blue Max was en route to Keating in no time at all.

About the time the Apaches reached Monti, they were told the insurgents had blown through our troops' last line of defense. The pilots were assured that all of our soldiers were inside the FOB, so anyone seen outside the wire was to be killed. As they continued on, they got another call from Bostic. They confirmed troops were all within the wire—pinned down in two buildings. Anything outside the wire—engage.

Lewallen and Bardwell came around the mountain, and the whole valley was filled with smoke. All the buildings were on fire. They couldn't believe it. On the way, they'd tried to make contact with the ground guys at Keating, but were unable to get through to them. They tried again and again, but no answer.

Finally someone responded from Keating and startled Bardwell. He replied, "You just scared the crap out of us!" Evidently the Keating operator had been talking by radio to someone else and had quite a lot on his plate at the moment.

As soon as they were overhead, they saw thirty insurgents coming down the switchbacks of a mountain that overlooked the COP. They called it in, and command replied, "Shoot 'em."

Lewallen and Bardwell saw people below, but they didn't feel like they should start shooting just yet—they weren't confident who was who.

"Confirm that you have no ANA outside the wire," verified Lewallen. He wanted to be sure. Usually pilots have to call in before they engage. This time that wasn't the case.

"We are in two buildings inside the wire. Everyone else is enemy—shoot!"

Wright and Bardwell were communicating via radio between their Apaches. They were looking at the same thing. They had hadjis in their sites. There were targets everywhere.

Insurgents were racing down the switchbacks. As soon as they saw the Apaches, they headed toward the ANA station, walked back, and then crouched behind a brick wall to take cover.

The Apaches engaged.

The Apaches were flying in orbit, dumping all three hundred rounds into these guys. There were so many casualties they were piling on top of each other. Those who escaped poured around the dead and ran down to the raging river below to find cover. There was a large group of hadjis climbing on top of each other in the river. In response, the Apaches shot at this great big moving wad of enemy.

Lewallen and Bardwell had seen insurgents inside the wire, but they didn't feel comfortable shooting into the FOB. They didn't have absolute confidence that American and ANA troops were only in the two buildings mentioned, and they didn't want to risk it. This was the right call—they learned later there were coalition forces that were defending from other places in the FOB.

It was only a few minutes before Lewallen and Bardwell were out of 30 mm. They were about to head back to reload when someone said, "Inside the mosque."

There was a mosque located on the other side of the FOB. Our guys were getting hammered from inside the mosque with DShK and RPG fire. The Apaches were given the command, "Engage with hellfires."

Randy and Chris flew around and put a hellfire into the mosque. Lewallen and Bardwell were following them in to do the same, but then Randy and Chris took a round to the aircraft. They immediately peeled off to reposition.

Lewallen stayed in the fight. He flew around through another valley, planning to hit the mosque from the other direction. Bardwell put a hellfire into the other side of the mosque. It hit perfectly, first sucking the walls in and then exploding outward. The mosque and its occupants blew apart in all directions.

Lewallen pulled out. About that time CW2 Gary Wingert and CPT Matthew Kaplan had launched from Jbad and were on their way.

"Ross, we'll come and replace Randy so you can stay on station," they radioed.

About that time Lewallen's gauges indicated a problem. Their Apache was out of hydraulic fluid in the utility system. They'd taken a round too.

Lewallen radioed back, "Ahh, never mind. We're all going back."

Lewallen and Bardwell flew back to Bostic to see what was wrong with the aircraft.

As they left, the A-10s were swooping in to rain hell on the insurgents. About that time, the weather started in. Large clouds formed around the mountains, and they looked angry.

The guys and I had been in Afghanistan for ten months, and our work was done. We'd planned, trained, taken ownership, and tracked data for the study, and then gave our heart and soul during the killing season. We'd worked on thousands of patients and tried our best to train up the new rotation, despite their training deficiencies.

It was time for our final formation in country. The commanders were acknowledging our contribution to the war effort.

We were in formation in the hangar in Bagram, listening to a speech by the Brigade Commander, Colonel Lewis. Al Smoot had just been awarded a Bronze Star when they stopped the ceremony.

"Keating has been overrun. Several soldiers have already died. There are multiple casualties."

I felt myself move.

It felt like someone had just kicked me in the balls. I literally moved, for the first time ever, in formation. I moved because I wanted to sprint for the fucking aircraft and go.

Everyone was visibly shaken.

"Thanks for your service, men..."

My thoughts went to Doc Kavanagh, who I knew was in the mix.

Doc felt very alone. He'd been in Afghanistan for ten months, but in the previous two weeks, everything had changed. We had been replaced by EMT-Basics and one former civilian paramedic. They were a great group of guys, but Doc knew they didn't have the experience needed to deal with the critical-care needs of the wounded. Before the new rotation arrived, it was optional to have a doctor on board with us because of our level of experience. Once active-duty came in, however, it was required that either Doc or the former paramedic ride on every flight. The level of training wasn't there to manage critical-care patients. The differences were stark.

Doc had visited Keating a dozen times. It was a small outpost in a hostile area and very isolated. He had gotten to know the guys up there. Early that morning, Doc received a nine-line call that Keating had been attacked effectively. There were multiple casualties.

He launched to Bostic with an EMT-Basic and positioned in preparation to transport casualties. They arrived about 0700 and sat on the flight line with helmets on. The wait was tense; they needed to get there now! The rotor blades spun for a while, and then they were told to power down. It wasn't safe for a Medevac mission. The enemy had effective positions in the area.

Come on!

The mechanics repaired Lewallen and Bardwell's aircraft by wedging the hydraulic lines together. They could fly it with a hole in the tail rotor. No big deal.

There were two weather holds. Thunderclouds were coming in over the top of the thirteen- to fourteen-thousand-foot mountains. They really wouldn't have a way to get out once in, so the commanders wouldn't let them launch. During that time, the air force dropped guided missiles into radioed grids.

Commanders were also organizing everyone from Bostic and moving them to Fritsche. Then they were given Overdrive from Bagram—two birds were brought up. Lewallen showed them the area to avoid on a map.

"This is where you're gonna get shot if you fly down the river. That's where the DShKs are," he warned.

They took off, and not ten minutes later, they returned. They had flown exactly where Ross had told them not to—right past the DShKs—and were shot. When the pilot landed at Bostic, he had nothing electrical left.

After the weather holds were lifted, Lewallen and Bardwell flew about nine more assaults throughout the day. They went Winchester three times. They shot everything they had.

Each trip in, they took a different route. They went out the back side over a twelve-thousand-foot mountain. At one point, a door gunner from a Black Hawk warned, "Hey, that guy is shooting RPGs at us!" The Black Hawk fired into this one little area on the mountain. Lewallen came in, and at first Bardwell couldn't see him. Then Lewallen banked around, and suddenly Bardwell was eye to eye with a hadji in a white shirt, pointing an RPG in his direction.

"Hey!" Bardwell yelled in surprise. Then, in response, he shot him with the IHADDS[49].

It turned out to be two Taliban in a tent a good six- to seven-thousand feet above Fritsche. It was clear they'd been setting up for this for a while. They knew the ways the aircraft got in and out, and they sat out there in the middle of nowhere shooting RPGs.

On the second trip in, Bardwell identified a DShK. He knew generally where it was because of where they'd taken rounds from. Then they learned there were three DShKs in there. The insurgents had no direct view of the FOBs from their location; their purpose was to shoot down helicopters.

During the battle, there were multiple requests from Medevac to go in and retrieve the casualties. They were told by the Battalion Commander that the decision would be made by Lewallen.

They flew down to take a look. The landing zone was down by the river, and it was completely engulfed in flames. We didn't control any of that land—it was overrun. The pilots were flying at eight to one hundred

---
49 Integrated helmet and display sight system

knots, not even slowing down for good shots, and yet they still were getting hit.

Lewallen made the call: no Medevac missions until dark.

Smoot was beside himself. He'd seen people die at the hands of untrained flight medics. He'd raised his voice, he'd trained, he'd politicked, he'd finagled and disobeyed and masterminded plans so that somehow, some way, he could ensure soldiers on the ground received the absolute best care available. Yet here he was.

Insult was added to injury when, just after they'd awarded him his Bronze Star, they'd sprung the news on us of Keating. It was a crushing blow.

There were twenty-nine casualties up in Keating that Smoot felt somehow responsible for. These were kids he'd seen from time to time as they rotated through Jalalabad. He had an emotional investment there for almost a year. He wanted to board an aircraft and go to them. Several had already died while he sat in Bagram.

Yet he couldn't do a fucking thing about it.

It was early evening before Medevac was cleared for launch.

Eleven excruciating hours of waiting.

Doc had received updates on the condition of the patients on the ground throughout the day. There were several heroes. There were multiple seriously injured patients who were receiving body-to-body blood transfusions from other soldiers still on the outpost. Doc got their vitals from a physician's assistant on the ground and detailed updates on their conditions.

By the time DUSTOFF launched, there was only one critically ill patient left alive. He had gunshot wounds to the abdomen and thigh. Under cover of darkness and with Apache escorts, Doc landed and picked up Scott[50]. The PA had done everything he could while they waited—gave him oxygen, put a tourniquet on his leg, and dressed the abdomen wound appropriately. Scott's blood pressure was profoundly low, his heart rate was elevated, and he was awake, speaking only a little.

DUSTOFF transported him to Bostic. The second the wheels touched ground, there were four people who scooped him up and ran full speed for the OR to do an exploratory laparotomy. He was critically ill.

Doc went with him. He stood for a moment at the head of the bed just before Scott was intubated. Scott asked questions about his buddies.

Doc changed the subject.

"Hey, Scott—you're going home, buddy. I'm heading out of this hellhole soon, too. Let's have a beer when we get back onto friendlier soil."

"OK," Scott whispered.

"What kind of beer do you like, Scott?"

"Coors Light."

"OK, Scott. It's agreed," Doc promised.

---

50 This is a pseudonym.

Scott went under anesthesia, and then they intubated him.

Doc headed out and got back into the aircraft. DUSTOFF launched for Keating to pick up more casualties.

When Doc returned an hour later, he learned that Scott had passed away during surgery.

The eighth hero from Keating.

SSG Spraktes and his children, William, Kaitlin and Joseph, along with his mother, Violet Johnson. Taken at award ceremony for DUSTOFF 24 in June, 2010.

SSG Angela Brennan, Medevac CE

CHP Flag Ceremony with Commissioner Joe Farrow, Deputy Commissioner Max Santiago, and Assistant Commissioner Kevin Green. This is the leadership that approved the CHP Military Deployment Program (MDP) to assist their military employees in reintegration after deployment.

Courtesy of Joe McHugh, Senior Photographer, CHP

REINTEGRATION

"No truly great man ever thought himself so."
William Hazlitt

"For war is not just a military campaign but also a parable. There were lessons of camaraderie and duty and inscrutable fate. There were lessons of honor and courage. Of compassion and sacrifice. And then there was the saddest lesson to be learned again and again. That war is corrupting. It corrodes the soul and tarnishes the spirit. That even the excellent and the superior can be defiled, and that no heart can remain unstained."
Rick Atkinson

Northern California
October 2009–Present

My boy, Joseph was crouched on his knees on the deck of the helicopter. He was hunched over his homework, like I'd seen so many times before. He had blocked out everything around him, even the strong wind that blew his blond hair to and fro.

He was unaware of the panic that wracked my insides.

William, my oldest son, was slightly forward, sitting on his knees very quietly, looking out the window. He knew exactly what was about to happen.

I was there in the aircraft too, holding on and amazed at how my sons deal with stress in the midst of catastrophe.

Brandon Erdmann was flying. The helicopter was spinning around and around, out of control, down toward the ground.

"Hey, Brandon!" I called out. "My sons are on board!"

I knew he was aware of this; we were all going to die. There was nothing he could do.

Helpless...

Spinning...

Death...

The ground grew closer... closer...

I jolted out of bed, still screaming. Soaked in sweat.

Terrified.

This was my new normal.

Coming home is awkward.

It was amazing to see my children again. I hugged them, put Joseph on my shoulders. It was so good to receive a warm welcome from friends and family, even my ex-wife. There were many friendly faces that were really glad to see me, and I them.

America is beautiful. My God—the grass was green, the sky was so blue, and the women were beautiful.

The grocery stores were stocked with more choices than needed.

America. Beauty. Safety. Love. Abundance.

I'd seen a lot in Afghanistan.

I'd had my hands inside dying soldiers.

I'd smelled fresh blood mixed with the aroma of fuel and burnt flesh and medicine.

I'd seen humanity at its worst. Hatred. Pain. Panic.

I'd brushed by death, sparking deep feelings of anguish and loss.

I wanted to take up where I'd left a year earlier. But everyone had changed.

I had changed.

My kids had grown, especially Joseph.

I'd gotten a Dear John e-mail in country, so I had no woman.

And then there was my job.

When I came back, maybe after a couple months, my coworker and close friend was all over me about my military career and deployment. In my mind, I was fresh off a helicopter with blood everywhere and people dying. Psychologically, I hadn't even thoroughly washed the blood from beneath my fingernails. Yet he was giving me shit about my service and how I wasn't going anywhere again. He went on to say how difficult it had been without me there. Pure hell.

I was ready to blow.

Oh, did you get a fuckin' paper cut or something? Did you not collate the packets correctly? Did you have to replace the ink cartridge, you son of a bitch?

I blew up at him in front of the CHP academy. I told him to go fuck himself. I wanted to hit him. I was angry, shaking mad.

He walked away, so it didn't come to blows. The next day he apologized. Then, over a long period of time, it eased up. Over time, we sort of went back to the place we were ten years prior, working the beat, catching bad guys, and depending on each other again.

Looking back, I think there were legitimate feelings of abandonment. But I was not in a place to accept them.

CHP Flag Ceremony

After I returned, Max Santiago talked about a flag ceremony. I thought, "OK. Whatever you need." I realized I had a responsibility to represent not myself, but every highway patrol employee that served, whether in combat or an ancillary position. I was honored to present this flag back to the CHP.

I was amazed at what Max set up. We rehearsed the ceremony a couple of times. The academy honor guard came out, and invitations were sent to the CNG, my company, people from headquarters, and the academy.

Commissioner Joe Farrow and Brigadier General Mary Kight spoke. I presented the flag back to the CHP. A lot of pictures were taken, and then we went outside and hoisted the ensign[52] in front of headquarters. I saluted the flag with my children next to me, and that was it.

This ceremony is something that I remember when there was so much pain that I don't want to get out of bed. I remember this honor, and I get up. I'm so very grateful.

A Silver Star

I was still in Jalalabad when I found out about the Silver Star. Smoot told me that they had put me in for a big award.

"Who's 'they'?" I asked.

"I don't know. Mountain Warrior, I guess."

Mountain Warrior was the land owner, responsible for a specific area of operation (AO). There was a chain of command within the AO, and Mountain Warrior was the task force that was in charge. The commander was the land owner, and he owned, for lack of a better term, the soldiers that we rescued on July 17. Mountain Warrior was so adamant about this award that they wanted to write up and submit the paperwork themselves.

It came down the pike that they had submitted DUSTOFF 24 for these big awards. I asked, "What are we talkin' about here? Air Medal with Valor?" But then somebody let it slip—they were talking about a Silver Star. I was stunned.

---

52 Navy term for flag

Really? After how I felt about my performance? About being a man? A soldier? A father?

I know people see themselves differently. I get that. I saw my foibles; they saw my forte. They saw strength; I saw weakness. I didn't know what to think.

I checked into it periodically. I'd be lying if I said I wasn't somewhat excited about the prospect, because I knew the medal brought credibility. It brings the spotlight, deserved or not. I could do a lot of good things with it. I could bring to light all of the amazing things our task force accomplished. Not just medics, but crew chiefs, Pathfinders, Apache pilots, Kiowa pilots, and Black Hawks—I would have a platform from which to speak on their behalf.

I was also keenly aware of the challenges of Medevac.

I was excited, but I was aware of the pressure such recognition would bring. I knew my own challenges because of the things I'd seen and experienced. Post-traumatic stress disorder. Relationship issues. Nightmares. Triggers. Reliving Afghanistan would be difficult, but I would share my story, because people want to know.

The medal process took awhile. It was something that somebody else felt strongly about, somebody else submitted, and somebody else reviewed. I had no input. It was impartial; I had no say. Those involved in this process were the people who wrote it along with several layers of review. My understanding is that the request went to a human resource command where high-ranking officials reviewed the write-up. They were to either accept it, upgrade it (which is rarely the case), or downgrade it (which happens). They looked at what took place and if it aligned with the standards for the award.

I learned I had been awarded the Silver Star in spring 2010. It first came with mixed emotions, and then I was swept away with the energy it generated. It felt like everyone wanted a piece of me. I had a lot of good people around me, but it was crazy.

I wanted to do the right thing. Those who supported me before the medal deserved support in return. I did everything that people asked me to do. I never turned down a presentation or a newspaper or magazine interview, not one. I felt they had given me a platform to speak, so I took the opportunity to communicate how magnificently these soldiers had performed and shared our struggles. They wanted to hear the sexy stories, like Watapur Valley on July 17. But I always brought in the uncomfortable stuff too.

Silver Star Ceremony
Northern California
June 2010

There were a lot of people at the ceremony. In the history of the California National Guard, they cannot find a soldier who has been awarded the Silver Star. I was quite disappointed by this, because I know that there are people who gave much during war, even their lives, but they weren't given this award.

The ceremony hosts made sure my family was in the right spot at the right time. We sat up front with the crew. General Kight was very gracious. She was a wonderful human being that understood the protocol but was also low-key.

Everybody did his or her part. They read the citation. They acknowledged the soldiers. They presented the medals. I thought it was a kindness that I could have my children and mother stand with me. The ceremony had an open invitation—others were allowed to attend, including the California Highway Patrol and the US Navy. I appreciated that as well.

I was slightly frustrated in that Governor Arnold Schwarzenegger didn't attend. He was the Commander in Chief of the California military, and I thought it was a missed opportunity to bring light to the Medevac issue. I didn't need to see him. I'd seen him while working many times. He treated everyone nicely—there was a lot of star power there—but it wasn't a big of a deal for me. It was a missed opportunity to focus on how his Guard performed. I thought it would've brought more attention to the issues.

I conducted a number of interviews with the press. There were a few things I wish I would've said differently, because I didn't want to come across as arrogant or that it was all about me. Being a standard-bearer is representative of what Medevac does. I'm just a regular guy within that community. What do these awards represent? That California should feel damn good about what we've got goin' on.

I asked if we were able to speak during the ceremony, and they said no. I was to say nothing. Damn. Opportunity missed to acknowledge my fellow service members. They, along with my supporters and family, really deserve the credit. The Silver Star is a representation of people working together on the mission, and in my mind, I am simply its guardian.

In addition to my family, many of my coworkers from the Highway Patrol attended. Charlie Company from the Guard and representatives from the US Navy in their white uniforms were present as well. My sister Barbara and her daughter Rebecca came up from Southern California. LTC Jimmy Blackmon and CSM Eric Thom flew out from Kentucky to attend. It was an incredible day.

I am not the only one who had honors bestowed upon me. Our unit and task force were exceptional and were recognized for excellence with awards, medals, and citations. We were given many awards, including several Rescues of the Year, aviation awards, medical awards, and unit citations. Many of our individuals earned Bronze Stars, Bronze Stars with V, Distinguished Flying Crosses, Air Medals with V, and Purple Hearts, and almost everyone came away with a Combat Medical Badge, including Doc.

Greeting the Governor

Down the road, the DUSTOFF 24 crew of 7-17 was to meet Governor Schwarzenegger at the capitol. This was a meet-and-greet for not just us, but for many others. I asked if I could bring my children and mother with me. I was granted permission.

All the way down to the capitol, my oldest son, William, and I were doing our Arnold impersonations. Joseph was cracking up in the back. It went on and on. "OK, we're going to stop talking like Arnold when we get to…"

But we couldn't stop.

We parked and walked to the governor's complex. My mom said nothing the whole time. She was giggling a bit at our jokes but mostly quiet. After we were ushered into the waiting area, Arnold arrived. While we took pictures with St. Aubin and Gifford (Erdmann was unable to make it), I put my arm around the governor's waist and quipped, "Distract him! I'll grab his wallet!"

My family took pictures with the governor, too. I wonder if he even knew why he was greeting the DUSTOFF crew from 7-17.

We shared some small talk. My mom approached Arnold, and, looking up at him, she beamed, "I never thought in my life that I would be here and that I would meet you."

Without hesitation he replied, "Well, I never thought in my life that I would be here and meet you, either." They had a wonderful human moment, and they giggled together like little girls. It was hilarious!

I gave him a National Guard coin. He called over to his assistant and chided, "What is wrong with you? Bring over one of the coins right now!" They scurried into action, laughing. He presented each of us with a Governor Challenge coin.

It was a cool memory.

A War in the Soul

During this time I was drinking too much, in a series of horrible relationships, and not sleeping. However, I did protect my kids. I didn't let anything come between me and my children. Nothing touched that, not even my own human frailties. I had to do that right.

Random people were thanking me for my service. I didn't want to be thanked. I had feelings of guilt and pain, and no one really had a clue what they were actually thanking me for. I wasn't about to tell them.

Many members of Task Force PaleHorse have had their issues since we've come home.

Al Smoot told me once that when he talks about what he's been through, his emotions are tied to the stresses of the years. Events of 2009 bring up the 2003 deployment. The memories of 2003 bring up 1998. Memories from 1998 bring up 1990, when he was at Fort Bliss and had to split some people off to deploy to Central America. He was supposed to go, but a woman he knew went instead. That crew flew into the side of a mountain when they decided to push everything to fetch an appendicitis patient. It killed three and critically injured an active-duty crew chief.

"I was supposed to be on that aircraft. I was supposed to be there. I was supposed to be in her spot," he says. Smoot looks at it now as if he got an extra twenty-two years. That bothers a man who saves lives for a living.

Awhile later I talked with Elizabeth Kimbrough, who after her second deployment, left military service. "When I watched men die on my screen that I had shot, I thought I would cry because I'd taken three lives. I thought I would lose sleep. But I didn't. And then I felt guilty that I didn't feel guilty. I didn't feel anything."

Some of the men have said that when they hunt, the smell of an open deer takes them back to Afghanistan. I understand that.

Doc Kavanagh had trouble with reintegration. In some ways, it is still hard for him. Sights and smells are still with him. But his life in residency for orthopedic surgery has him in survival mode. He keeps busy.

Many of us drink too much.

I also learned that forty-two people from our task force divorced after deployment.

Adapting

Post-traumatic stress is cyclical. I've talked with a police psychologist, and I've gone through the counseling. I've been saturated with war and its carnage. There's so much residue. From time to time, it just shakes out, and I have to deal with it.

My friend, Rich Nicholoff, a retired CHP officer and former SWAT teammate, shared some poignant thoughts with me in a low moment. He was also a Marine Corps sniper and Vietnam veteran who suffered silently for forty years before he was able to speak of what he witnessed.

I was driving alone one night, struggling with feelings and memories, and Rich just happened to call. I explained what I was dealing with and asked him if it ever went away.

"No," he replied, "it won't. It's not supposed to. It'll always be there."

Believe it or not, this was a huge relief. It gave me comfort in a strange way. I didn't feel sorry for myself anymore. I finally realized post-traumatic stress from the war wasn't going away, and I made peace with it.

Anxiety-filled memories and nightmares come back once in a while. I say, "Oh, there you are, I've wondered where you've been. I haven't seen you in a while, old friend."

The other key piece for me was talking with my friend and police psychologist, Dr. Todd Langus, who is a former cop and has been through many traumatic events. One night he said to me, "Emmett, we're rescuers. That's how we're wired. We want to be able to fix things. We're fixers. We rescue; we fix; we want to make things better. But sometimes you can't, because it's a shitty situation. And it's OK to feel shitty about a shitty situation. That's normal."

I feel shitty. But I can live through it, knowing that it's normal.

We blame ourselves for things we had no part of, didn't cause, and had no control over, because we're rescuers. We blame ourselves for woulda, coulda, shoulda. It's normal to feel shitty about a shitty situation.

I think many of us felt like we had abandoned the soldiers. The pain of Keating just intensified it. We knew we had done some good things while in theater, but we wanted to do more. We still had our battle with the army, and in some ways, that drove us onward.

And then, a dose of medicine. We got the results from Bagram.

Blood-soaked boots, helmet and uniform on the floor of Jalalabad FST. There were countless heroic efforts by FST personnel during difficult conditions to bring our soldiers home.
Courtesy of Sebastian Rich, Photojournalist

RESULTS FROM BAGRAM

"When you can't make them see the light, make them feel the heat."
Ronald Reagan

"Doc, anyone who will listen is welcome to the data/info. I'm more than happy to talk with anyone who will listen."
CW2 Jason Penrod

**United States
2010-2012**

Jason Penrod was a civilian paramedic, a National Guard flight medic, a doctor of pharmacology, and a Medevac pilot. He had a well-rounded platform from which to observe what worked and didn't work for Medevac. Penrod is also a genuine human being; he cares about people. He's a lot like Al Smoot in the depth of his compassion and deep emotion, but he displays it differently.

Soon after we returned from Afghanistan, Jason's partnership with Major Mabry began to move forward. The letter that Jason had sent to Colonel Dorlac was forwarded to a number of people, which began communication. The Schoolhouse read Jason's letter and took it as an indictment on their performance. It didn't go over well. But Major Mabry took special notice and started a serious conversation with those who were involved.

He sent an inquiry to Doc Kavanagh, who, at the time, was yet to depart Afghanistan. Doc's experience since we left had only intensified his fervor for change. The difference between our team and the team who had replaced us was vast. "I see the fear on the faces of my medics when they are handed off multiple sick patients from the FSTs in the area, when they realized how far in over their heads they are," he wrote. "I think that both our medics being charged with this mission and the patients for whom they are responsible, deserve better."

There was significant push back in the months that followed. The idea that there was a problem significant enough to cause the deaths of soldiers on the field was a bitter pill to swallow for those overseeing Medevac training. Acknowledging that their efforts weren't good enough was unthinkable, and they chose to deny the problem existed, deflect blame, and demonize the messengers. The battle lines were drawn.

Tactical Combat Casualty Care Conference
February 2010

Mabry invited Penrod and me to speak before the Department of Defense committee on Tactical Combat Casualty Care in Texas. We were to present our experiences in Afghanistan and the impact our paramedics had in theater as case presentations. For the first half of the presentation, I was asked to do a vignette, which was a problem because I didn't know what the hell that was.[54] I learned it was a PowerPoint presentation about an event in a specific format provided by the committee. They asked me to speak about the 7/17 rescue in the Watapur Valley. The second half I was to assist Penrod, who would address our findings and recommendations.

---

54 I thought a vignette was something to put on a salad.

There were hundreds of people in the audience from all services. We began discussing training deficits, and I made the statement that no one was actually at a paramedic level. "They go through a Whiskey One course[56] but not even the PJs who were pushed into the Medevac mission were actually operating at a paramedic level," I declared.

At that point, a man stood up and introduced himself as the USSOCOM[58] Command Surgeon. "The PJs are trained to a paramedic level. They are paramedics," he asserted.

"Sir," I answered, "I understand that your PJs are initially trained to be paramedics, but they want to be operators, not Medevac. They want to be Delta Force. They do two weeks per year on medical training to get the requirements done, but they don't regularly use the skills. They don't practice so that they know how to do what they need to, and yet they are expected to take on a Medevac mission and do it successfully. People die that way."

"I get it; our PJs are terrible medics," he said and then he just let it hang there.

I didn't know how to respond. He wasn't being sarcastic. I was at a loss.

Next, a Whiskey One representative for 160th SOAR[60] raised his hand and said he felt that they needed to have nurses on board.

Penrod responded, "It seems like a good idea, but it just isn't gonna happen. Being a flight member takes a significant amount of time to learn. It takes hours and hours just to learn how to operate on a helicopter crew. Now, nurses have their own job. To take them away

---

56   This is the course all combat medics must undergo. It is equivalent to an EMT-Basic in the civilian sector.
58   United States Special Operations Command
60   Special Operations Air Regiment

from that is almost impossible, because there is a significant shortage of nurses. We need them to fill the spots in the emergency rooms—we don't even have enough nurses to fill these spots, let alone take them out and put them on a helicopter. The only answer is to have a flight paramedic on board. We need a systemic fix; not a Band-Aid approach."

Many of those in attendance were receptive. Initially, the committee chairman seemed receptive to what we were saying, but then he turned confrontational. He seemed to be on an island all by himself. He went so far as to say that he'd take a combat medic over a paramedic any day of the week. But when you've worked field medicine long enough like we had, you know this is bullshit. It became a political show. The support was certainly on our side. Unfortunately, we were a little hamstrung because we didn't have our numbers yet. The study wasn't complete, so we were limited in our claims.

The committee chair had a different idea of what a paramedic was and dismissed our presentation. He stated that technology would ultimately improve patient outcomes, not paramedics. Colonel Dorlac emphatically disagreed, along with others. He characterized the current training and employment of army flight medics as grossly unethical and equivalent to criminal malpractice in the civilian setting. People went back and forth.

That presentation stirred the pot. We were making some serious claims that had significant ramifications. Some supported what we said; others did not.

Dorlac stepped in again right before we concluded. "The way we are implementing Medevac today is completely negligent and substandard," he said. "If this was occurring in the civilian world, it would be deemed to be medical malpractice, and people would be prosecuted and thrown into prison for it, and they would be sued civilly."

He emphasized that if we continued down this road, we were all complicit.

We never finished our presentation. The committee chair did not allow us to continue, choosing instead to break early for lunch.

Following this outcome, Mabry and Penrod decided to push forward with the study and wrote up the paper.

They submitted the manuscript to two prominent journals. During this time, Congress became aware of the study, and staffers began calling the Pentagon looking for answers regarding the study's findings. The journals both declined publication. Penrod believes this because at least two of the reviewers found it hard to believe that the Department of Defense (DoD) would allow such a damning study to be made public.

I tend to think they were right. A little bit of mold in an ancillary building in Walter Reed caused a national uproar and heads rolled. Nobody died. It was mold. They could bleach it, paint over it, and call it good. Who gives a shit? But this—this was the mortality rate of our soldiers! We're talking about sons, daughters, fathers, mothers—people who matter to our nation, our communities, and our families. The seriousness of this was staggering.

In the meantime, there were others that were talking as well. Smoot had grown more savvy over the years as he spread his Medevac message. Walters and Ferguson took opportunities to communicate their views to those who would listen. Ben Higgins wrote a paper and submitted it to the American Association of Critical-Care Nurses[ii]. Even some of the active-duty flight medics had joined in the the fight—one getting into trouble for some articles he'd written. He was removed from a nice position in the Schoolhouse and sent back to Afghanistan.

The Schoolhouse

Soon thereafter, Doc and I went back to Fort Rucker when he was awarded the 2009 AAAA Flight Surgeon Award, and I was recognized as 2009 Flight Medic of the Year. We went to the Schoolhouse of Flight Medicine and met with the medical director, who was an aerospace physician. He had many of his enlisted personnel sitting at the table with us.

Our purpose for the meeting was to use Penrod's letter to discuss the necessity for in-country flight surgeons to be emergency room docs and surgeons, because of their experience with trauma. We shared what our training was, what we saw in Afghanistan, our strengths and weaknesses, and how we thought the training could be improved.

You'd think that we had killed Christ.

We got significant push back. They told us they didn't need ER docs or paramedics. They were insistent they could fix this problem with minimal adjustments. Doc sat there with me shoulder to shoulder as he argued, "NO! That's not right! The medical directors overseeing Medevac training and standards should be emergency physicians or trauma surgeons, not physician's assistants or physicians without formal residency training in trauma care!"

The Lieutenant Colonel answered, "No, no, no. It doesn't have to be that." He minimized our concerns. He treated us like we didn't know what we were talking about. He blew us off.

The Schoolhouse idea was to create an EMT-M and call it the Super Medic. The Super Medic was to be the flight medic. This level would provide some enhanced training, but it was still a minimal commitment.

I'd worked with medics in Iraq that didn't even know how to start an IV. We're gonna have people work on a soldier with his legs blown off who've never even started an IV?

I spoke up, but Doc was on fire. He knew what they were saying was total bullshit and told them so. I'd had my turn in Afghanistan when I stood face to face with the army's Surgeon General. This time, it was Doc's turn. He was very vocal in that meeting—borderline insubordinate.

They also criticized Penrod and his paper. They claimed he didn't know what he was talking about. Doc and I were in support of his paper and its remedies; therefore we were dismissed.

I was angry the enlisted guys were in lock step with the officers. They didn't know what they didn't know; I can forgive their ignorance. But there were people around that table who knew the problems, knew that people were dying, and yet were indifferent. They wouldn't even sit and talk about some possible solutions. That I can't forgive.

When Doc and I walked away from that meeting, we didn't have the support of the Schoolhouse. It was like trying to shove a wet noodle up a bobcat's ass! But we moved forward anyway.

Proof

Major Bob Mabry called Jason Penrod in late summer 2010 with the initial results of the data analysis. It showed a 66 percent reduction in mortality when our Medevac paramedics were compared to all other Medevac providers. When compared against strictly army flight medics, the mortality difference jumped dramatically. A patient aboard a helicopter who was cared for by a standard army flight medic was at least three and a half times more likely to die than if he or she was cared for by one of our paramedics.

In Jalalabad, the rotation before ours lost sixteen out of a hundred patients. During our rotation, that number was reduced to eight per hundred. After we left, the number returned to sixteen. The difference was eight patients for every hundred—eight families that didn't lose their loved ones because there were paramedics in the back of the helicopter. To give you an idea of the math, I alone had 184 documented patients during my deployment.

We knew there would be a difference in the numbers. We saw it with our own eyes. But we had no idea it was this significant. We had the proof we needed.

These results brought a whole new dimension to our cause. It wasn't just our opinion anymore. We had the numbers to back it up. We were now armed for the battle ahead. The next step was to get this information to those who made the decisions.

2010 AMEC (Army Medical Evacuation Conference)

Smoot and Walters attended the 2010 AMEC. This time they had the study data together. It hadn't been published yet, but it was only a matter of time. They went to the Schoolhouse people, who had heard of the study findings. They stayed up night after night, facilitating communication between different factions on what was right for the patients. Some ideas were accepted in the Fort Rucker community and within the community of 67Js[62].

One afternoon, Smoot cornered the Chief of Staff to the Surgeon General and one of his aides. He told them that they did the study and

---
62 Pilots that are medical service corps

it was out there. "In three days I am going back to being a civilian," he warned. "I can take this to senators. After twenty years, I am sick of watching the neglect. This is not so much a threat as much as a promise."

Published

The study was published by the Journal of Trauma and Acute Care Surgery on August 8, 2012, and for presentation at the Military Health System Research Symposium in the same year. It was finally out there, but other than in the army, it received little attention. The delay helped in some ways because the army was able to get most of the solution in place before it was released. The Surgeon General of the Army intervened and directed the army Medical department to develop a program that provided flight medics with the same training our paramedics had taken into combat.

Army Critical Care Flight Paramedic Program

Once the Surgeon General gave the go-ahead, the army started the Critical Care Flight Paramedic program at Fort Sam Houston in Texas, much to the frustration of Fort Rucker's flight medic course.

The class has moved forward. The army graduated its first class in October 2012. The first national registry paramedic test had a 90 percent pass rate. The national levels are high seventies to low eighties for initial pass rate. So, we're obviously doing something right—we're picking the right people to do the job. The first class with this passing rate out the door is remarkable.

After that, the class moved on to the critical-care piece, which is more involved. It's an eight-week course that includes classroom training, hands-on training, and clinical training. This is the training that really matters, the training that will give these guys success.

This new program gives the army flight medic thirty-nine weeks of training to reach a nationally recognized data-driven standard. It also provides that these medics will have hands-on experience in American emergency rooms before they are deployed. This new standard was directed by the House of Representatives (FY13 NDAA, H. Rept. 112-479).

A Political Chess Game

Smoot had been talking about this since the late eighties, and Walters and others joined him a few years later. Penrod had come to the same conclusions in Nevada many years ago and voiced his concerns to deaf ears. After our 2009 deployment, Doc and I joined the choir.

When the study came forth with its results in 2010, our noise became truth. Then the political chess game began. As the results became known, it was clear that something had to be done before another Walter Reed incident arose.

We are not sure of the exact track this information took to finally make a difference. Penrod surmises it was the process by which the study ultimately became public. It was no secret this study was politically damning to those overseeing Medevac. The results of the study plus the initial phone calls from congressional staffers generated by several medical journal submissions, certainly raised the awareness level of those who made the ultimate decision.

"Until the study was on the verge of getting released, we were nothing more than a group of annoying Guard guys that didn't even show up on the proverbial food chain," Penrod says. "We were summarily dismissed and expected to dissipate with time. Instead, we blindsided them with explosive data...those who knew we were right and were afraid to risk their military careers to fight alongside us, finally had the concrete data they needed for protection."

Once they had our study in hand, the army finally had the proof they needed to make swift and corrective action. They committed tens of millions of dollars to put into motion a move that changed forty years of relative stagnation within the flight medic medical training. The new standard for army Medevac flight medics will be to train them as critical care transport paramedics. Hopefully they will develop a realistic policy to sustain that training as well.

Sustainment training is crucial. Paramedic skills have to be practiced on a regular basis, or they are ineffective. The PJs are trained to a paramedic level, but then they don't practice those skills, and they are lost. We can't afford to let the same thing happen to army Medevac—or the millions of dollars spent will be wasted. Medevac is not a part-time occupation; it must be continuous.

The mark is that by 2017, all Army flight medics will be paramedics. The total number between regular Army, Army Reserve, and National Guard will be 934 flight medics. This is life saving news for those on the battlefield.

The army has addressed the medical deficit. Now they need to address the continuous sustainment training.

HOW DID THIS HAPPEN?

"Limited medical treatment can be continued in flight if the casualty is evacuated in cargo-type helicopters. These helicopters may carry a medical attendant in addition to the pilot, who is also a qualified medical assistant. It must be realized that, although helicopter ambulance pilots are qualified medical assistants, their medical function in flight is limited to judgment because they are too occupied flying the aircraft to devote any direct attention to casualties."
LTC Spurgeon H. Neel, Jr., USAFMJ, Volume 5, No. 2, February 1954

"Senior folks spent decades doing it that way. It is hard to consider what they've mastered to be obsolete. There is also circular thinking associated. This must be the best way because this is how we do it. If there were a better way, that's how we'd do it."
MAJ Robert Mabry

After the battle, it is a wise move to debrief. What actually happened? What are the recollections of each participant? What circumstances and decisions do we want to repeat and not repeat?

After how we were treated, the guys and I were angry. We saw, felt, smelled, and touched the consequences of a relatively unchanged Medevac doctrine and system created during the Korean War[iv]. From our civilian-trained paramedic view, it wasn't good enough and needed to be changed for the sake of the patients. We couldn't understand why the army wouldn't listen. From our perspective, we assumed they didn't care about the men. We assumed they were only interested in protecting their careers. We made our judgments from our perspective, and they did the same.

Now that there is consensus on both sides on the level of training needed for flight medics, it's important to take a look at how this happened. How is it that the most powerful, technologically advanced military in the world was forty years behind the civilian standard of care?

There are several reasons, all intertwined in complex philosophies and perspectives.

Leadership

First of all, no one was overseeing battlefield medical care. There is a general in charge of dental care and a general in charge of vet care, but no physician or senior medical official in charge of battlefield medical care. Since everybody owned Medevac, nobody owned Medevac.

Those who are in charge of overseeing Medevac are medical-service corps officers (lieutenants and above). They are also pilots. In combat, the focus is on transport, as it has been from its beginning. The pilots, who are essentially in charge of the missions to evacuate the injured, are focused on transporting the wounded from the battlefield to the FSTs. Speed and safety are the prime goals[vi].

In country, most Medevac medical directors are flight surgeons working in the aviation clinic, not EMS trauma docs who can do what the medics do. Hence, their primary responsibilities were to oversee the medical needs of the flight medics.

This could've been the case with Doc Kavanagh. He was a flight surgeon with medical experience, yet he had a physician's assistant who wanted to work the clinic. This freed him up to fly with us, learning how to effectively work with trauma in the back of the aircraft. He knew he needed more experience to be effective, and he worked hard to gain that experience. This is why he was so adamant about the medical directors having EMS experience. There was so much more to do than rectal exams.

The Nature of Bureaucracy

The US Army is a bureaucracy, and therefore functions to complete complex tasks in efficient, standardized ways. We march the same and wear the same uniform, generation after generation, with not much deviation. We keep doing what we've been doing because it's proven to be the best way in the past.

Within a bureaucracy, change is difficult. Change disrupts the established order. When there was talk about taking flight medic training from aerospace medicine doctors and moving it somewhere else, this threatened to change roles within the organization. Making a statement that a medical director is not competent to run Medevac because he or she isn't an EMS trauma doctor is threatening. In fact, change in any organization will cause some to argue against the change because they are threatened in one way or another.

Because pilots are in charge, all things are aviation-focused rather than patient-focused. Think back to Ferguson's tail to tail experience early in the deployment. The pilot chided him for taking too long, while, unbeknownst to him, Ferguson and Cornell were saving a life. The pilot was working from an aviation-centric paradigm, while Ferguson and Cornell were patient-centric in their paradigm.

Battlefield Philosophies

Vietnam was the last war we fought, and Medevac was a solid asset. Then, over the years, EMS, prehospital care, critical care, and trauma surgery evolved within the civilian world. With no significant foreign conflict to drive innovation, the standards for Medevac and its battlefield medical care stayed the same. Now, with over a decade of war in Afghanistan and Iraq, we have realized we can do better.

The focus of Medevac by leaders was to move casualties off the battlefield as soon as possible so that the war could be fought. The focus was on the battle. Without a watchful eye overseeing the transport piece, it was viewed as transport from point A to point B, nothing more. This is referred to as the Fulda Gap philosophy—a battle-centric focus from the Cold War that Medevac was simply to clear the battlefield. There was no real thought to en route treatment at all. This is demonstrated by a piece of equipment on the helicopter called a carrousel, which held about four patients. The medic wasn't able to even reach them because it took up so much room.

Those of us who were civilian-trained didn't have this philosophy. We were trained to think of the patient first and base our actions around his needs. Our perspective was patient-centric. Our study showed that both philosophies can successfully coexist. If you do en route patient-centric care while clearing the battlefield, survivability dramatically increases.

Medevac was viewed as transport only with a single medic with no advanced capabilities designed to get the patient to the doctor. But when transport trips are sometimes twenty to sixty minutes long, treatment in the back of the helicopter can be the difference between life and death for a critically ill patient. Then, after surgery, they are post-operative ICU patients, and the same flight medics are expected to ride along and somehow keep them stabilized without knowledge and training on the equipment that is essentially keeping them alive. This part wasn't thought through, because it wasn't directly connected to the war effort.

The original philosophy of Medevac focused on speed, NOT en route treatment.

Lastly, because en route treatment wasn't the focus, documentation for the medical record wasn't required for patients until they arrived at the FST. There was no way to measure what was done in the field or on the helicopter. With no one tracking this, there was no quality improvement. You can't improve what you cannot measure. Therefore, there's no problem. This is why it was key that Ferguson's patient care reports were constructed. We had to show there was a problem.

When we initially brought our concerns to the Schoolhouse, this was the response. We had no evidence there was a problem, only our opinions. But after the study was conducted, we had the proof that there was indeed a significant problem, and we had effectively demonstrated the solution. Once the fact that a problem existed was established, decision makers were compelled to listen.

It was the emergence of the evidence that finally turned our battle for lives toward its solution. There were many people within the army and in our government leadership who cared about the mortality rate of our wounded. Through systematic re-education, introduction of new standards, and ways of implementing the new training without upsetting everything they had in place (only some things), we are now on the way to improving battlefield care for now and in the future.

Major General David S. Baldwin and CHP Commissioner Joe Farrow signing the Statement of Support for the Guard and Reserve in Sacramento, California, May 23, 2013. The California Highway Patrol pioneered a military deployment program (MDP) to properly transition their employees from service overseas. The CHP is a leader in the nation for their support of military employees.

Courtesy of Joe McHugh, Senior Photographer, CHP

THE SIREN'S CALL

"You lured my ship where I swore never to return and all so easily done. Again you make me weep as the tempest turns my ship and soul asunder; Lashing against the waves of emotion that surge against my dreams and my soul."
Nicky McNeil, Siren's Call

"At least I left shit better than I found it."
1SG Alva Smoot

War is seductive. It's a siren's call to the rocks. Some of the rocks we see; some are below the surface. We crash; we are devoured. The physical or psychological destruction comes, sometimes years later.

One is never needed so much as in war. No one is needed more than right then, right there. Many times on the deck of the helicopter, patients looked up at us, wanting, needing, trusting. In some ways they were like newborn babies—completely unable to care for themselves. They needed us to survive. Sometimes it was like that. Patients were dying and didn't want to die. They trusted us to intercede—to do what we could to help them get home to their families.

It's not a feeling of power; it's a feeling of worth. It's an ability to give and to be blessed to be able to give everything and make a difference for these soldiers. I am just part of a painful memory.

Prehospital medicine is never as rewarding or challenging as in war: flying in a helicopter, under goggles, at night, under fire, giving paralytics, performing procedures you can't do often or at all in the United States, and making quick decisions with hopefully good outcomes. Hoisting into hostile territory and shooting back—it's seductive. It's the Super Bowl of flight medicine.

Even though things get confusing, there's a clarity about the chaos. There is a long-lasting camaraderie with those I work with. Sure, we have our personality conflicts, but we also get past that—we have to so that we can work together. We allow that commonality to take precedent.

When I was in Iraq, I knew Afghanistan was the place to go. I needed my experience. As painful as it's been, I'm very grateful for it.

I'm also grateful for coming home. I'm grateful for the green grass. I'm grateful for women. I'm grateful for the nineteen kinds of cream corn in the grocery store. I am goddamned grateful. Many died for this.

I don't want to be an angry vet. I have my moments. Yet I was allowed to make a difference in some lives and participate with some amazing people, and I was able to do it in my late forties when many are looking at retirement.

Even now I still hope to make a difference. I hear the siren's call again.

A New Mission

My father died saving my life. I've spent most of my life paying it forward, first as a police officer, then as a paramedic. I'm now retired from the California Highway Patrol and have just a short time left with the Guard. I have one more selfish prayer—to tell the world.

When I set out to write this book, our deployment had given us the proof we needed to be taken seriously. The study was creating a stir but hadn't been published yet. There was a paramedic class in place, but there wasn't a sustainment policy, and only two classes were scheduled.

Call me a cop—but I didn't trust the army to keep this going without a sustainment policy. In the days of military budget cuts, my fear was that the next Surgeon General would cut the program—and everything we'd worked for would be lost.

At that point, I decided to invest in the saving of more lives. I wouldn't wrap my hands around the heart of an Afghan police officer, or hoist down in the middle of a firefight to rescue a soldier the age of my son. But I would do what I could to ensure all future flight medics would have the training they need to do it in my place.

The journey that unfolded since has been amazing. As Victoria and I interviewed those who were deployed with me, I learned a lot about who they were and what they'd been through. We'd experienced many of the same emotions and thoughts, but I would've never known had we not talked with them.

Facing Demons

During the research process, I traveled to Florida to finally meet the man who crashed into my family that fateful night of March 8, 1962. He hesitantly agreed to meet with me on the condition that I not use his real name in the book. I agreed to this stipulation. So Harry Blevins was born; a pseudonym, but a real man.

When I first found him, I thought of a promise I made to myself thirty-five-plus years ago: "Kill him; no one will know. There's no connection." Then I told my mother I had located him and that I was going to interview him. She replied, "You should, honey. I'm sure he's had a lot of pain these many years." Her tender, forgiving heart crushed my angry, hardened heart in an instant.

The man and his family had, in fact, suffered tremendous hardship over the years. Due to stress over the incident, they put their first child up for adoption, and then another pregnancy miscarried. There was a series of misfortunes afterward.

The meeting was surreal. He was a bent, shriveled man. His wife of all those years was in ill health and a wheelchair. Life had done more to him and, unfortunately, her than I could ever do. We did not part friends. I could not bring myself to say "I forgive you," but we had an understanding. I felt compassion for their pain, and that is that. I was able to move on.

In the process of hassling Smoot, Kavanagh, Penrod, and others that we interviewed for the stories, I realized we all have events that keep us awake at night. One such event was the Ganjgal ambush. There were many different facts and opinions that came with Ganjgal, and at one point I wasn't sure I wanted to include it. But in the process of searching for the truth, we came across camera footage that gave us unequivocal evidence we needed to publish our account. That footage led to a reunion of sorts here in Sacramento with Captain Will Swenson. In many ways, that weekend brought about healing for those who were present. I can't ask for more than that.

Lastly, I've had to deal with my anger toward those who we battled for the Medevac training change. The process of seeking support from others has forced me to look at the factors and perspectives in play, and I am beginning to understand why they did what they did. This understanding has cooled my fire for the time being, provided the army continues to look at what is needed for giving our soldiers the best battlefield care they deserve.

Retired?

As a CHP retiree, I am still involved in many ways. I donate my time to help train new officers in emergency medical response at the Academy. I also have been a voice for our employees who've been deployed to Iraq or Afghanistan. I hold up the CHP as a wonderful model of how to help service members returning from deployment reintegrate back into their jobs, and share this model with other departments.

In May 2013, the CHP put together a tribute to those who are both military and CHP employees at Headquarters. There is a mural, photographs, memorabilia, including my Silver Star. At the unveiling ceremony, California National Guard Major General Daniel Baldwin and CHP Commissioner Joe Farrow signed an agreement to work together to reintegrate men and women in the Armed Forces when they return from war. It was an honor to be in attendance.

My brothers and I set out to fight two battles as lifesavers; one on the battlefields of Afghanistan, one within the army itself. In many ways, there are pieces of this journey that have come full circle. There are also pieces that are yet unfinished. There are still other pieces that have crashed upon the rocks in response to the siren's seductive call.

That is the very nature of war.

ENDNOTES

i   AACN Advanced Critical Care, Volume 21, Number 3, pp. 288-297, copyright 2010, AACN

ii   "After a significant test conducted by Army and Air Force representatives on 3 August 1950 in the school yard of the Taegu Teachers College, Army helicopters were adopted for the evacuation of casualties and the first procedures were established. In January 1951 the first Army helicopter detachment with a primary mission of medical evaluation became operational, followed in rapid succession by two others." Page and Neel, Army Aeromedical Evacuation, US Armed Forces Medical Journal, Volume VIII, No. 8, August 1957.

iii   "The current concept for accomplishing the Army aeromedical evacuation mission... Specifically, the proposed concepts 1) place the welfare of patients *secondary* to other logistical considerations and missions, which is contrary to the national philosophy and detrimental to individual and unit morale;" Page and Neel, Army Aeromedical Evacuation, US Armed Forces Medical Journal, Volume VIII, No. 8, August 1957. Italics mine.

This was the original concept of getting wounded off the battlefield, and was addressed by implementing helicopters that were solely for medical evacuation.

GLOSSARY

A
ABP – Afghan Border Police
Active Duty Flight Medic – Medevac flight medic trained to an EMT-Basic level (MOS: 68W(F))
AIT – Advanced Individual Training
AK-47 – A selective-fire, gas-operated assault rifle
Ambulatory patient – Ill or injured patient able to walk on their own
ANA – Afghan National Army
ANP – Afghan National Police
Apaches – AH-64 Longbow Army Gunships
Asadabad – Town in Afghanistan where we had a FOB

B
BAF – Bagram Air Field
Barge Matal – Tiny little town in Northeast Afghanistan located along ancient trade routes
Bingo – Nearly out of fuel
Black Hawk – UH 60 aircraft, used as Medevac platform or gunship
Boot Drive – Fire Department fund raiser – Firefighters walk about intersections with a boot, people put in cash from their cars.
Blue Max – Apache company attached to the 7-17 for the 9-11 rotation

C
Capnography – Measurement of exhaled carbon dioxide from a human body
Cardiac Massage – Direct compressions to the heart by hand
Casualty – Injured Patient
CDC – California Department of Corrections

Chemically Paralyzed – Immobilizing a patient using paralytics
Chemically Sedated – Altering the level of consciousness using Versed or other like sedatives
Chest tube – Flexible tube introduced into the chest cavity through the chest wall to relieve a tension pneumothorax
Chinooks – CH-47s; Large transport helicopters
CHP – California Highway Patrol
Click – One thousand meters
CNG – California National Guard
Cold offload – Medevac helicopter completely shuts down
Cold onload – Patient put on the helicopter prior to starting it up
Combat Hoist – Lowering the medic to the ground while the helicopter is moving forward
Compliance – Complete inhalation during intubated bagging
Crew chief – The medic's wooch; flying mechanic
Crike, cricothyrotomy – Making an incision in the throat to place an airway tube
CSP – California State Police

D
Dart Bilaterally – Both right and left chest had been decompressed with large angiocaths.
Deranged – Irregular
Diazepine – Anxielytic/sedative
Distinguished Flying Cross – A medal awarded to member of armed forces who exhibits support of operations or extraordinary achievement while participating in an aerial flight.
Distinguished Flying Cross with V – See above; a V Device would indicate the award was for heroism.
Dopamine drip – A dopamine drip is generally used in emergency situations when blood circulation is compromised, causing an individual to go into shock.
DShK – Soviet heavy anti-aircraft machine gun

DUSTOFF – Medevac helicopters – Dedicated, Unhesitating Support to our Fighting Forces

E
EMT-Basic – Emergency Medical Technician – 120 hours of required training
EMT-Intermediate – Emergency Medical Technician – 500 hours of required training
EMT – Paramedic – Emergency Medical Technician – 1200-1800 hours of required training
End Tidal CO2 – Carbon Dioxide levels in exhaled breath
Epinephrine intravenous boluses – Constricts blood vessels, increases blood pressure
ERF'd out – Environmental Risk Factors – Once an air crew has worked so many hours in a row, they must get a minimal period of rest.
Etomidate – Psychotrobic sedative used to calm a patient prior to intubation
Eviscerate – Contents of abdominal cavity spilled out due to laceration or penetration of the abdomen
Extubated – To remove the endotracheal tube from trachea

F
FARP – Forward Area Refueling Point; where helicopters get gas in theater
FDIC – Fire Department Instructors Conference
FDNY – Fire Department of New York
FEMA – Federal Emergency Management Agency
Fentanyl – Opiate that typically does not have respiratory and blood pressure derangements
Flagpole – Headquarters command location (slang term)
Flight medic – Army EMT-Basic with additional air crew training
FOB – Forward Operating Base
FST – Forward Surgical Team: surgeons, nurses, medics

G
Ganjgal – Small village located southeast of Asadabad

H
Hellfire – Laser guided missile primarily used against buildings
Helmet Cam – Camera attached to a helmet that digitally records events
Hero – US service member who gave his/her life during battle
Hoist – Machine that lowers and lifts a cable to extract medics and patients
Hot LZ or HLZ – Landing zone under enemy fire
Hypertonic Saline – Saline with a greater density to draw fluid to it
Hypothermic – Abnormally low body temperature
Hypovolemic – A low volume of blood within the circulatory system
Hypoxic – Deficiency in the amount of oxygen reaching body tissues

I
IO – Intraosseus – Introducing a rigid catheter through bone via drill to introduce blood, fluids and medications into patients without a good IV site
ICS – Incident Command System
IED – Improvised Explosive Device
Innervation – How the nerves run through the body
Innocent – Person who is not involved in any way
Insurgents – Rising in revolt against established authority, especially a government.
In Theater – Area of operation
Intravenous catheters – Small pliable tube introduced via needle into the veins of a patient for meds, blood, etc.
Intravenous pump – Machine that regulates the amount of fluid/medication going into the venous system of a patient
Intubate – Insert a hollow tube into the trachea to create a patent airway
ISAF – International Security Assistance Force

Israeli Bandage – Pre-made pressure bandage to control bleeding
IV – Intravenous

J
Jalalabad – Located at the junction of the Kabul River and Kunar River near the Laghman Valley; Jalalabad is the capital of Nangarhar province
JTTR – Joint Trauma Theater Registry
Jungle Penetrator – A contraption one sits on that is attached to hoist to extract patients

K
Keating – Combat outpost located in northeastern Afghanistan, near Pakistan border
Kiowa 58s – Small attack helicopters used by Scouts
Korengal – Valley in Afghanistan

L
Laparotomy – Incision made by a surgeon into the abdominal cavity
Litter – Collapsible gurney used to carry patients
LZ – Landing Zone

M
M-4 – Primary weapon of service members, Assault Rifle
Mass Casualty – Numerous patients injured in a single event
Medal of Honor – Highest military honor awarded for heroism above and beyond the call of duty.
MIA – Missing in Action
Mortars – An indirect weapon that fires explosive projectiles at low velocities, short ranges and high-arcing ballistic trajectories.
Motor – Peace officer that rides a motorcycle
MRAP – Mine Resistant, Ambush Protected Vehicle

N
Navy Cross – Second highest military honor for valor for extraordinary heroism in combat; Awarded to navy and marine personnel
Navy Specwar – Naval Special Warfare Command
NCOIC – Non-commissioned officer in charge
Neurogenic Shock – A loss of sympathetic stimulation to the blood vessels. This causes them to relax resulting a sudden decrease in blood pressure.
Night Vision Goggles – Devices that service members use to see at night
Nine-line – Request for Medevac Support based on nine questions: 1) Location of pick up site, 2) radio frequency, 3) number of patients by precedence, 4) special equipment needed, 5) number of patients by type, 6) security at site, 7) method of marking pickup site, 8) patient nationality and status, 9) Nuclear, Biological or Chemical (NBC) contamination.
Not responsive – Subdued level of consciousness, don't respond to pain

O
OP – Observation Point
Outside the wire – Outside the perimeter of defense

P
Packaging a patient – Prepare for Medevac transport
Pain Management – Managing a patient's pain through opiates
Paralytics – Drug to keep a patient from moving.
Para-jumpers – Air Force Special Forces
Pavehawks – Air Force UH-60s
PCR – Patient Care Report
Perfusion deficits – Challenged circulatory system
Pneumothorax – Chest cavity penetration that collapses the lung
POI – Point of Injury
POPPS – Public/Policing and Problem Solving Program

Protocols – Predetermined medical policies and procedures that medics follow guidelines
PRT – Provincial Reconstruction Team – American organization that help Afghans with their infrastructure
Pulse oximetry – Measures levels of oxygen attached to the hemoglobin of the red blood cell

R
Rapid Sequence Intubation – Sedate, paralyze and intubate a patient rapidly in exigent circumstance
RIP/TOA – Relieve in place, transfer of authority. Incoming crews are introduced to area of operation.
RPG – Rocket Propelled Grenade
RSI – Rapid Sequence Intubation

S
SCBA – Self-Containing Breathing Apparatus
Schoolhouse – An Army training facility that has responsibility for a specific discipline, e.g., the flight medic course is located at Fort Rucker, Alabama
Scooters – Slang for Kiowa 58s
Sepsis – Systemic blood infection
SERT Team – Special Emergency Response Team
SF – Special Forces
SFPA – Special Forces Physician's Assistant
Shrapnel – Broken pieces of a projectile that causes penetration to the human body
Shura – The Quran and Muhammad encourage Muslims to decide their affairs in consultation with those who will be affected by that decision.
Silver Star – Military award given for gallantry in action
Sked© – Foldable thick plastic gurney designed to place and secure a patient to carry them from the battlefield; Sked is short for the company that manufactures the stretcher – Skedco.

Stick – Slang for introducing an IV catheter into a patient's venous system
Sticks, Wiggle the – Slang for cyclic or collective controls the pilot uses to control the aircraft
Succinylcholine – Powerful, short term, nondeplorizing paralytic
Suppressive Fire – Bursts of gunfire toward the enemy to slow advance
SWAT – Special Weapons and Tactics Team used by law enforcement agencies
SWCC – Special Warfare Combatant – Craft Crewman

T
Taliban – Fundamentalist Muslim group that controlled much of Afghanistan from 1995 until U.S. military intervention in 2001
Task Force – Grouping of military units or forces under one commander for the performance of a specific operation
Tenth Mountain – A unique mountain warfare unit in the US Army specializing in fighting in mountainous and arctic conditions
Terrace – Flat area of ground carved out of a steep mountainside, used for agricultural purposes by local populace
Titrating – Adjust the introduction of medications or fluids based on physiological responses of patient
TOC – Tactical Operations Center

U
USAR Team – Urban Search and Rescue Team

V
Vascular Access – Introduce a catheter to a vascular space - i.e., vein
Ventilator – Mechanical device designed to control respiratory effort of a patient
Versed – Sedative
Vitals were deranged – Outside the typical vital value – e.g., respiration, heart rate, blood pressure

W
Warrant Officer – An officer of one of five grades ranking above enlisted personnel and below commissioned officers, generally not required to stand in formation
Winchester – Out of ammunition

Z
ZOL – A monitored defibrillator

BIBLIOGRAPHY

Chapter 1 – My Father's Legacy

Car Crash in Chase Kills 1, Injures 6, Sacramento Bee, March 9, 1962.

Diane Spraktes, 4, Dies of Car Crash Injuries, Sacramento Bee, March 10, 1962

Recorded interview with Violet Johnson

Interview with Harry Blevins

Chapter 2 – Police Officer, Patrolman, Paramedic

Spraktes eyewitness recollections

Cops flush out, seize suspect after standoff, Jim Mikles, Sacramento Bee, April 27, 1996.

Grenade assault ends Orland siege; fugitive captured, Kirsten Mangold, Chico-Enterprise Record, April 27, 1996.

Chapter 3 – A New Mission

Spraktes eyewitness recollections

Recorded interviews with Alva Smoot, Mike Ferguson, Robert Walters, Jimmy Blackmon

Chapter 4 – Righting Wrongs

Spraktes eyewitness recollections

Recorded interviews with Alva Smoot

America's Sons and Daughters in Good Hands in Afghanistan, Dave Cornell, Flt Medic, San Rafael Fire Department News, Vol. 2, Issue 1, December 2008.

Story of rescue gone bad: Mountain Rescue Association, www.mra.org HU U © 2008, Charley Shimanski/Mountain Rescue Association – All rights reserved, pages 5 & 6. http://www.montereysar.org/SARMembersDocs/AMRO_rev08.pdf

101st CAB hands over Afghan region to 159th, Jake Lowary, The Leaf-Chronicle, January 9, 2009.

Copter Spotlight, Jake Lowary, The Leaf-Chronicle, February 23, 2009.

Chapter 5 – We're Not in America Anymore

Spraktes eyewitness recollections

Recorded interviews with Ruben Higgins, Mike Ferguson

Medevac unit deploys for Afghanistan, 2nd Lt. Will Martin, Grizzly, November 2008, p. 4

Soldiers save infant girl, Pfc. Christina Sinders, Freedom Watch Afghanistan Magazine, March 2009, p. 12.

Chapter 6 – Study at Bagram

Spraktes eyewitness recollections

Recorded interviews with Jason Penrod, Mark Kavanagh, Rob Walters, Alva Smoot, Mike Ferguson

Impact of critical care-trained flight paramedics on casualty survival during helicopter evacuation in the current war in Afghanistan, Robert L Mabry, MD, MC, Amy Apodaca, MS, Jason Penrod, PharmD, Jean A. Orman, ScD, MPH, Robert T. Gerhardt, MD, MPH, and Warren C. Dorlac, MD. Fort Sam Houston, TX. Copyright 2012, Lipponcott Williams & Wilkins.

Chapter 7 – Combat Hoists

Spraktes eyewitness recollections

Recorded interviews with Alva Smoot, Donald Baker, Marc Dragony

Chapter 8 – Building Trust

Recorded interviews with Alva Smoot, Michael Ferguson, Ross Lewallen, Gary Parsons, Elizabeth Kimbrough, Jimmy Blackmon, Mark Kavanagh, Rob Walters, Jason Penrod

Spraktes eyewitness recollections

Chapter 9 – Afghan Police Officer

Recorded interview with Marc Dragony

Spraktes recollections

Chapter 10 – Critical Care Transport

Recorded interview with Ruben Higgins

Medevac – Critical-Care Transport from the Battlefield. R. A. Higgins, SGT, ARNG, AABA. AACN Advanced Critical-Care, Vol. 21, No. 3, pp. 288-297, AACN.

Chapter 11 – Seven Minutes in Hell

Recorded interviews with Alva Smoot, Mark Kavanagh, Jason Penrod, Donald Baker, Marc Dragony

Helmet Cam, Alva Smoot

Chapter 12 – Spinning Plates

Recorded interview with Rob Walters

Chapter 13 – Chapadera

More Than Horse Shit and Gun Powder, published photographic collection circa 2009

Spraktes recollections

Chapter 14 – Stetsons and Spurs

Recorded interview with Alva Smoot

Spraktes eyewitness recollections

Photos, 2009

Chapter 15 – Ten Miles from Jbad

Recorded interviews with Donald Baker, Mark Kavanagh, Alva Smoot

Spraktes eyewitness recollections

More Than Horse Shit and Gun Powder, published photographic collection circa 2009

Cal Guard Aviation Company Earns Army Medevac Award. Sgt. Jonathan Guibord, 1-168th General Support Aviation Battalion, Grizzly, March 2010, p. 6-7.

Photos, 2009

Chapter 16 – Loss at Barge Matal

Spraktes eyewitness recollections

Recorded interview with Mark Kavanagh

Chapter 17 – Walmart and Other Morale Builders

Recorded interviews with Donald Baker, Elizabeth Kimbrough, Ross Lewallen, Alva Smoot, Chad Bardwell

E-mails from Carmel Cammack, Angela Nolan

Spraktes eyewitness recollections

Photos, 2009

The Quote Book

Chapter 18 – Selfish Prayer

USA Sworn Statements by CW2 Ryan E. Neal, CW4 Brandon Erdmann, SSG Thomas Gifford, SSG Emmett Spraktes, O3 Shaun Conlin, CW2 Scott St. Aubin, SSG Jonathan Wedemeyer, E5 James K. Price, SPC Travis Adkins, O3 Chad Marzec, CW2 Donald Cunningham, O2 Brandon Jackson, CW3 Scott Stradley, CW3 Charles Folk, Unclassified

Spraktes eyewitness recollections

Valorous Unit Award summary

Napan and Crew Win Military Honors for Heroic Rescue in Afghanistan, Napa Valley Register, June 27, 2010, pages 1, 3.

Cal Guard Aviation Company Aviation Company Earns Army Medevac Awards, Sgt. Jonathan Guibord, 1-168th General Support Aviation Battalion, p. 6-7.

Selfless Service Leads to Silver Star, Brandon Honig, *Combat Tested – Medics Shine in Battle*, Julie Zeitlin, GX, The Guard Experience, Sept/Oct 2010, Vol. 7, Issue 5, pp. 38-45.

Daring Rescue: Medevac Pilot earns medal for risky mission, Stephanie Inman, GX, The Guard Experience, Nov/Dec 2010, Vol. 7, Issue 6, pp. 20-21.

Chapter 19 – Routine Career Call

Recorded interview with Michael Ferguson

Chapter 20 – Riding the Hero

Recorded interviews with Alva Smoot, Marc Dragony

Chapter 21 – Sauvetage

Recorded interview with Ruben Higgins

Dustoff Crews Assist French Armed Forces, Grizzly, March 2010, page 7.

Chapter 22 – Benson and Stead

Recorded interviews with Ross Lewallen, Jimmy Blackmon, Donald Baker

Spraktes eyewitness recollections

Family Flies High in Sendoff, September 16, 2011, Fort Campbell Courier, Heather Clark

Recognizing the Valor of a Hero, June 2, 2010, al.com, Kelley Lane Sivley

Army Pilot receives Distinguished Flying Cross, William T. Martin, November 23, 2011, Huntsville Newswire

Chapter 23 – Ambush at Ganjgal

Into the Fire, Dakota Meyer

Recorded interviews with Jason Penrod, Mark Kavanagh, Marc Dragony, Kevin Duerst, Jimmy Blackmon

Verification by William Swenson

Helmet Cam, Kevin Duerst

Helmet Cam, Jason Penrod

Written account by Jason Penrod

Battle of Ganjgal, Wikipedia.org.

http://www.mcclatchydc.com/2009/09/12/75301/for-reporter-no-doubt-id-use-the.html

http://www.mcclatchydc.com/2012/09/13/168356/afghan-survivors-of-ganjgal-battle.html

Chapter 24 – Landings, Lasers and a Ronald Reagan Moment

Recorded interview with Jason Penrod

Helmet Cam, Jason Penrod, Kevin Duerst

Spraktes eyewitness recollections

Chapter 25 – Let the Terrorist Fly

Recorded interview with Alva Smoot

Written account by Rob Walters

Verification by Mark Kavanagh

Chapter 26 – Keating

Recorded interviews with Ross Lewallen, Mark Kavanagh, Chad Bardwell, Elizabeth Kimbrough, Alva Smoot, Rob Walters, Jimmy Blackmon

Memorandum for Record: Recommendation for Flight Medic Stay Behind Program, CPT Mark Kavanagh, July 12, 2009.

The Outpost, Jake Trapper

Battle of Kamdesh, Wikipedia.org

Probes Overlook McChrystal's Role in Costly Afghan Battles, ?, February 20, 2010

McChrystal's Barge Matal Flashback, Examiner.com, June 3, 2010

Wounded US Soldiers Refused to Leave Taliban Fight, Karen Russo, ABC News, October 5, 2009.

http://youtu.be/CPtxxWIzea0

Chapter 27 – Reintegration

More Than Horse Shit and Gun Powder, published photographic collection circa 2009

1-168th Evacuates 3,400 wounded during Afghan tour, Brandon Honig, Joint Force Headquarters Public Affairs.

CHP Flag Brings Medic Comfort in Afghanistan, Grizzly, May 2010, page 6.

Cal Guard Aviation Company Earns Army MEDEVAC Awards, Grizzly, March 2010, Cover Story, page 6-7.

Combat Tested: Medics Shine in Battle, Julie Zeitlin, GX, Sept/Oct 2010, Cover Story, pages 38-45.

Daring Rescue: Medevac pilot earns medal for risky mission, Stephanie Inman, GX, Nov/Dec 2010.

159th Combat Aviation Brigade sweeps Army awards, Posted April 29, 2010.

Recorded interviews with Alva Smoot, Rob Walters, Mark Kavanagh, Elizabeth Kimbrough, Jason Penrod, Marc Dragony, Michael Ferguson

Interview with Dr. Todd Langus

War's Horror Still Haunts Area's Wounded Warriors, Sacramento Bee, December 4, 2011; pages 1, 20-21.

Chapter 28 – Results from Bagram

Spraktes eyewitness recollections

Recorded interviews with Mark Kavanagh, Jason Penrod, Rob Walters, Alva Smoot

Phone calls and e-mails with Robert Mabry

U.S. Military Medevac Comprehensive Issues and Solutions, paper by CW2 Jason M. Penrod, PharmD. (Study)

Flight Medics get Paramedic Training: New course add more lifesaving skills, Army Times, August 29, 2012.

Top-flight medics: Army training moves to next level, Gregg Zoroya, USA Today, September 6, 2011.

Chapter 29 – How Did This Happen?

E-mail contact with Robert Mabry, 2012-2013

US Armed Forces, Medical Journal, Vol. 10, No. 2, February 1954. Medical Considerations in Helicopter Evacuation, Spurgeon H. Neel, LTC, MC, USA

US Armed Forces Medical Journal, Vol. 6, No. 5, May 1955. Helicopter Evacuation in Korea, Spurgeon H. Neel, LTC, MC, USA

US Armed Forces Medical Journal, Vol. 8, No. 8, August 1957. Army Aeromedical Evacuation, Thomas N. Page, COL, MC, USA, Spurgeon H. Neel, LTC, MC, USA

The Future of the Flight Medic, CSM Tod L. Glidewell, Army Aviation, January 31, 2010. pp. 16-19.

Chapter 30 – The Siren's Call

Spraktes eyewitness recollections

Study: 25% of war deaths medically preventable, ArmyTimes, Patricia Kime, Jun 28, 2012.

New Army medics to receive enhanced training, Gregg Zoroya, ArmyTimes, Sept 6, 2011.

Top-flight medics: Army training moves to next level, Gregg Zoroya, USA Today, Sept 6, 2011.

Flight medics get paramedic training, Joe Gould, ArmyTimes, August 29, 2012.

Other related articles:

Band of Brothers, The Herald Magazine, 13 Jun 2009, Cover story, pages 6-12.

Organized Chaos at Bagram, Stars and Stripes, Vol. 7, No. 78, June 27, 2009, p. 4.

Sharpening the Edge: Paramedic Training for Flight Medics, LTC Robert L. Mabry, MC, USA, COL Robert A. De Lorenzo, MC, USA, http://www.cs.amedd.army.mil/dasqaDocuments.aspx?type=1.

Regaining Our Edge: Evolving Air Medical Evacuation to Meet the Demands of the Contemporary Operational Environment, LTC Robert L. Mabry, MC, USA, Army Medical Department Journal, April-June, 2011.

MEDEVAC; Critical Care Transport From the Battlefield, R. A. Higgins, SGT ARNG, AABA, Copyright 2010, American Association of Critical Care Nurses.

Army Dustoff Medics Unprepared, Michael Yon, February 23, 2012, Military.com's News and National Policy Blog

Military medical revolution: Deployed hospital and en route care, Lorne H. Blackbourne, MD, David G. Baer, PhD, Brian J. Eastridge, MD, Evan M. Renz, MD, Kevin K. Chung, MD, Joseph DuBose, MD, Joseph C. Wenke, PhD, Andrew P. Cap, MD, Kimberlie A. Biever, MS, Robert L. Mabry, MD, Jeffrey Bailey, MD, Christopher V. Maani, MD, Vikhyat Bebarta, MD, Todd E. Rasmussen, MD, Raymond Fang, MD, Jonathan Morrison, MD, Mark J. Midwinter, MD, Ramo'n F. Cestero, MD, and John B. Holcomb, MD; Copyright 2012, Lippincott, Williams & Wilkins.

Study: 25% of war deaths medically preventable, Patricia Kline, Army Times, June 28, 2012.

http://couriersebastian.wordpress.com/: Sebastian Rich's blog – dispatches from the field. You can read his archived posts from 2009 when he was imbedded with us in Afghanistan.

Aviation units transfer authority, Sgt. Charles Brice, Fort Campbell Courier, Jan 15, 2009, p. 9A.

Cover photo: Toru Yakota, Japan
Back cover photo: SGT Michael Schofield

ACKNOWLEDGEMENTS

The good idea fairy tapped her filthy little wand on those surrounding me upon my return from Afghanistan. The idea was to write a book; tell the story. It's been a hell of a ride! This idea dragged me to places I wouldn't have predicted nor necessarily wanted to go. It's not curbed my enthusiasm for drinking too much, hasn't helped my sleep, and I continue to burn through one bad relationship after another. But through the haze I saw a need and felt compelled to speak for those I care about. This task fell to me. Those who were involved have honored me with their trust, their friendship, and their pain.

Beyond this book and its few stories, there are people, places, institutions and events that deserve to be acknowledged. They made a contribution to change; they were dedicated to saving lives. There were thousands of individual events, hundreds of characters and many compelling stories. I couldn't possibly chronicle them all - the few stories here are just representative of what many Medevac crews did and do.

It wasn't just the California National Guard that took part in the fight for change; Nevada and Wyoming National Guards were also involved. They fell under Charlie Company 1-168th GSAB, and were a part of the study during the 9-11 rotation in Afghanistan.

There were many active duty officers and enlisted personnel that supported our cause. They saw the value; they saw that lives would be saved when the standards changed. These men and women informed, politicked (silently and loudly), provided information to the right people, wrote articles, sent detailed emails and frustrated some decision makers. They worked within and without the army system and often risked their careers. I either do not name them or use a pseudonym to further protect them. This piece gave me fits - I wanted to shout out their names from the rooftop and give them credit.

It wasn't just flight medics that were responsible for the change. Pilots, crew chiefs, maintainers, and operations personnel all made the study possible.

Service members will always hold a special place in my heart: you are magnificent. You fight for us and give us our freedoms. You give up parts of yourselves; sometimes you give it all, everything. Bless you.

I would like to acknowledge and thank the Westbrook family and of course, Captain Will Swenson. I traveled to Tennessee, Kentucky, Texas, Nevada, Florida and up and down California to conduct interviews and research. During my review of supporting materials I found we had helmet cam videos of the Ganjgal battle. Within these videos I found the last moments Swenson and Westbrook shared on the battlefield; it was a poignant moment. The video also gave clarity to who was where and when. I understood its meaning.

I contacted Captain Swenson and told him of the video's existence. I felt it should fall to him to present this to the Westbrook family because they were friends and SFC Westbrook was his senior enlisted in theater.

I also requested that Swenson come to California to meet the soldiers on that Medevac call. These men had suffered greatly having listened to the calls for help from the marines while they fought and ultimately died. They also had risked their lives picking up wounded Afghan soldiers and SFC Westbrook, only to have Westbrook die later due to a bad blood transfusion. Captain Swenson indeed visited us and there was much healing.

I was not at Ganjgal; I was hauling Afghans from camp Joyce to Jbad. However, years after this call that haunted the crew, I was able to help. I deeply appreciate Captain Swenson for staying with us and talking about it.

I need to acknowledge and thank many in the California Highway Patrol (CHP) that supported me and put up with my absences and bullshit. The CHP has been there for me and many Veterans. They were gracious and patient, even when I came back a little different.

Special thanks to my *old friends* Booze, Guilt, Pain, PTSD, Nightmares, Flashbacks, and Failed Relationships. Without you, I would not be the man I am today.

Victoria and Brent Newman and their family have kept me on track as much as they possibly could. I am deeply grateful for them and their guidance and all they have done for me.

It may seem odd that I would acknowledge my family last, since they are most important to me. You get the last words…I love you.

SSG Emmett William Spraktes
Courtesy of Sebastian Rich, Photojournalist

AUTHOR INFORMATION

Author Biography: Emmett William Spraktes

Emmett Spraktes served for ten years in the US Navy Reserve with Special Boat Units (SBU) and Special Boat Teams (SBT). He held the rate of Gunners Mate Guns Second Class (GMG 2), completed the US Navy elite Special Warfare Combatant-Craft (SWCC) course and was assigned to SBU 11, Mare Island, and SBT 22 Det. 122, Sacramento. In 2002, he deployed with SBT 22 to Central and South America where he participated in Foreign Internal Defense/Maritime Interdiction Operations/Protective Services Detail Missions.

He enlisted in the California Army National Guard in 2004, and in 2007 volunteered to serve as a ground medic with the 1-143 Field Artillery as they deployed to Balad, Iraq.

Staff Sergeant (SSG) Spraktes returned home to his family in 2008, and five months later he was activated and deployed to Jalalabad, Afghanistan as lead flight medic with Charlie Company, 1-168th GSAB. During his ten month tour in Afghanistan, he evacuated/treated 184 patients, flew 250 combat flight hours, and participated in twelve individual hoists.

SSG Spraktes is the recipient of the Air Medal, Air Medal with V device for valor, Army Commendation Medal, Army Commendation Medal with V, Combat Medical Badge and Silver Star for gallantry in action. He also received two Army Aviation Association of America Awards – Medic of the Year – 2009, and Rescue of the Year – 2009. He is a graduate of Flight Medic Course and Joint En Route Care Course, among numerous other military courses.

Spraktes honorably service-retired in 2011, after 25 years of law enforcement. The agencies he worked for were the California Department of Corrections, California State Police, Vacaville Police Department, and the California Highway Patrol (CHP). His past assignments included ten years as a SWAT operator and medic, Governor's Protective Detail/Dignitary Protection, Flight Officer/Paramedic, Drug Recognition Expert, Bicycle Patrol, Public Oriented Policing and Problem Solving Officer, Emergency Medical Services instructor at the CHP Academy, and many other positions.

Spraktes is currently a Nationally Registered Paramedic and California State licensed paramedic that is an associate academy instructor for the CHP Emergency Medical Services unit. He also is a firearms instructor for a California-based company called Team3Tactical. Spraktes is a private consultant for California Peace Officers Standards and Training (POST) evaluating certified courses and instruction.

Spraktes has done countless presentations for charity and community organizations. He has also presented to such groups as the Oregon Association Chiefs of Police, the FBI National Academy Graduates and California POST on topics regarding the challenges of reintegration for law enforcement personnel after military deployment.

Victoria M. Newman
Courtesy of Benjamin Newman

Author Biography: Victoria M. Newman

Victoria M. Newman is Founder of How2LoveYourCop, an operation that provides resources, support, and encouragement for police families. Married 25 years to an Assistant Chief with the California Highway Patrol, she authored *A CHiP on my Shoulder – How to Love Your Cop with Attitude*, a realistic but positive book to help police wives in their marriages. She now speaks and leads seminars throughout the country and abroad on police marriage. Mrs. Newman is emerging as a known Advocate for law enforcement personnel and marriages through networking, speaking for cop families to civilian audiences and partnering with departments and other like-minded organizations.

Mrs. Newman has operated a book consulting business for the past ten years, collaborating, editing, and rewriting works on business practices, prison survival, special needs children, marriage, and a memoir from a World War II prisoner of war.

Mrs. Newman descends from a long lineage of military ancestors dating back to knights in medieval England. Her strong, passionate support for military personnel and their families was ignited by conversations with her grandfather, a mechanic on the Flying Tigers during World War II.

Mrs. Newman has four children, and resides in Sacramento, California.

She can be reached via her website, www.how2loveyourcop.com.

Made in the USA
San Bernardino, CA
19 September 2013